Music of My Future

The Schoenberg Quartets and Trio

Music of My Future

The Schoenberg Quartets and Trio

edited by

REINHOLD BRINKMANN

& CHRISTOPH WOLFF

Isham Library Papers 5
Harvard Publications in Music 20
Harvard University Department of Music
2000

Distributed by Harvard University Press
Cambridge, Massachusetts, U.S.A. · London, England

Printed and bound in the United States of America

Typesetting and printing by Puritan Press, Hollis, New Hampshire
Photograph of David Lewin by Jane Reed, Harvard News Office

Library of Congress Cataloging-in-Publication Data

Music of my future : the Schoenberg quartets and Trio / Edited by
Reinhold Brinkmann & Christoph Wolff.
p. cm.
Papers presented at a symposium held in John Knowles Paine Concert
Hall of the Harvard Music Dept., Feb. 26-27, 1999.
"In honor of David Lewin."
Includes bibliographical references and index.
ISBN 0-9640317-1-X (alk. paper)
1. Schoenberg, Arnold, 1874-1951. Quartets, strings. 2. Schoenberg,
Arnold, 1874-1951. Trio, strings, op. 45. 3. Chamber music--History and
criticism. I. Brinkmann, Reinhold, 1934- . II. Wolff, Christoph.
III. Lewin, David.
ML410.S283 M87 2000
785'.7194--dc21

00-012392

The authors and the Harvard Department of Music
dedicate this volume
to
David Lewin

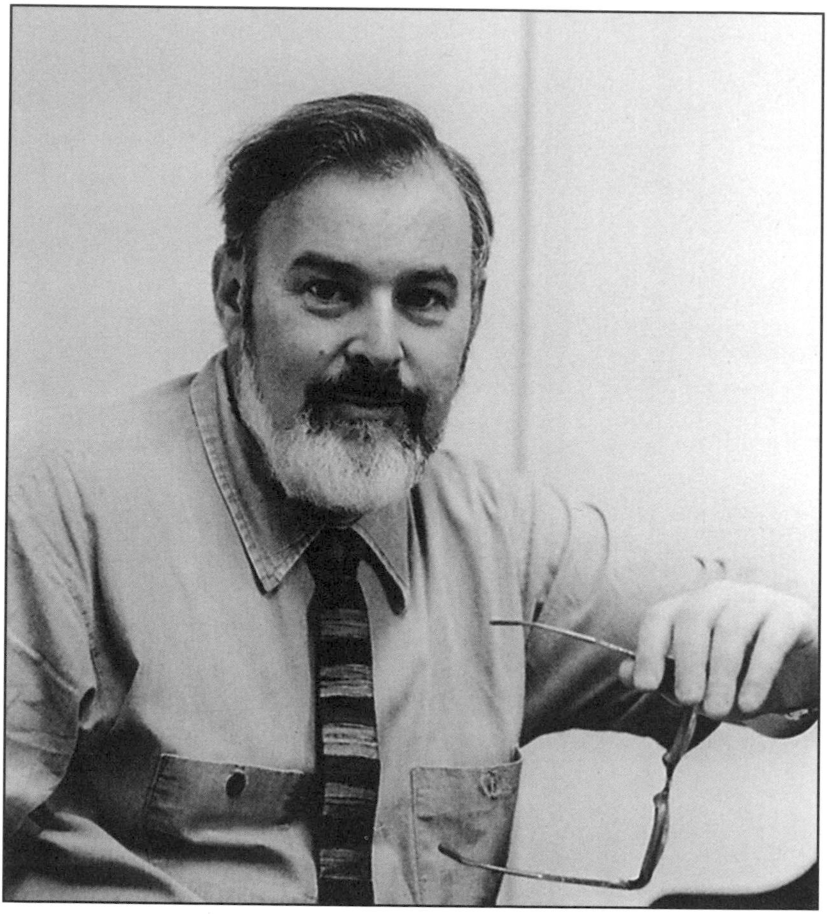

David Lewin

Contents

Preface

In a letter of 12 February 1927 to Henri Hinrichsen, owner of C. F. Peters and the grandseigneur among the music publishers, Arnold Schoenberg paraphrased the term *Zukunftsmusik* (music of the future) as 'music of my future'. It seems that for David Lewin, our colleague and friend, Schoenberg's string quartets assumed this role—after concerts by the Juilliard Quartet with all four quartets had b[illegible]ative experience and contributed to the decision of the young mathe[illegible]ncentrator from Harvard College to devote himself permanently to the [illegible] of music. And indeed, Schoenberg's music and his ideas about music we[illegible] a source of never-ending inspiration for David. Thus it was only logical when we approached him on behalf of the Harvard Music Department with our plan for a conference in his honor, that he proposed a series of concerts with Schoenberg's music for strings instead. The joining together of both plans led to a combination of three concerts with a symposium on February 26 & 27, 1999, in Paine Hall of the Harvard Music Department. Opening the event, six students from Music 180, the chamber music and analysis class taught by Robert Levin, played Schoenberg's sextet for strings, *Verklärte Nacht*, op. 4—a stunning performance, technically as well as musically of the highest quality. A roundtable, chaired by Thomas F. Kelly, on the music-historical context of Schoenberg's quartets, featuring Harvard's musicology faculty followed. The evening concert by the Mendelssohn String Quartet, our Blodgett Artists-in-Residence, with Susan Narucki, soprano, presented intense and exciting performances of the first two Quartets, op. 7 in D Minor and op. 10 in F-sharp Minor. On the second day, six individual studies on compositional aspects of the works and a philosophical meditation were scheduled in two sessions. An evening concert by the Juilliard Quartet, with the last two Quartets op. 30 and 37 and the Trio op. 45, concluded the event. It might be noted that the Trio was commissioned by our Music Department, for a symposium on music criticism held at Harvard in 1947, and was premiered in Sanders Theater by members of the Walden Quartet.

Thanks go to Lesley Bannatyne, Nancy Shafman, Ann Steuernagel—all of the Harvard Music Department—who participated in the organization of the conference and in the preparation of this volume. Thomas Peattie served as a competent and dependable assistant to the editors, Alan Gosman did the proofreading, Aaron Allen the indexing, Anne Canright was the expert copy editor. We also wish to express our gratitude to the participants in the conference for allowing us to publish their contributions and for submitting them in a timely fashion.

Reinhold Brinkmann
Christoph Wolff

Historical Context:
Four Sketches

REINHOLD BRINKMANN

Schoenberg's Quartets and the Viennese Tradition

Genre

Responding to the "laws" of the genre and its "Viennese" history since Haydn, Schoenberg's four mature quartets fall clearly into two groups. To begin with the easier of the two: the Third and the Fourth Quartets, Opus 30 and Opus 37, in every respect fulfill the expectations for a quasi-"classical" string quartet:[1]

- there are four movements, clearly defined and separated;
- the first movement follows the sonata scheme;
- one of the middle movements is an "Intermezzo" (not a Scherzo!);
- the last movement is a lighter, Haydnesque rondo

The neoclassical orientation of both twelve-tone quartets is obvious. And it is significant that Schoenberg's models for Opuses 30 and 37 are not the late Beethoven quartets (as is the case for Bartók's quartets) but rather Haydn and Brahms. They are neoclassical quartets also with regard to their musical language and texture; in their orientation toward working with themes and motifs, both realize the well-known metaphor of a discourse among "four reasonable people."

[1] For a general characterization of Schoenberg's quartets, see Ludwig Finscher, *Streichquartett*, in *Die Musik in Geschichte und Gegenwart*, 2. Auflage, Sachteil, vol. 8 (Kassel: Bärenreiter; Stuttgart: Metzler, 1998), 1965–1966.

With regard to the norms of the genre, however, the first two quartets, Opus 7 and Opus 10, are different. A brief comparison of one specific compositional agent can highlight this distinction. In the classical understanding, pitch and duration are considered primary parameters, whereas dynamics, color, and articulation are seen as secondary ones. It is well known that for music around 1900 these "secondary" parameters increasingly assumed a "primary" function. In Schoenberg's Opuses 7 and 10, the tempo is almost a primary parameter as well. Whereas in the classical sense of musical form, tempo changes generally serve to clarify the relation between sections of a movement, in Opus 10 nearly the opposite occurs: in certain passages the "flow" of the music, the quasi-natural "breathing" of its unfolding in time, becomes a formal device in its own right; here it is the tempo that seems, as the governing principle, to determine the place and character of sounds, motifs, themes, and sections. Consider, for example, the opening twelve measures of the first movement: with *Mäßig* (moderato) (♩ = ca. 100) as the first tempo indication, the movement in fact begins "a bit slower" than this tempo, arriving in m. 8 at "a bit faster" than 100—that is, 120–126—only to slow down again with the *rit.* from m. 11, and finally picking up the *Hauptzeitmaß* (𝅗𝅥. = ca. 52–56) with the transition theme in the viola of m. 12. Even more differentiated are the tempo modifications for the same passage that Schoenberg entered into a copy of the first edition of the score to influence a performance planned for 1909 or 1910 in Paris.[2] Here the tempo for the first measure is given as ♩ = 72; it reaches 76/80 in m. 6, a bar that itself is marked *poco accel. . . .*, then already in m. 7 changes to the slower 66, with an additional *molto rit. . . .* for this one bar; m. 8 then has the again abruptly faster ♩ = 92; m. 10 slows down again to 80; and finally m. 12 picks up the motion at 96.

Such a design of the tempo as an independent compositional force is not to be found at all in Opuses 30 and 37. There the few tempo indications content themselves with shaping and clarifying the formal architecture.

[2] Christian Martin Schmidt, *Arnold Schönberg. Streichquartette 1. Kritischer Bericht, Skizzen, Fragmente*, in *Arnold Schönberg, Sämtliche Werke*, vol. 20b (Mainz and Vienna: Universal Edition, 1986), 206–17. The annotated score is now among the holdings of the Paul Sacher Stiftung, Basel; see Hermann Danuser, "Im Unterricht bei Arnold Schönberg. Eine Quelle zum Streichquartett Nr. 2 in fis-Moll," *Mitteilungen der Paul Sacher Stiftung* 10 (March 1997): 27–31. The implications of Schoenberg's annotations for both a reflection on historical performance practice and the artistic practice of today are discussed by Hermann Danuser, "Instruktion durch den Autor—Zur Vortragsästhetik von Schönbergs 2. Streichquartett op. 10," in *Musikwissenschaft zwischen Kunst, Ästhetik und Experiment. Festschrift Helga de la Motte-Haber zum 60. Geburtstag* (Würzburg: Köningshausen & Neumann, 1998), 75–87.

(Characteristically, the development sections display more tempo changes than the expositions and recapitulations.) The first movement of Opus 30 is a good example: the basic tempo at m. 1 is given as Moderato 𝅗𝅥=100, and it remains unchanged until m. 42, when the *poco rit....*serves to introduce the transition section, which after the one-measure *ritardando* returns to the main tempo, 100. About twenty measures later, another slowing down, with two measures of a more forceful *poco rit....molto rit.*, introduces the second theme, which in itself is (marginally) slower throughout (*Etwas ruhiger, molto cantabile*) and marks the first real deviation from the stable *Haupttempo* of 100.

In the two twelve-tone quartets, the same principle is applied for the placement of textural fields and the use of certain specific colors (*sul ponticello, col legno, tremolo...*). In Opus 7, mm. 1261–1267, the "alienated" texture and colors mark the climax of the entire work; in tone they are the quasi-"negative" result of an utmost dynamic expansion, the collapse of an extreme surmounting of dynamics into the opposite—like similar passages in Mahler's symphonies, which Erwin Ratz and Theodor W. Adorno have called "negative fields." The "textural fields" in the first movement of Opus 37, however—mm. 63–65 and 89–94, for example—are used to articulate and clarify the sectioning of the sonata form; that is, they are employed in exactly the same way as the tempo modifications: as signposts. To be sure, this is part of a larger reorientation of Schoenberg's aesthetics during a period of general "stabilization" (Adorno) in the 1920s. Another indication of this change is Schoenberg's famous idea of a *Klangfarbenmelodie,* which, confined to the end of the *Harmonielehre* from 1911, indeed marks an extreme position in Schoenberg's development. About fifteen years later, in the composer's "Interview mit mir selbst," we witness the complete return to the traditional view: here the "idea" of a work is again given in the traditional relationship between pitches and durations, with color serving as a secondary device.

Opus 7, despite its dense thematic construction, is driven by a latent musico-dramatic impulse. Its continuous form (a combination of a four-movement design with the one-movement sonata form) comes from the tradition of the symphonic poem, that is, Liszt and Strauss. It is a monumental quartet, its grand tone distinctly symphonic. In addition, Opus 7 is program music (Schoenberg's hidden program has been published by Schmidt).[3] Thus, it does not belong in the Haydn-Brahms classical tradition of the quartet as the most prominent realization of the aesthetic paradigm of

[3] Schmidt, *Arnold Schönberg,* 109–10.

an "absolute music." On the contrary, Opus 7 is a *neudeutsch* tone poem in the guise of a chamber work and as such continues the idea of *Verklärte Nacht*, op. 4.

Opus 10 returns, as Schoenberg himself emphasized, to four movements, the first two being purely instrumental, though the scherzo movement is programmatic in terms of the specific ironic use Schoenberg makes of a popular song, "O du lieber Augustin." The third and fourth movements, however, introduce a soprano—that is, a fifth voice—with a poetic text, thus rendering the work no longer a "quartet" in the strict sense. Christian Martin Schmidt has touched upon this expansion of the genre.[4] Certainly Mahler's influence plays a role here—to combine the symphony with the lied, the human voice, is a Mahlerian formula; and Opus 10 directly follows, in Schoenberg's output, the Chamber Symphony, op. 9, a work that deliberately compressed Mahlerian symphonic dimensions into the small body of a chamber ensemble.

Thus, the central elements of the traditional definition of a string quartet—the homogeneity of the string sound, the pureness and perfection of the four-part setting, and the structural metaphor of a discourse among four reasonable people—no longer apply. Instead the four instruments accompany the human voice, which becomes more and more dominant and so changes the function of the instrumental ensemble, particularly at the climactic recapitulation of the finale. This indeed is a "literarization" of music, a procedure against which conservative Viennese critics like Hirschberg wrote in their polemics. But the historical significance of Opus 10 relies on exactly those "literary" elements that alter the genre, that are foreign to the essentials of a string quartet.

Social Character

With regard to the social character of Opuses 7 and 10—that is, their public reception—we must not forget that these works participated in Schoenberg's development of an atonal language and structure, the Second Quartet in particular. Schoenberg approached and defined his free atonality entirely within the realm of chamber music; it is of utmost significance that this important step, which in music history has been assigned the status of an aesthetic revolution, was not taken within the large and popular genres, such as the symphony or symphonic poem, genres for the broad public that

[4] Ibid., xvi.

around 1900 were considered aesthetically and sociologically progressive and were designed to define the "world" in a paradigmatic sense. On the contrary, the step was taken deliberately within the intimate realm of chamber music: a string quartet with voice, songs, lyrical piano pieces. The subject of Viennese atonality was a decidedly lyrical one.

Around 1900, however, the cultural devotees of chamber music, and of string quartets in particular, were members of the higher bourgeoisie. And the dominant taste of this audience was classicist. Leon Botstein, in his vast study of the Viennese musical culture around 1900, even speaks of an ideology of classicism: "A coherent ideology of musical classicism was nurtured. Classicism—formal symmetry and balance—was what the Viennese encouraged and appreciated so well; what they thought they could readily discern and appreciate."[5] The aesthetics of Schoenberg's two quartets, Opuses 7 and 10, however, are decidedly anticlassicist. Thus, Schoenberg forced his "revolution" of the musical language on an audience that was neither prepared nor willing to accept this new paradigm.

Historical Significance

It is reasonable to distinguish between compositional and historical significance of works of art. Although it seems unlikely that a work of minor aesthetic quality could ever achieve historical significance, not every work of high artistic distinction will be or will become historically significant. Brahms's *Ein Deutsches Requiem* seems a case in point.

Schoenberg's Opus 10 is the only one among the four quartets that has "made history" in a major sense. Opuses 30 and 37 are fine and important examples of Schoenberg's twelve-tone writing, but they never became models for a specific compositional reception within the genre, nor are they in any general sense historically significant. Opus 30 belongs to Schoenberg's second phase of twelve-tone composition, during which he freed the new technique from its initial application to baroque forms and employed it within various chamber ensembles, before moving on to the large orchestra and the operatic stage. Opus 37 is an example of his mature twelve-tone style in his first American phase. And Opus 7 is also an important work, though mainly within Schoenberg's individual compositional development, in that it marks the transition from the large symphonic orchestra (*Pelleas und Melisande, Gurrelieder*) to chamber music as the focus of his turn to atonality.

5 Leon Botstein, "Music and Its Public: Habits of Listening and the Crisis of Musical Modernism in Vienna, 1870–1914" (Ph.D. diss., Harvard University, 1985), 851.

Opus 10, however, goes beyond Schoenberg's individual development, occupying a prominent place at the center of a paradigmatic change within the history of music in general. And in truly modernist fashion, the work displays the new atonal realm even as it reflects on its historical place. There, for example, we find the "Augustin" quote, an ironic use of the popular Viennese song in the trio of the Scherzo movement, reflecting on the perceived state of tonality both as a compositional principle and as a symbolic representation of the Western musical tradition. We also find the use of Stefan George's poetry in the last two movements, the finale in particular. Characteristic for the harmonic language of the Second Quartet in general is the juxtaposition of key-centered and nontonal passages. As Walter Frisch has shown, at the historically important sections the traditional meanings of these principles are reversed: tonality/consonance is now associated with instability and atonality/dissonance with stability.[6] The famous introduction to the finale, with its systematically applied mixture of fifths and whole-tone progressions, is the most prominent place where this new paradigm is presented. Compared to these measures, the entry of the soprano voice with the famous line "Ich fühle luft" is harmonically rather traditional, with E♭ major, C minor, then F♯ major at the metrically accented places; the progression is more defined through voice leading (contrary motion in mm. 21–23, chromatically gliding augmented triads, then six-four chords in mm. 24–25) than through structural harmony. The work's main key, F♯, enters somewhat unprepared, particularly after the strong C minor—a tritone away—of m. 23, and is in itself unstable as a chord in second inversion, that is, a lasting dominant pedal without being resolved into the tonic. In general, however, this is a passage with strong tonal implications and, as such, it is quite normal for Schoenberg's works at the borderline between tonality and atonality. It seems to me that the text here is in fact commenting on the preceding music, heard in the instrumental introduction. The poetry is thus not set to music in the traditional sense of an interpretive act; rather, the words are used as a means of presentation, of representation. The text "pronounces" the idea of the music, explains in poetic images what is going on compositionally; the text is a commentary on the music and its historical position: self-reflectivity as a truly modernist stance.

[6] Walter Frisch, *The Early Works of Arnold Schoenberg, 1893–1908* (Berkeley and Los Angeles: University of California Press, 1993), 258–72.

Schoenberg's Opus 10 and Webern's Opus 5

The historical place of Schoenberg's Opus 10 and his idea of atonal structure can be determined also by another approach, using Webern's Five Movements for String Quartet, op. 5, composed in 1909, immediately after Schoenberg's Opus 10. These "movements" can be seen as Webern's commentary on Schoenberg's Second Quartet, its structures and historical position. Heinz Klaus Metzger, in a brief paragraph from 1955, stated that in the third movement of his Opus 5, Webern used the thematic substance from the Scherzo movement of Schoenberg's Opus 10, drawing quite different consequences from the material.[7] Although Metzger did not support his thesis through a detailed analysis, the reference can easily be demonstrated for eye and ear.

Webern's "reductive version" keeps the basic textures of the beginning and ending of Schoenberg's Scherzo, with the repeated bass note in the violoncello (the "leading tone" C♯ instead of Schoenberg's D); the dynamic intensification toward the end, culminating in ostinato figures and "unisons" (seventeen measures in the Schoenberg, two in the Webern); and Schoenberg's extensive "trio," represented only in miniature by Webern through a lyrical three-note phrase (*sehr zart*, m. 14).

I would like to extend this case of an intertextual relation to Webern's Opus 5, no. 4, which to me is a study about the Schoenbergian motif "Ich fühle luft." In particular, I see Webern's treatment of this motif as a compositional critique of Schoenberg's principles in his definition of an atonal language, a critique from a more structuralist point of view. At the same time, in my view, Webern's critique, which indicates the limitations of Schoenberg's "atonal theory" at quite an early moment, assigns Opus 10, and Schoenberg's free atonal language in general, a secure place within the evolving history of atonality.

Webern's reception of Schoenberg's Opus 10 must have had a biographical and inspirational background similar to that which underlay his reaction to the Chamber Symphony, op. 9. Webern reports: "In 1906 Schoenberg came back from a stay in the country, bringing the Chamber Symphony. It made a colossal impression. I'd been his pupil for three years, and immediately felt 'You must write something like that, too!' Under the influence of the work I wrote a sonata movement the very next day. In that movement I reached the

[7] Heinz-Klaus Metzger, "Webern und Schönberg," in *Die Reihe. Information über serielle Musik*, vol. 2: *Anton Webern* (Vienna: Universal Edition, 1955), 48.

farthest limits of tonality."[8] Behind the "something like that, too!" one senses Webern's desire to be more radical, more systematic than Schoenberg, to surpass his teacher and step to the forefront of historical development (based on an enthusiastic affirmation of "new" modes of artistic expression). And just as easily, one can imagine Schoenberg's own reaction, his anxiety over losing the privilege of historical priority.

(A philological note in parenthesis. No autograph scores exist for the two pieces in question that could shed light on Webern's critical perspective and procedures: no sketches, no earlier versions, no first drafts. The autograph manuscript of the complete set of the five pieces in the Paul Sacher Stiftung is a fair copy. The only major difference between this autograph and the printed version concerns the third piece, which in the fair copy is notated *alla breve.*)

Webern's Opus 5, no. 4, has been competently analyzed by George Perle and Elmar Budde, both of whom proceed from beginning to end, thus following the aesthetic experience of the listener.[9] My interpretation, in contrast, is generic. To me, the upward-gliding figure that appears within the piece three times (in m. 6, from c´; then in m. 10, from f; and finally in mm. 12–13, from g♯´) and articulates its three-part form, each time unaccompanied and after a ritardando, is the point of departure for Webern. In its first four notes, this figure is a version of the motive that, in various intervallic shapes, occupies a prominent place in movements two and three of Schoenberg's Opus 10 and finally carries the programmatic words of its finale: "Ich fühle luft." My analytical example shows its derivation and unfolding into Webern's aphorism. In Schoenberg's quartet the different appearances combine, in either upward or downward order (also forward or retrograde motion), a third (major or minor) with a second (major or minor, always as the middle interval) and a fourth (or tritone): its overall shape thus encompasses a minor or major seventh.

The Webern version consists of a major third, major second, and fourth upward: C-E-F♯-B (in Schoenberg's quartet this spelling can be found as retrograde in m. 264 of the second movement); and is enlarged to seven digits by another whole-tone step, B-C♯, and two concluding notes, G-B♭. But the first four notes become the intervallic center of the piece, in a characteristically

[8] Anton Webern, *The Path to the New Music*, ed. Willi Reich (London: Universal Edition, 1963). 48.

[9] Elmar Budde, "Anton Weberns op. 5/IV. Versuch einer Analyse," in *Erich Doflein Festschrift zum 70. Geburtstag* (Mainz: Schott, 1972), 58–66; George Perle, *Serial Composition and Atonality,* 4th ed. (Berkeley and Los Angeles: University of California Press, 1977), 16–18.

Example 1

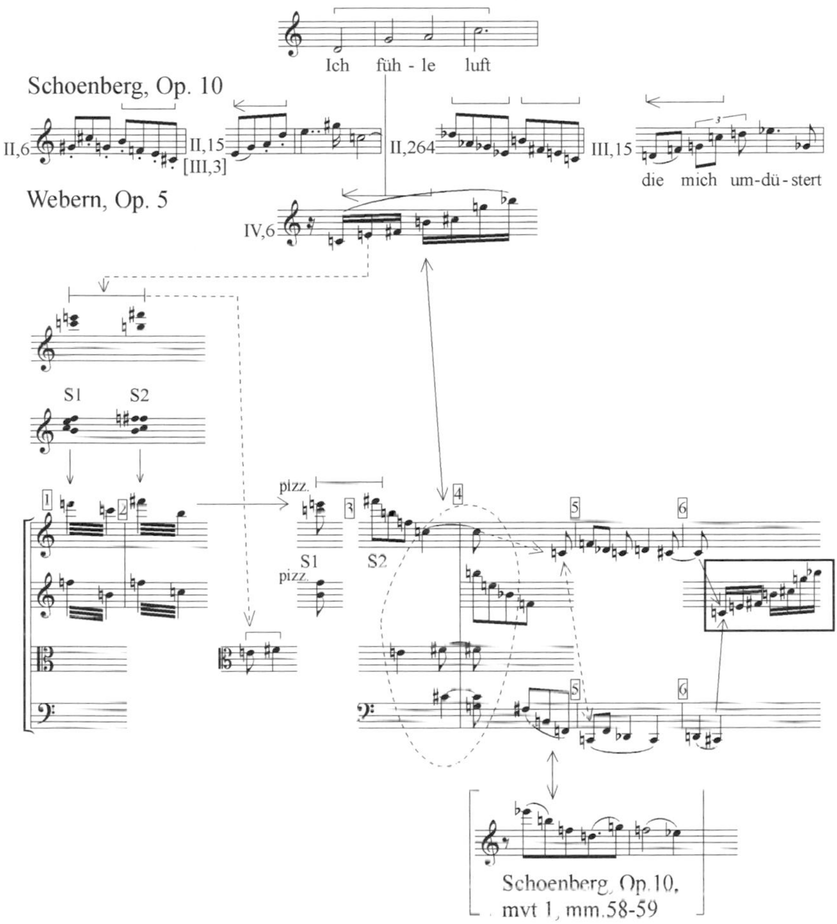

Webernian mode. The two dyads C-E and F♯-B are separated and given to the first violin (m. 1); to both another dyad is added in the second violin, thus forming a sequence of two tetrachords that, taken as pitch class sets (4-8 and 4-9, respectively, in the Fortean system), are symmetrical: B-C-E-F (S1) and B-C-F-F♯ (S2). The only new pitch class of S2 is F♯, thus emphasizing the important whole-tone step E-F♯ from the initial figure. The as-if fundament E♭ in mm. 1–2 of the violoncello, placed as an echo after S1 and S2, is alien to these chords; just as, at the beginning of Webern's George song "Dies ist ein Lied," op. 3, no. 1, the left-hand note E is alien in relation to the symmetrical chord of the right hand: in both cases the isolated bass note does not function as a fundament.

As shown in the lower half of the music example, the second symmetrical tetrachord is then used both vertically and horizontally and is subjected to contrapuntal procedures, in transpositions by the "tonal" interval of a fifth, and the first appearance of the "source" figure in m. 6 is introduced as if it were a result of these procedures. The imitative lines of the first violin and the violoncello in mm. 4–5 "break off" with the C♯ (D♭), while the expected continuation with C appears in the heptachordal figure. The upward motion of this figure is in distinct contrast to the lines of the first six bars, though it is initially prepared through the E-F♯ motive in the first violin (m. 1, then again mm. 2–3) and the viola (mm. 2–4), before the pending halftone F♯-G-F♯ in mm. 4-6 of the viola takes back the upward direction. Played *äußerst ruhig, ppp* and with a light decrescendo at its end, the figure transcends the realm of the first section with its symmetrical and polyphonic orderings and disappears, as if with a sigh, in the "air of another planet." The same gesture closes and opens up the middle section (m. 10), and finally also the shortened recap of the first section, which forms the end of the piece.

Thus, the initial invention, taken from Schoenberg, is "figure." Webern then turns "figure" into "structure."[10] This displays Webern's own and very personal idea of an atonality structured through intervallic relationships, and through symmetries in particular, an approach Schoenberg will not take. This is more than only a local compositional difference between two works that otherwise share the same historical challenge: it is a mode of thought that distinguishes Webern from Schoenberg in general. We find the same distinction later in the specific way Webern constructs symmetrical contrapuntal relations for the internal organization of his twelve-tone rows and unfolds these relations both horizontally and vertically into the structure and form of the entire composition. His Symphony, op. 21, is the *locus classicus* of this approach.

Thus Webern defines his own position in relation and in contrast to Schoenberg; his compositional commentary on Schoenberg's "figural" music as "air from another planet" is a critique on structuralist grounds.

[10] See Harold Kaufmann's methodologically brilliant cross-dressing of categories in his essays "Struktur in Schönbergs Georgeliedern" and "Figur in Weberns erster Bagatelle," in *Neue Wege der musikalischen Analyse*, Veröffentlichungen des Instituts für Neue Musik und Musikerziehung Darmstadt, vol. 6 (Berlin: Verlag Merseburger, 1967), 53–61, 69–72.

CHRISTOPH WOLFF

Schoenberg, Kolisch, and the Continuity of Viennese Quartet Culture

As we approach the final days of the twentieth century, let us try to imagine the following: exactly one hundred years ago, in 1899, Arnold Schoenberg was twenty-five years old. Like us today, he was in a position to look back at a virtually completed century. In 1827, less than three-quarters of a century earlier, and in more or less a single stroke, Beethoven had published his last quartets, opp. 130–133 and 135. In so doing, he closed, in many ways, the first and immensely important chapter of a musical genre: "in many ways" meaning in terms of structural design, compositional technique, social function, and aesthetic intent. For the Schoenberg of 1899, Beethoven was a figure from a not too distant past, and I don't find it farfetched to observe that for us, in 1999, Schoenberg is a figure from a not too distant past as well. Indeed, his Third Quartet of 1927 is chronologically separated from us by exactly the same time span. And at least in some sense, that piece, too, closed a chapter in the string quartet genre—a chapter, however, that did not have a sequel comparable to that which followed the first. For after Beethoven came Mendelssohn, Schumann, Brahms, Dvořák, and many more, whereas after Schoenberg the genre of the string quartet lost much of its prominence. Nevertheless, in terms of compositional and aesthetic choices, Schoenberg did manage to place the "quartet idea" on an entirely new level, not only by way of his unique musical conceptions and convictions but also by capitalizing on the extraordinary and unbroken tradition that quartet composition and quartet playing enjoyed in his native Vienna. What he had no control over, of course, were external events, such as the dramatically changing musical landscape in the decade after World War I in general, and the devastating political events of the 1930s, which eradicated, once and for all, the continuity of Viennese quartet culture.

What does "Viennese quartet culture" mean? I do not intend to suggest that the quartet genre was born in Vienna (it was not) nor that Vienna ever functioned as a center of quartet publishing (it did not). Still, one cannot find any other place in Europe—take London, Berlin, Paris, or Rome, whether in 1800, 1850, 1900, or 1925—that could even remotely compete with Vienna when it comes to the overall importance of the quartet genre. This can be measured not only by the remarkably steady commitment to the genre of composers working and living in Vienna and the number of influential quartet ensembles based in Vienna, but also, significantly, by the devotion to the genre of audiences in Vienna. Even after Archduke Rudolph and the Kinskys, Lobkowitzes, Razumovskys, Lichnovskys, and other aristocratic patrons of Beethoven's and Schubert's Vienna were long gone, and private concerts at the nobility's city palaces and mansions had been replaced by bourgeois concert series at the Musikverein and elsewhere, the more intimate, devoted, and often professionally focused settings for quartet playing remained. The non-negligible dimension of musical entertainment was always balanced by an aspect of musical connoisseurship. When in 1784 Leopold and Wolfgang Amadeus Mozart engaged in quartet playing with Haydn at Mozart's Viennese apartment—primarily for themselves, but also in front of friends—that scene was not fundamentally different from that of the Joachim Quartet (essentially a dislocated Viennese ensemble based in Berlin) studiously reading the latest Brahms or the various quartet configurations—including, among others, the Galimir Quartet and the group that later became the Kolisch Quartet—playing new works in Schoenberg's Verein für musikalische Privataufführungen.

Viennese performers, notably first violinists, whether or not they were themselves composers, played a remarkably decisive role in this unfolding, beginning with Ignaz Schuppanzigh (1776–1830), whose quartet—the first truly professional ensemble of its kind[1]—premiered virtually all the

[1] From 1794 to 1795 Schuppanzigh's quartet performed in the service of Prince Karl von Lichnovsky, from 1808 to 1814 in the service of Count Andrej Razumovsky, and thereafter in public subscription concerts. After Schuppanzigh's death, the quartet continued until 1849 under the leadership of Leopold Jansa (1795–1875). He, in turn, was succeeded by Joseph Hellmesberger, who renamed the quartet after himself.

Beethoven quartets as well as Schubert's A Minor Quartet (dedicated to Schuppanzigh).[2] This role continued with the quartets led by Joseph Helmesberger (1828–1893), with premieres of Brahms's Opus 51 and the Bruckner Quintet. The quartet led by Arnold Rosé (1863–1946), Gustav Mahler's brother-in-law, initiated a significant series of first performances in Vienna, from the Brahms Quintet, op. 111, and works by Hans Pfitzner, Max Reger, and others, to Schoenberg's *Verklärte Nacht,* op. 4 (1903), and his first two quartets, opp. 7 (1907) and 10 (1908).[3] Under the leadership of Rudolf Kolisch (1896–1978), Schoenberg's Third and Fourth Quartets, opp. 30 (1927) and 37 (1937), were premiered in Vienna and Los Angeles, respectively; Kolisch's Wiener Streichquartett (later renamed the Kolisch Quartet) also presented first performances of, among other works, Berg's *Lyric Suite* (1927), Webern's String Trio (1928), and Bartók's Quartets nos. 5 (1935) and 6 (1941).

A Context for Schoenberg's Opus 30

Two specific points of context need to be stressed in regard to Schoenberg's Opus 30 of 1927. First, there is the remarkable hiatus of nearly twenty years that separates the Third Quartet from its forerunners, Opuses 7 and 10 of 1907–8, a hiatus that placed the later work in an entirely different musical world. The fundamental changes in the composer's method of composition and aesthetic orientation that had evolved during the preceding two decades, reaching their first culmination in Opus 25 of 1921, now in the Third Quartet were carefully and deliberately applied to, indeed translated into, the most classic of all instrumental genres, a genre from which Schoenberg seemed to have distanced himself for so long.

Second, during this very era—that is, the two decades before 1927—string quartet production continued to flourish in Vienna. There is no question that Schoenberg paid attention to what was being composed in this realm, though the extraordinary profuseness of quartet composition during his own "quartetless" period may well have reinforced his reluctance to become involved himself. In the unusually rich quartet repertory created at

[2] The history of the string quartet ensemble has not yet been written. See W. Ehrlich, *Das Streichquartett in Wort und Bild* (Leipzig, 1898), and, most recently, L. Finscher, "Streichquartett-Ensemble," in *Die Musik in Geschichte und Gegenwart,* 2d ed., ed. L. Finscher (Kassel: Bärenreiter, 1998), vol. 8, cols. 1977–1989.

[3] It is noteworthy that Adolf Busch (1891–1952) founded his quartet 1913 in Vienna (originally Wiener Konzertvereins-Quartett; from 1919, Busch Quartet).

that time,[4] one can differentiate between a more conservative circle of composers, such as Josef Foerster, Felix Weingartner, Guido Peters, Alexander Zemlinsky, Julius Bittner, Richard Stöhr, Johanna Müller-Hermann, Franz Moser, Karl Weigl, Franz Ippisch, Hugo Kauder, Hans Gál, Egon Kornauth, and Erich Wolfgang Korngold, and the "avant-garde" represented by Alban Berg, Anton Webern, Egon Wellesz, Paul Amadeus Pisk, Josef Matthias Hauer, and Alois Hába. Schoenberg, it must be noted, had personal relationships with individuals in both "camps."

Schoenberg's Third Quartet was first performed on 19 September 1927, on the second of two evenings of chamber music at the Mittlere Konzerthaussaal in Vienna featuring premieres of works commissioned by Elizabeth Sprague Coolidge, one of the greatest chamber music patrons of all time. The first evening's program comprised works by Frank Bridge, Gian Francesco Malipiero, and Leo Weiner, and that of the second, compositions by Charles Loeffler, Frederick Jacobi, Ottorino Respighi, and Arnold Schoenberg. Schoenberg's new quartet was presented by the Wiener Streichquartett, led by the composer's brother-in-law, Rudolf Kolisch, the other members being Felix Khuner, Jenö Lehner, and Benar Heifetz. The performance received high praise (reports specify that Schoenberg personally received much applause when appearing on stage and taking a bow),[5] but the Viennese press generally printed sharp, vitriolic attacks on Schoenberg. The *Neues Wiener Tagblatt* of 3 October 1927, for example, relates the new quartet to "the fashion for making sense of the incomprehensible, for taking the antimusical for music and true music for antimusical." [6] Among the prevailingly negative reviews, however, one mildly positive review stands out. Josef Reitler wrote that, in contrast to those atonal composers who take "expressive mist for truth, perseverance for logic, and accumulation of bizarre musical thoughts for a view of the world [*Weltbild*]," Schoenberg in his Third Quartet

[4] Wolfgang Oberkogler, *Das Streichquartettschaffen in Wien von 1910 bis 1925,* Wiener Veröffentlichungen zur Musikwisenschaft, 22 (Tutzing, 1982).

[5] Reviews are collected in Rudolf Kolisch Papers (bMS Mus 195), Houghton Library, Harvard University, no. 2095. See also Claudia Maurer Zenck, "'Was sonst kann ein Mensch denn machen, als Quartett zu spielen?' Rudolf Kolisch und seine Quartette: Versuch einer Chronik der Jahre 1921-1944," *Österreichische Musikzeitschrift* 53 (1998): 8–57, which makes extensive use of the Kolisch Papers and presents a detailed overview of Kolisch's quartet activities.

[6] "Heute ist es Mode, das Unverstehbare zu verstehen, das Widermusikalische für Musik, und wirkliche Musik für widermusikalisch zu halten."

"reestablishes musical architecture by returning to old forms of composition [*alte Satzformen*] and to the artifices of old contrapuntal style."[7]

By emphasizing the reestablishment of musical architecture and the return to old forms and contrapuntal devices, Reitler clearly articulates Schoenberg's idiosyncratic response to the "neoclassic" trends of the 1920s—for it had indeed been the composer's intention to apply his new dodecaphonic language to the traditional quartet genre. Also, Kolisch's concert tour in the fall of 1927, which featured Opus 30, puts the work in a genuinely classical frame, as the programs presented at various places in Germany demonstrate: in Aachen (30 September), it was performed together with Berg's *Lyric Suite* and Beethoven's Opus 59, no. 3; in Cologne (7 October), again with the *Lyric Suite,* as well as Webern's Bagatelles, op. 9, and Beethoven's Opus 59; and in Ludwigshafen (17 October), with Hanns Eisler's Duo for violin and violoncello, op. 7, and Beethoven's op. 59, no. 3. The repeat performance in Vienna on 20 November included Bach's A Minor Partita, played by Eduard Steuermann, and Schubert's *Trout* Quintet.[8]

Although the contents of the concert programs were primarily determined by Rudolf Kolisch, Schoenberg must have felt comfortable with the violinist's decisions. In Opus 30, then, he finds himself musically much more closely linked with the quartet classics from Haydn to Brahms than was the case with his first two quartets. Or to put it differently, when we compare his early quartets with the third (and fourth), we see Schoenberg distancing himself from the tradition of the string quartet genre in two fundamentally different ways: earlier, by changing conceptually both formal design and technical-compositional premises; later, by changing tonal approach, musical vocabulary, and grammar while preserving the essential constructive pillars of form and counterpoint. It is hardly a coincidence, then, that Schoenberg turned to a quintessentially classical genre in order to consolidate the twelve-tone system bound up with his new musical language.

[7] "Stellt man sich 'atonal' ein…so mag man im Zustande der Tonbewusstlosigkeit auch irgendwelchen Ausdrucksnebel für Wahrheit, Beharrlichkeit für Logik, die Häufung verzerrter Tongedanken für ein Weltbild nehmen. Schönbergs neues Quartett bekennt sich zu der Wiederherstellung musikalischer Architektonik in der Rückkehr zu den alten Satzformen wie zu den Künstlichkeiten alter kontrapunktischer Satzweise dabei."

[8] MS Mus 195.

Composer and Kolisch Quartet Working Together

The collaborative relationship between Schoenberg and the Kolisch Quartet,[9] which cannot be underestimated, is well documented in the Rudolf Kolisch Papers housed in the Manuscript Department of Harvard University's Houghton Library.[10] They provide an enormously rich resource particularly for the study of the Schoenberg quartets—their compositional history, many details of performance-related matters, and in matters pertaining to the establishment of a philologically accurate text. For example, the published study score of the quartet Opus 7 from Kolisch's library (Verlag Dreililien, Berlin-Lichterfelde) contains corrections, as is specified by an autograph note on the title page: "Dieses Exemplar enthält Korrekturen. Sch."[11]

The following references highlight some relevant points with respect to Opus 30: Kolisch's rehearsal diary (*Probenjournal*)[12] records that the rehearsals for the Third Quartet, which was completed on 8 March 1927, began precisely two months later, on 8 May. Rehearsals on 8 June, from 9 A.M. to 1:30 P.M., were held in the presence of Schoenberg, who worked with the quartet on the first two movements ("Schönberg anwesend / [Satz] I, II stud[iert]"; Fig. 1), after they had read through the quartet the previous evening, from 6 to 7:15 ("Schönberg III. Quartett dsp [durchgespielt]"). Schoenberg joined them two days later, from 5 to 7 P.M., for rehearsals of the last two movements. Rehearsals intensified—interrupted only by concerts—between 17 July and 4 August and between 13 August and 15 September; at rehearsals on 11–12 September, Schoenberg was again present. The premiere followed on 19 September.

Kolisch and his quartet were reading and performing Opus 30 from a set of parts copied from Schoenberg's autograph score by the professional copyist Wewerka and proofread by Felix Greissle.[13] The sample pages reproduced in Figures 2–3 indicate noteworthy details such as

- the importance of cue staff notation, entered during the rehearsal process to emphasize musical connections;

[9] For a detailed discussion, see Alexander Ringer, "Joachim Stutschewsky und das Wiener Streichquartett," *Österreichische Musikzeitschrift* 39 (1984); and Maurer Zenck, "'Was sonst kann ein Mensch denn machen.'"
[10] bMS Mus 195.
[11] fMS Mus 195 (1899).
[12] fMS Mus 195 (2118).
[13] bMS Mus 195 (1675).

- the addition of dynamics, also entered during rehearsals and not found in the published score;
- the addition of other markings such as the indication "Pesante" (1st movement, m. 339) or "molto espressivo" (2d movement, m. 11), again not found in the published score.

The Kolisch Quartet used to perform from memory and, for rehearsal purposes, often made use of paste-up scores, that is, large-format card boards, each providing a synopsis of several pages from small-format study scores pasted next to each other. A paste-up score for Opus 30 has survived (Fig. 4), but it apparently originated from rehearsals of the piece in later years, after 1927. It contains numerous entries in pencil that relate to various details, ranging from text corrections to dynamics, fingering, articulation, emphasis of individual phrases, tempo modifications, and analytical observations relevant for performance.[14]

In closing, let me return to the "Viennese quartet culture" and its historical continuity over almost two hundred years. I realize that these brief remarks can in no way do justice to the phenomenon of that culture, nor to Kolisch or Schoenberg. However, an unforgettable personal experience I had reflects directly on my thoughts here. About ten years ago I attended, at the New England Conservatory, a quartet coaching session conducted by the venerable Jenö Lehner, long-time violist of the Wiener Streichquartett and the Kolisch Quartet. The well-prepared students were struggling mightily with Schoenberg's Fourth Quartet, but then a turning point in their approach to the music came when Lehner—much to their amazement—told them, "Play it as if it were a Haydn; that's what Schoenberg aimed at when working with us."

Perhaps not surprisingly, Lehner's helpful recollection is in a sense reiterated in the statement found at the end of Reitler's review of the 1927 premiere of Opus 30: "The Wiener Streichquartett, led by Rudolf Kolisch, reproduced the work with a freedom and security that suggested they were dealing with a Haydn and not the latest Schönberg."[15] Clearly, the continuity of the quartet genre and its performing tradition, going all the way back to its founder,

[14] There exists also a paste-up score for the Fourth Quartet, originally prepared for a performance in Los Angeles in 1937: pfMS Mus 195 (1953).

[15] "Das Wiener Streichquartett, geführt von Rudolf Kolisch, hat das Werk mit einer Freiheit und Sicherheit reproduziert, als handelte es sich um einen Haydn und nicht um den letzten Schönberg."

Franz Joseph Haydn, mattered a great deal to the Schoenberg of Opus 30. We need to consider, of course, that Schoenberg's Haydn was not necessarily our Haydn, much less Beethoven's Haydn, and definitely not Haydn's Haydn. What Schoenberg absorbed, rather, was the inspiring musical atmosphere and its deep roots in specifically Viennese culture. Just as Schoenberg saw Haydn's spirit alive in Mozart, Beethoven, Schubert, and Brahms, he wanted to make that spirit work for his later string quartets as well.

Figure 1

Kolisch, *Probenjournal,* fMS Mus 195 (2118), pp. 000–000.

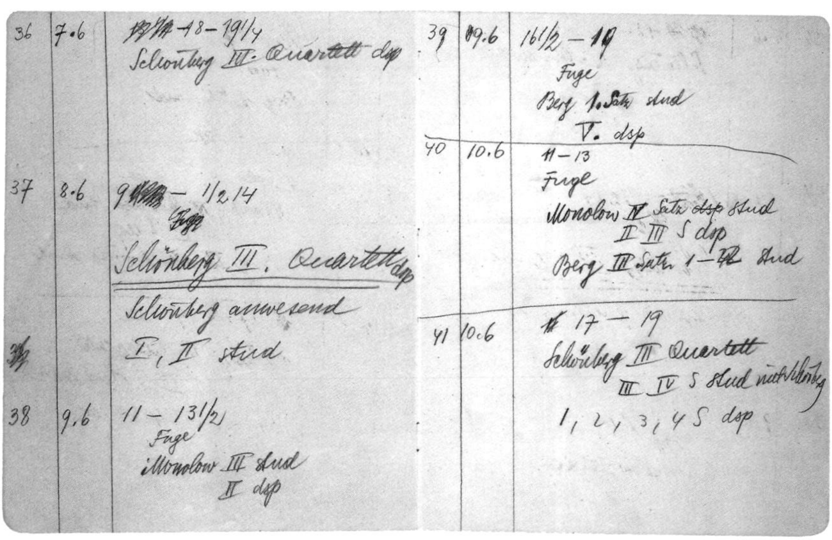

Figure 2

Schoenberg, op. 3, manuscript part of violin I, bMS Mus 195 (1675), p. 1.

Reproduced by permission of the Houghton Library, Harvard University.

Figure 3

Schoenberg, op. 3, manuscript part of violin I, bMS Mus 195 (1675), p. 2.

Reproduced by permission of the Houghton Library, Harvard University.

Figure 4

Schoenberg, op. 3, paste-up score, pfMS Mus 195 (1952), board 3.

Reproduced by permission of the Houghton Library, Harvard University.

KAREN PAINTER

Form, Innovation, Modernism: Early Responses to Schoenberg's First Quartet

For both composer and his critics, Schoenberg's D Minor Quartet, op. 7, which premiered in 1907, was a turning point: the most traditional genre, but a composition whose harmonic innovations push up against the very boundaries of tonality; the conventional movement types, but a bold execution of a formal plan that undermines the psychological and cultural basis of musical structure. The consequences of its innovations were not always apparent to Schoenberg, who developed a vocabulary for discussing his break from tonality and conventional form only in the works *following* Opus 7. But the quartet forced Schoenberg's contemporaries to question long-held assumptions about the importance of structure in art. Their perceptions extended beyond the traditional vocabulary of music theory, capturing through metaphors some of the fundamental experiences of modernism. The nature of this discourse changed in significant ways from the initial performances in 1907 to the Berlin premiere in 1912, by which point a vocabulary of scientific modernism had entered the public realm. While atonal music or abstract painting would incite wrath often without insightful observations, Opus 7 challenged listeners to experience a new relationship between subject and object, space and time.

I am grateful for the assistance of Therese Muxeneder of the Arnold Schönberg Center, Vienna, and the staff at the Geheimes Staatsarchiv, Berlin, as well as to Joseph Auner for directing me to the Steininger Sammlung housed there. The Schoenberg reviews from the Steininger Sammlung will be published in a volume edited by Auner and Klaus Kropfinger.

The infamous riots at the initial performances of Opus 7 had impetus both musical and ideological. It is difficult to find a reviewer who was untroubled by the work's harmonic innovations or contrapuntal writing, or who was unconcerned about the consequences for the future of the string quartet or of concert life as a whole. But despite the diatribe against modernism and the attendant cultural ills, critics did address a basic aesthetic problem: the conflict between listening to music as process or as structure. Tension between these two poles of experience is often inevitable in musical listening, but Schoenberg's quartet brought this issue to the fore. The title that appeared in the early programs, "Quartet in One Movement," seemed to insist that listeners comprehend the fifty minutes of music under one rubric. Certainly the thematic connections between sections (or movements) and recall of earlier themes encourage such holistic perception, as a single structure. Yet at the same time, the liveliness of the counterpoint and the timbral "effects" thrust listeners into the vibrant moment, the immediacy of process.

Since the early nineteenth century, the cultural and aesthetic importance of instrumental music often depended on grasping a work as a unified structure, with the themes and other aspects of the musical unfolding heard in relation to a larger formal scheme. By the turn of the new century, compositional praxis turned more on the immediacy of sonority in ways that could not be conceptualized into a whole. With Mahler's music, vain attempts to "overview" (*übersehen*) symphony movements led to a criticism of excess—the number of instruments, the manner of scoring, the overdevelopment of "impoverished" thematic material. One month after Mahler's Sixth Symphony brought this issue to the fore in Vienna, Schoenberg's Opus 7 prompted critics to understand the perceptual failure in terms similar to what Judith Ryan, in her study of developments within literature and psychology in the decades around 1900, calls "the vanishing subject."[1] Even though the four movement types were clearly recognizable in the quartet's four sections, the manner of the formal articulation defied expectations to the point that no coherent subject was perceptible. At the initial performances in 1907, as I will show, the clash of synchronic and diachronic modes of listening provoked violent tropes—in effect, the dissolution of the subject (whether in the sense of the expectation of rational dialogue among the four players or the more abstract sense of human logic projected by the listening subject). By the Berlin premiere of 1912, a vocabulary of scientific modernism had developed that captured this same clash in more productive ways.

[1] Judith Ryan, *The Vanishing Subject: Early Psychology and Literary Modernism* (Chicago: University of Chicago Press, 1991).

Not unlike his worst critics, Schoenberg could seem more concerned with the historical position of Opus 7 than with its innovations. When he finally witnessed a warm reception of the work in 1920, Schoenberg complained to his students that the success was based on its "timbral effects" and that "the audience here seems a long way from grasping the 'symphonic' and melodic qualities." Mood and poetic meaning, in his opinion, were criteria for the lowest level of listening.[2] Schoenberg would later emphasize the symphonic nature of the quartet in a more public forum. For the first time, now thinking of the work in the context of his four quartets, Schoenberg suggested in 1936 that analysts would find interesting the fact that Opus 7 had as its model the first movement of Beethoven's *Eroica* Symphony.[3] It is surprising that Schoenberg gave no specification as to the nature of the influence, especially since he had recently enumerated the specific ways that five composers had influenced his writing.[4]

Schoenberg's remarks are too brief to offer insight into the kind of formal listening he had in mind with Opus 7. Remarkable, however, is that reviewers in 1907 perceived nothing symphonic in the quartet—or at least did not identify it as such. More relevant to their experiences is, ironically, Schoenberg's utterances about his work in the years immediately following the completion of Opus 7. He avoided challenging the notion of the symphonic associated with critics at liberal papers, even as he rejected the strictures of the conservative ideal for orchestral writing.[5] When requesting that Strauss in 1909 conduct the Pieces for Orchestra, op. 16, Schoenberg explained, "There is absolutely nothing symphonic about them. In fact the opposite is the case: there is no architecture, no structure. Merely a bright, unbroken alternation

[2] The letter, dated 6 December 1920, was addressed to his students and friends; see Juliane Brand, Christopher Hailey, and Donald Harris, eds., *The Berg-Schoenberg Correspondence: Selected Letters* (New York: W. W. Norton, 1987), 294–295. The letter is discussed in Christopher Hailey, "Between Instinct and Reflection: Berg and the Viennese Dichotomy," in *The Berg Companion*, ed. Douglas Jarman (Boston: Northeastern University Press, 1990), 227.

[3] Arnold Schoenberg, "Notes on the Four String Quartets" (1936), quoted from *Schoenberg, Berg, Webern: The String Quartets—A Documentary Study*, ed. Ursula Rauchhaput (Hamburg: Deutsche Grammophon Gesellschaft, 1971), 38–39.

[4] Arnold Schoenberg, "National Music" (24 Feb. 1931), in *Style and Idea: Selected Writings of Arnold Schoenberg*, ed. Leonard Stein, trans. Leo Black (Berkeley and Los Angeles: University of California Press, 1984), 173.

[5] These viewpoints are laid out in my forthcoming article "Symphonic Aspirations, Operatic Redemption: *Mathis der Maler* and *Palestrina* in the Third Reich," in *Musical Quarterly*.

of colors, rhythms, and moods."[6] This sense of release pervades Schoenberg's letters in 1909 to Busoni. He spoke of a wish for "complete liberation from all form, from all symbols of cohesion and logic," from such things as "motivic working out," "harmony," and "cement or bricks of a building." Schoenberg formulated an aesthetic of intuition and personal expression, denying any structural force to his harmonic language ("Harmony is expression and nothing else").[7] His correspondence with Wassily Kandinsky explored the aesthetic ramifications of the move away from representation and form—with Kandinsky reaching his most fluid compositions, the Improvisations, as Schoenberg developed an atonal idiom. Schoenberg recognized the many common elements in their approach but did not join the painter in rejecting logic in his work (a long tradition in musical thought), instead preferring to dissolve consciousness. "I am sure that our work has much in common—and indeed in the most important respects: In what you call the 'unlogical' [*Unlogische*] and I call the 'elimination of the conscious will in art.'...But only unconscious form-making, which sets up the equation 'form = outward shape,' really creates forms." Kandinsky responded, "This human tendency toward the fossilizing of form is shocking, even tragic."[8] Even in his 1912 speech on Mahler, Schoenberg defined the symphonic without any claims of holistic structure: "the individual sections are organic components of a living being, born of a creative impulse and conceived as a whole."[9] Especially in his professional capacity, writing to Strauss and speaking on Mahler, Schoenberg attributed a coherent subject to the musical work, in terms of compositional voice or what the listener experiences.

Reviewers of Opus 7 recognized the conventional four-movement structure but neither praised nor better understood the music as a result. The most symphonic of procedures—thematic recall from earlier movements—went unnoticed. Unmoored from secure tonal foundations, Schoenberg's Opus 7

[6] Letter to Strauss, 16 July 1909, quoted from Reinhold Brinkmann, "Arnold Schoenberg. Fünf Orchesterstücke, Op. 16," in *Komponisten des 20. Jahrhunderts in der Paul Sacher Stiftung*, ed. Hans Jörg Jans (Basel: Paul Sacher Stiftung, 1986), 63.

[7] Schoenberg to Busoni, Aug. 1909, in *Ferruccio Busoni: Selected Letters,* ed. Antony Beaumont (London: Faber & Faber, 1987), 389, 392–397; see also the excerpts in Oliver Strunk, ed., *Source Readings in Music History*, gen. ed. Leo Treitler (New York: W. W. Norton, 1998), 1283–1289.

[8] Schoenberg to Kandinsky, 24 Jan. 1911, and Kandinsky to Schoenberg, 6 Feb. 1911, in *Arnold Schoenberg, Wassily Kandinsky: Letters, Pictures, and Documents,* ed. Jelena Hahl-Koch, trans. John C. Crawford (London: Faber & Faber, 1984), 23, 27.

[9] Arnold Schoenberg, "Gustav Mahler" (13 Oct. 1912; revised 1948), in *Style and Idea,* 462.

would incur the wrath of conservatives who sought in music a validation of structure, hierarchy, and tradition. This ideal for symphonic structure required of the composer, and was supposed to capture in the music, a firm sense of self. As the Viennese critic Robert Hirschfeld explained, to "produce symphonic structure" a composer must "possess inner strength, composure, and the immense spiritual calm of shaping" and must think in terms of "continuity and progress on a straight course, following a line."[10] However, in a move that would make the quartet all the more difficult for such listeners, Schoenberg did not altogether reject the conditions of structural form. Rather, in a brilliant critique of tradition, he builds large forms from the very materials that were traditionally seen as resisting synthesis—counterpoint and complicated rhythms—and undercuts those forms at important points of juncture. Symphonic goals are virtuosically prepared, but never achieved in the expected manner.

Opus 7 fared no better in the liberal press, for it did not conform to that symphonic ideal either. Liberals celebrated logicality and directed debate in the Brahmsian tradition. Symphonic music meant counterpoint and thematic working—the "compelling interpenetration and disputation among musical ideas," in Julius Korngold's terms.[11] The abstraction of logic and tightly wrought and unified procedures could not be reached through the virtuosic independence of the contrapuntal lines found in Opus 7. Furthermore, its formal layout did not correspond to the notion of a symphonic "striving," a Goethean term connected with the emerging bourgeois musical culture in the first half of the nineteenth century.[12] By the end of the century, liberal critics had special claims on this notion, and they personified musical procedures, even individual movements or passages, as goal-oriented, praising the composer's approach in terms of its "striving." By contrast, conservative critics would denigrate a composer or musical work for giving the impression of striving. Only in specific contexts, such as the Bruckner revival and later under National Socialism, would the trope of

[10] Review of Mahler's Third and Seventh Symphonies, *Wiener Abendpost*, 5 Nov. 1909, from the Vondenhoff Nachlass, Music Division, Austrian National Library, Vienna.

[11] Review of the Viennese premiere of Mahler's Fifth Symphony, *Neue Freie Presse*, 12 Dec. 1905.

[12] The trope of "striving" was very important to the writings of Friedrich Rochlitz in the *Allgemeine Musikalische Zeitung*, the preeminent example of bourgeois musical culture in the early half of the nineteenth century; the trope also figures prominently in a Viennese essay that develops the precepts for an educated musical public, "Über Musik-Pflege," *Morgenblatt für gebildete Stände* 2, no. 9 (11 Jan. 1808).

striving assume wider political significance. In Opus 7 Schoenberg abandoned the end-accented formal archetype expected for symphonic striving. He favored a classical model much like the *Eroica,* with a weighty first movement and the lighter rondo-finale. An extraordinary buildup of tension reaches no structural pillar, but assumes the immateriality of energy, which suddenly dissipates. The quartet thus defied the liberal notion of a striving across the symphony, such as the archetypal musical progressive Paul Bekker propounded in his writings beginning in the 1910s. It would only be from the vantage point of 1912, after Schoenberg had severed ties with tonality, that Korngold decided Opus 7 should have been harmless to early listeners, as "a one-movement form, striving after certain symphonic orchestral forms, encircles the usual four sonata movements in a free blending."[13] Yet even this constrained appreciation of the symphonic as a kind of form rather than as a set of procedures was not echoed among colleagues.

Most critics, conservative and liberal alike, did not perceive any symphonic qualities in Opus 7. Without an aesthetic framework, the shifts between synchronic and diachronic perception in the quartet (between grasping the work as a whole and experiencing the immediacy of its materials and procedures) had an explosive result. Schoenberg was not alone in his attempt to break down artistic materials into their basic components. Picasso's *Demoiselles d'Avignon,* the prototype of cubist art, was first exhibited a few months after the premiere of Schoenberg's quartet. Was the attempt to grasp Opus 7 as a single movement perhaps as frustrating as trying to process the jagged planes of a cubist painting as representational? Critics at liberal newspapers would often expect a quartet to confirm the individual as subject by developing ideas as a demonstration of logic and a sustained expression of emotions in a way that upheld objective communication. Thus for the reviewer at Vienna's *Sonn- u. Montags Zeitung,* the stipulation of a single movement "signifies that loss of self-control to the highest degree, no longer subjectively controlled by formal considerations"—no matter that the four "usual" movement types were easy to identify within the one. The "idea of sonata form," this reviewer continued, is contradicted in the development of material and the proportions between sections "in a way that scorns the idea of chamber music." Opus 7 lacked the moral qualities of predictability and constancy (in pulse) and moderation (the "rhapsodic" mode of expression, the dissonance and registral extremes). "Rough contrasts

[13] Unidentified clipping dated Apr. 1912, Arnold Schönberg Center, Vienna [hereafter cited as ASC]. In all likelihood the source is the *Neue Freie Presse.*

bursting onto one another, the continuous ripping and joining together" focus attention on the detail, not the whole ("a disunified, disjointed expression").[14]

Subjectivity, immediacy, and disunity were also common points of attack in the reception of Mahler's symphonies and Strauss's *Salome* during these very years. But the problem was intensified in the case of Schoenberg's Opus 7. The quartet remained the last bastion of tradition in the new century, a genre still associated with *Hausmusik* and performed in a smaller public forum than symphonic music or opera. The projection of a subject, a logical mode of thought, was especially important in the quartet, where the traditional model was a conversation among rational persons—unlike the corresponding model for the symphony, of a sublime that overwhelms and uplifts the listener. When the Vienna Hellmesberger Quartet moved from a small hall into a larger one in the 1880s, and added powerful accents to their earlier delicate playing, the critic Theodor Helm lamented the loss of "true, pure, thoughtful chamber music."[15] Under the circumstances, it is not surprising that the cultural and aesthetic problems with the emancipation of timbre disturbed critics all the more in the "simple" genre of the string quartet. As Riemann's *Lexikon* warned, in chamber music the instruments should not be treated "orchestrally"; rather, the "chamber style" entails that detail work compensate for the limited range of sonorities and the "sameness of instrumentation."[16] The reviewer for the left-liberal *Illustriertes Wiener Extrablatt* reported of Opus 7: "It lasts an hour without interruption, tries to bring about orchestral effects in the simple string quartet, and also has no trace of logical unity of thematic development, and explodes the quartet movement into a thousand pieces."[17] For Albert Kauders, critic at the Viennese *Fremden-Blatt*, which was associated with the Ministry of External Affairs, the timbral effects seemed to threaten the very nature of the genre, and by extension the institution of music. Especially because quartet players must, more than other musicians, avoid "the attendant material sounds of tone production," Kauders said, the scoring in Opus 7 threatened to reduce music to mere noise.

14 *Sonn- u. Montags Zeitung*, 11 Feb. 1907, ASC.

15 Theodor Helm, concert report from Vienna, *Musikalisches Wochenblatt* 14 (1883): 388, quoted from Margaret Notley, "*Volksconcerte* in Vienna and Late Nineteenth-Century Ideology," *Journal of the American Musicological Society* 50, nos. 2–3 (1997): 443.

16 See the "Kammermusik" entry in the 1900 edition (retained in subsequent editions), quoted from Erich Reimer, "Kammermusik," in *Handwörterbuch der musikalischen Terminologie*, ed. Hans Heinrich Eggebrecht (Wiesbaden: F. Steiner, 1971–), 12.

17 *Illustriertes Wiener Extrablatt*, 6 Feb. 1907, ASC.

"The string quartet is flogged to reproduce orchestral effects in a cramped manner, even raped [*vergewaltigt*], inasmuch as such coloristic emanations should be achieved only through totally different tonal bodies.... Every use of individual sonority goes beyond the boundaries of its expressive possibilities, and its sonic peculiarity can serve only the cult of the ugly [*des Hässlichen*]."[18]

Listeners of Schoenberg's quartet faced two barriers to holistic perception. First, they experienced the scoring and the thematic treatment as *physical* procedures, so immediate in effect that no conceptualization of a schematic plan or larger structure was possible. Second, without the rubric of conventional tonality, without clear harmonic goals to showcase the thematic material, the motifs and even longer themes seemed to slip away, elusive as they shimmered in vibrant color or contrapuntal tension. For August Püringer, Opus 7 lay on the border between music and noise, as "a wholly smashed mosaic of short and small bits of phrases, rubbing one another and falling through one another."[19] Metaphors of painting, colors, even mosaics, proliferated among Viennese supporters of Mahler and Strauss, but with Schoenberg the colors would not coalesce. The quartet was doomed to be experienced as individual voices interacting in a way that was rawly physical and hence unproductive.

Violent images of a mosaic shattered or a quartet sonority raped were perhaps encouraged by the programming of Opus 7 in Vienna with Schubert's C Major Quintet. Schoenberg's quartet would seem all the more fragmented as critics such as Kauders compared it to the "heavenly" music by Schubert that followed. Critics attending the 1907 festival of the Deutsche Tonkünstlerverein in Dresden did not perceive a violent clash in the diachronic and synchronic facets of Opus 7, but precisely how the form should be experienced remained a problem nonetheless. If Opus 7 was an "unequivocal failure," as the reviewer at *Die Woche* suggested, the reason was less the "extravagance" in harmony and counterpoint than "its formal impossibility."[20] Although Schoenberg used the usual theme types, the critic at the *Berliner Börsen-Courier* explained, his attempts to intertwine them into a "unified, uninterrupted movement—so the composer himself says" could not be justified. The fundamental laws of form must be observed; the "formlessness" of Opus 7, all agreed, was dangerous. "No one processes [*verarbeitet*]

[18] Albert Kauders, *Fremden-Blatt*, 11 Feb. 1907, ASC.

[19] August Püringer, "Musikbrief aus Wien," *Allgemeine Musik-Zeitung*, no. 12 (22 Mar. 1907), ASC.

[20] "Musikwoche,"*Die Woche*, no. 28 (1907), ASC.

with impunity the material of a four-act drama into *one* act"—perhaps an allusion to the one-act *Salome* from the previous night at the festival.[21]

The programs at the Dresden festival were devoted to new music, where formal listening would be more difficult than with classical repertoire in any event. Opus 7 opened a program of lieder sets by Walter Courvoisier and Wilhelm Kienzl and a trio by Wilhelm Rohde. In this context, Schoenberg's quartet posed a very different challenge from the superabundance of aural stimuli that Viennese critics perceived as violent. The review by the Leipzig critic Alfred Heuß shows how programming decisions may have influenced interpretation. Heuß, rather than evaluating each program in turn, discussed together the three most noteworthy works from the festival. These include the work most enjoyed by audiences, orchestral variations entitled *Kaleidoscope,* composed by a man unknown to the festival critics, Heinrich Noren; Heuß's own favorite from the festival, Bernhard Sekles's Serenade for Eleven Solo Instruments; and Schoenberg's quartet, which caused a "sensation." Despite its unrefined title, *Kaleidoscope* was "one of the most brilliant modern orchestral works," wrote Heuß, "full of exuberant joy," a composition both "concentrated" and yet "improvisatory in the good sense." With chamber music, however, Heuß had very different expectations. "If surprise plays a large role with [*Kaleidoscope*],...then with [the Serenade] one lives with a still, beautiful *Musizieren*, one can breathe fully and totally." Sekles succeeded in the enrapturing effect of the sonority (flute, oboe, clarinet, horn, bassoon, string quintet, harp), along with "the thoroughly careful, clean working [*Arbeit*] and his strong love for diatonicism." For both works, the terms of praise derived from a subject-centered aesthetic experience—surprising the listener or representing the fullness of human consciousness. By contrast, according to Heuß, Schoenberg's quartet was inscrutable, its problems emblematic of the modern condition. The "monochrome sonority wears on one's nerves." As if unable to decipher a larger course to the music, Heuß felt that "above all, what is entirely missing in the string quartet are issues which it seems to take on and wants to solve."[22]

Heuß's monochrome impression was more than an example of bad reception, more than a failure to cede Schoenberg's vivid timbral effects. He

[21] F. Z., "Aus dem Musikleben," *Berliner Börsen-Courier*, 3 July 1907, ASC, Vienna.

[22] Alfred Heuß, "Musikberichte," unidentified source, ASC. See also Hans-Joachim Gehrke, ed., *Alfred Heuß, Ansichten seines Lebenswerkes. Beiträge des Symposions "Alte Geschichte und Universalgeschichte, Wissenschaftsgeschichtliche Aspekte und historiseh-kritische Anmerkungen zum Lebenswerk von Alfred Heuß," Göttingen, 16. und 17. Mai 1996* (Stuttgart: Steiner, 1998).

drew on a trope of modernism as an indecipherable mass. In a pedagogical text from 1902, Felix Draeseke (b. 1835) explained that excessive innovation in harmony or in timbre leads to a loss of discrimination, as if colors are mixed into an "indeterminate gray." Modern music thus faced the same danger as urban society, captured by the common analogy of "an age of traffic"—not unlike the opening scene of Musil's *The Man without Qualities,* a novel about the Vienna of 1913. Instead, Draeske argued, music should be in primary colors.[23] Yet even as an older generation warned that excess and overstimulation lead to the dissolution of values and structure, a younger generation was discovering within the modern gray an abundance of color. Opus 7 inspired this very response in the twenty-six-year-old Arnold Zweig in his prose fragment "A Quartet Movement by Schoenberg" (1913). In it, Eli Saamen, a Russian Jew raised in Germany, prepares to leave a Europe that he finds stifling and empty in order to seek a more integrated life in Palestine. His final night in Leipzig, Saamen finds himself at a concert in which a Haydn quartet offers pleasant respite and a work whose composer he does not know (but is readily identifiable as Opus 7) suggests a new way of experiencing modern life. The music initially sounds "acerbic," until Saamen senses a sweetness in the acerbity, "just as the gray of a crowded street will under scrutiny decompose into a myriad of colors."[24]

Zweig must have heard the Berlin premiere of Opus 7 in 1912. By that point, neither sympathetic reviewers nor detractors lamented the absence of a subject in the music; rather, Schoenberg's novel articulation of form now provoked explanation through metaphors of science and physics. Zweig himself attempted to mirror Schoenberg's structural devices in prose. Saamen is introduced as a character alien in the old world. He finds the static monumentality of the architecture and statues in Leipzig to be stifling but enjoys the train station, which was then Europe's largest, as a large space with motion and space intersection ("its huge curved hall from iron gave him a pleasant surprise," 333). As a virtuosic example of the vitalism in the years before the World War I, the story shows that truth value exists only in action—in verbs, which capture the essential experiences of the performance of Opus 7. Images are proffered, but only as the material to explain the movement and action. There is no single subject, no hero in this music. Rather, it pulsates with life to the point of explosion. "It flows and flows, life breaks in

[23] Felix Draeseke, *Der gebundene Styl. Lehrbuch für Kontrapunkt und Fuge,* vol. 1 (Hannover: Louis Oertel, 1902), 5–6.
[24] Arnold Zweig, "Quartettsatz von Schönberg," *Novellen,* vol. 1 (Berlin: Aufbau, 1961), 336.

on all sides, hits in a cascade from violin to violin, lasts without rest, without end, without sleep, leaps over a precipice from cello to viola....It rejoices; the sounds; it breathes; their lungs; to moans, the rhythms of work rupture" (337–338).

In Zweig's account, the three most vivid images of modern life are each interrupted by the violin's lyricism, a refrain ("the violin sings, the violin") that structures the temporal flow of the quartet. The first image is visual, the modern counterpart to the nature scenes inspired by the Haydn quartet: "the electric cars on the asphalt of streets full of rushing traffic." Here the refrain leads to a melancholic state, which exposes the complexity of the music: "The light falls onto the foreheads, which furrow over the mathematical signs and rows of numbers, the rows of words of published books, and phrases are built in the brain which show logic, recognition, and truth." The second time the refrain interrupts a more advanced, scientific image: "Electric waves encircle the towers as an audible word around the globe." The final refrain, now in the form of an exclamation, shows the power of science to conquer a diseased world, much as Saamen aspires a release for the Jews living in an anti-Semitic Europe: "The doctor, stooped over wild sickness, researches tenaciously to eradicate them: the test tube, knife, dark-streaming ore—ah, the violin sings, the violin!" (336–337). The abrupt return of the violin refrain, as an infusion of humanity into the energy of the modern world, brilliantly represents Schoenberg's special use of performance indications in Opus 7. The extraordinary energy and complicated interaction of the four instruments led to a multitude of instructions for the execution of rhythm, tempo, and dynamics. But in the first movement he avoided any terms of emotional expression except at the second theme group (beginning with its lead in m. 57) at its three appearances (in the exposition, development, and recapitulation); the prominence of the violin at each of these thematic entrances corresponds perfectly to Zweig's focus on the violin singing. Here one finds various combinations of *zart bewegt, ausdrucksvoll,* or *espressivo, weich,* and *innig*—often intensified (*sehr*). Even in the middle movements, Schoenberg resorted to expressive markings merely to highlight the *Hauptstimme*—except, of course, when the second group is recalled within the third movement (L52). The final movement has no expressive markings whatsoever until the coda, which is marked *ausdrucksvoll.* The so-called hidden program of the quartet, discovered in sketches after Schoenberg's death, is no hermeneutic tool that contradicts this "subjectless" world; its fragmentary state, along with the avoidance of traditional expressive performance indications, suggests a displacement of musical meaning away from the human subject.

The programming of Opus 7 with late Beethoven (Opus 130) for the Berlin premiere may have encouraged critics to consider the experimental and novel course of the music. Although Zweig's enthusiasm was not shared by Berlin critics, through scientific metaphors they could more effectively capture the experience of listening to the music than did reviewers in 1907. The multiple perspectives in the quartet, with attention shifting from one instrument to the next in a buildup of momentum and energy, encouraged spatial descriptions. Spatial metaphors in general in the early twentieth century captured the intensity and complexity of musical perceptions that were not merely emotions or the abstraction of logic or a more spiritual transcendence. Insofar as spatialization involved motion *through* space, the listening experience became more all-encompassing than had been the case with the older metaphors of form as a process of spinning out or the segmentation of a schematic form. No longer, as in the century of the bourgeoisie, did musical listening promote a confirmation of the individual through such experiences as transcendence, emotional narratives, and visualization. Now the listener's state of consciousness, including sensations of movement and physicality, was reflected in the musical experience. At the same time, a spatial conception did not depend on the listener's perception to the degree that visualization did. Critics now discussed the musical work in terms of its "dimensions," as if the composition had an existence of its own, within space, independent of the listener.

By the Berlin premiere in 1912, therefore, a safe distance between listening subject and musical object could be explained in terms of dimensions, rather than by the old tropes of gesticulation and shimmering colors: instead of the flat planes of blended sonorities and logical development, Schoenberg presented a world shattered into different perspectives. One reviewer criticized Opus 7 for its lack of "wide stretches of two-dimensionality" but sarcastically conceded that such an ideal was "narrow and old-fashioned."[25] Einstein's theorizing introduced the idea of four-dimensional space-time. A critic at the *Berliner Börsen-Courier* suggested that Schoenberg's quartet was almost an application of "the modern principle, according to which each instrument is developed according to its independently speaking individuality until it is pushed to the extreme, where the conflict becomes completely aimless and breaks all form. The four-dimensional music exceeds our ability to perceive." But the critic ultimately resisted the scientific trope, which would become popular among the practitioners and French critics of

[25] "Quartett von Schönberg," unidentified clipping, Apr. 1912, ASC.

cubism, seeking refuge instead in the plain German of Goethe's *Faust:* "The inaudible is not heard."[26] More was at stake than a pun on the four players and their respective "dimensions" or parts. The fourth dimension, as was widely recognized by this point, is a mathematical construct that represents in diagram more than the three physical dimensions.

The metaphor of "breaking form" and shifting into a new dimension captured an important way in which Opus 7 diverges from the nineteenth-century tradition of combining the sonata form with the four-movement form (as exemplified, for example, by Schubert's "Wanderer" Fantasy, Liszt's B Minor Piano Sonata and symphonic poems, even Strauss's orchestra poems). The two formal archetypes are not so much blended but function as two planes between which radical shifts occur. Consider the shocking yet exciting point at G104 when Schoenberg uses harmonics and unusual, static patterns to divert the music from the conventional formal plan (Scherzo-Trio-Scherzo) into another realm—namely, into the developmental and recapitulatory sections based on material from the first movement. After the extraordinary symphonic buildup across the preceding eighty measures (G20–103), the pizzicato into which the final gesture dissipates seems to push the listener from the standard progression of sections into a new dimension where forty-five minutes can be encompassed in one movement.

Schoenberg superimposed two formal schemes, a complicated one-movement plan and a conventional four-movement archetype, without sealing the joints, without aligning the structural points into a single ongoing course. No listener, regardless of training or ability, could follow the music without expectations being overturned. The violent tropes of early critics captured the vitality of Opus 7 more effectively than did Schoenberg's own musings on its innovations and conventions. The power of their images validated the music even as their final judgments turned against it. Only gradually would this fragmentation of the subject in music, as in the other arts, be accepted down to its final ramifications: the recipient cannot gain full control over an artwork; total comprehension would flatten the vitality and complexity of the artist's creation. "In the course of years," one critic recalled in 1917, "[Opus 7] has lost all its terror.... Today this music no longer unnerves.... Its architecture has become crystallized. One perceives in the calm a noble work

[26] F. Z., "Aus dem Musikleben," *Berliner Börsen-Courier*, 3 July 1907, ASC; reprinted in *Breslauer Morgen Zeitung*, 4 July 1907, ASC. On the reception of Einstein and the possible connection with cubism, see Stephen Kern, *The Culture of Time and Space, 1880–1918* (Cambridge, Mass.: Harvard University Press, 1983), 145.

that takes Beethoven's late quartet style as its point of departure." Yet the writer sensed an important point: "This music has less power to overcome the clearer it becomes, the more its provocative problems dissipate."[27]

Still in 1920 Schoenberg criticized "modern-minded" listeners who "cling to the abstruse and only enjoy it if it remains unclear to them."[28] Only in 1933, that critical juncture for Schoenberg as German and Jew, artist and human, striving to make sense of political chaos and terror of the future, would the composer embrace incomprehensibility, returning to the image that encapsulated his First Quartet years earlier, in Berlin: "I am very happy that I understand Einstein as little as Kant, because then I can believe that there is something to it."[29] The artistic ideal long ago captured in his virtuosic adaptation of traditions would finally be recognized in theory, not only in practice.

[27] Unidentified review, 6 May 1917, Steininger Sammlung, Geheimes Staatsarchiv, Berlin.
[28] Letter to his students, 6 Dec. 1920.
[29] Arnold Schoenberg, "Neue und Veraltete Musik, oder Stil und Gedanke" (10 Feb. 1933), in *Stil und Gedanke. Aufsätze zur Musik*, ed. Ivan Vojtech, vol. 1: *Gesammelte Schriften* (Frankfurt am Main: S. Fischer, 1976), 477, quoted in Albrecht Riethmüller, "Hermetik, Schock, Fasslichkeit. Zum Verhältnis von Musikwerk und Publikum in der ersten Hälfte des 20. Jahrhunderts," *Archiv für Musikwissenschaft* 37, no. 1 (1980): 54.

LEWIS LOCKWOOD

On Schoenberg's View of the Beethoven Quartets

In 1891, after his father's death, the seventeen-year-old Arnold Schoenberg went to work in a bank. Suffering under the painful routine of banking duties, he soon found a way to cope by entering into the account books as a new customer the name of "L. van Beethoven."[1] The stratagem worked: he was fired. By enlisting Beethoven as an ally in his campaign to defend the inner domain of art against the crude pressures of the outer world, Schoenberg opened a lifelong dialogue with Beethoven that continued throughout his career as composer and teacher.[2] Through all the transformations of his artistic life, Schoenberg kept his sense of history perpetually before him, self-consciously defining his role as a misunderstood revolutionary whose work and thought were deeply rooted in the classic masterworks that he never ceased to study and to explicate to students and to the musical public in his teaching and writing. His relentless sense of artistic mission and of the need to raise the standards of musical comprehension within as well as outside the professional world of music only reinforced his identification with Beethoven as, of all his major predecessors, the one most dramatically associated with the transformation of traditional tonal language and the broadening of the framework of musical expression in his time, in ways that were still fully relevant.

[1] Alessandra Comini, *The Changing Image of Beethoven* (New York: Rizzoli, 1987), 20.

[2] On this aspect of Schoenberg's creative creed, see Reinhold Brinkmann, "Schoenberg the Contemporary: A View from Behind," in *Constructive Dissonance: Arnold Schoenberg and the Transformation of Twentieth-Century Culture,* ed. Juliane Brand and Christopher Hailey (Berkeley and Los Angeles: University of California Press, 1997), 197.

As Schoenberg's career unfolded, to be marked by ever-increasing public resistance, he could also identify with Beethoven's celebrated artistic isolation in his last years. Alexander Wheelock Thayer's emerging biographical portrait presented the mature Beethoven as primarily the deaf genius cut off from ready communication with the world around him, immersed in the creation of works too difficult to be understood by his contemporaries.[3] The parallel was obvious, and for Schoenberg the dilemma of isolation remained an *idée fixe* that sometimes found expression in anger, sometimes in irony. Thus he wrote in 1927, "I usually answer the question why I no longer write as I did at the time of *Verklärte Nacht* by saying, 'I do, but I can't help it if people don't yet recognize that fact.'"[4] We see the same Beethovenian isolation, as Reinhold Brinkmann has shown, in a self-portrait that Schoenberg painted of himself in 1911, in which he is seen from the back while walking on the streets of Vienna—exactly as Beethoven had been portrayed, walking in the same city, around 1820.[5] In fact, it is not too much to say that the modern view of Schoenberg that is epitomized in the writings of Adorno and Dahlhaus not only projects the themes of artistic isolation and public rejection as a basic parallel between Schoenberg and the late Beethoven, but that this powerful and magnetic Schoenbergian image itself has become a major influence on the ways in which many modern critics and scholars see the life and work of Beethoven, above all in his last years.[6]

[3] The first volumes of Thayer's biography, dealing with Beethoven's life up to 1816, appeared in German in translation by Hermann Deiters in 1866, 1872, and 1979; after some complications, the first version of Thayer's work that carried the biography to the end of Beethoven's life came out in Hugo Riemann's edition of volumes 4 and 5 of 1907–1908. See Elliot Forbes, preface to his edition of *Thayer's Life of Beethoven* (Princeton: Princeton University Press, 1967), v–xviii.

[4] Letter no. 95, of 12 February 1927, to H. Hinrichsen, head of C. F. Peters; in *Arnold Schoenberg Letters*, ed. Erwin Stein (Berkeley and Los Angeles: University of California Press, 1987), 124.

[5] Brinkmann, "Schoenberg the Contemporary," 196–220.

[6] See, e.g., Theodor Adorno, *Philosophie der neuen Musik* (Tübingen: J. C. B. Mohr, 1949, and later editions); and his fragmentary writings on Beethoven assembled as *Beethoven: Philosophie der Musik*, ed. Rolf Tiedemann (Frankfurt am Main: Suhrkamp, 1993), published in English as *Beethoven: The Philosophy of Music*, trans. Edmund Jephcott (Stanford: Stanford University Press, 1998). Dahlhaus's numerous writings on Beethoven include his book *Ludwig van Beethoven und seine Zeit* (Laaber: Laaber Verlag, 1987), published in English as *Beethoven: Approaches to His Music*, trans. Mary Whittall (Oxford: Clarendon Press, 1991). Both authors essentially portray Beethoven's late style and ambience as alienated from the traditional modes of artistic presentation familiar in Beethoven's earlier phases of work.

Growing up in Vienna in the 1880s and 1890s, Schoenberg came of age in a musical world uncomfortably divided between Brahms and Wagner, whose dominating roles were now being challenged by the emerging figures of Richard Strauss and Mahler. In the further background, what we now see historically as the classical triumvirate of Haydn, Mozart, and Beethoven was then radically biased toward the glorification of Beethoven, thanks to decades of image-making and virtual deification. As musical god and hero, Beethoven was the dominating master of the modern forms of expression in instrumental music—above all in his symphonies, sonatas, and chamber music—which now had either to be challenged or emulated, according to one's point of view, but either way remained basic. The Beethoven cult was reaching its heights: witness the many nineteenth-century Beethoven statues and monuments, perhaps most striking among them Max Klinger's celebrated marble sculpture of the naked, godlike Beethoven on a throne, created for the famous Vienna "Secession" exhibit of 1902, which Schoenberg certainly must have seen at first hand.[7] I can imagine that Klinger's sculpture could have presented Schoenberg with a paradox: on the one hand, it shows him as a superhuman figure; on the other, it presents the physical figure of Beethoven to a public that could value Beethoven's true musical significance only dimly and intuitively, not with the inner understanding of which Schoenberg dreamed.

Schoenberg reports that as he grew up he first played the violin; wrote a few violin duets modeled on Viotti and Pleyel; bought as his first scores the *Eroica* and Fourth Symphonies, the Opus 59 quartets, and the *Große Fuge;* and began to play chamber music under the aegis of Oskar Adler. Adler, though not a professional, was a gifted musician and quartet leader. Schoenberg later laughed at his early attempts to play the cello using violin fingering, but we also hear from Hans Keller, who played and studied with Adler, that at one session the teen-age Schoenberg dared to play Beethoven's Opus 18, no. 4, on a second-hand cello, but when it came to the high-register solo in the first movement he suddenly switched to a viola he had hidden nearby.[8] This might have more than comic overtones, as shown by the recent suggestion, by Anne Stone, that the finale of Opus 18, no. 4, could have been the model for the finale of Schoenberg's Wind Quintet, op. 26, of 1924.[9]

[7] See Comini, *Changing Image of Beethoven*, dust jacket front and back, pl. 10, and 388–410.
[8] Hans Keller, *The Great Haydn Quartets* (New York: George Braziller, 1986), 14ff.
[9] Anne Stone, "A Beethoven Model for an Early Twelve-Tone Work of Schoenberg" (paper read at the annual meeting of the American Musicological Society, Oakland, Calif., 1990).

That the young Schoenberg rapidly assimilated the modern language of extended tonality is clear from his early programmatic works. But when he turned to the string quartet he was accepting a historically greater challenge, namely, to stand up to the tradition that stretched back from Brahms to Haydn, with Beethoven's quartets as the central foundation of the nineteenth-century phase of the development. In the 1890s Beethoven's late quartets were only beginning to be accepted and appreciated, and another generation had to pass before they began to gain a real foothold in recitals. As Adolf Loos put it in a satirical article in 1913, in Beethoven's time audiences had ascribed the dissonances of his late works to his illness and his bad ears, but now, a century later, audiences themselves must have developed the same bad-ear illness because they were now ready to accept these dissonances as normal.[10] But what they certainly could not yet accept were modern radicals like Schoenberg who claimed to be in the mainstream but wrote at levels of harmonic complexity that could cause hostility and even riots, as at the first performances of Schoenberg's first two quartets.

Schoenberg came to grips with the Beethoven quartets in three ways: as performer, as pedagogue, as composer. The first way, as performer, was vital in the early years and no doubt always remained in his consciousness, but it soon gave way to his stronger vocations as composer and as theorist and teacher, areas in which Schoenberg's activities were probably more comprehensive than had been the case for any major composer since Rameau.[11] In his voluminous theoretical and critical writings, Beethoven, as we would expect, plays a substantial role, and passages from the quartets appear repeatedly as primary compositional models. As early as his *Harmonielehre* of 1911, Schoenberg includes significant references to both middle and late quartets, especially to Opus 59, no. 2, Opus 127, and Opus 130. In his chapter on "Fluctuating and Suspended Tonality," for example, Schoenberg cites the opening of the finale of Opus 59, no. 2, of which he writes: "Beethoven begins in a sort of C major which, however, keeps reaching over toward E minor....Indeed (because C is somewhat distant) it reaches over for the most part even as far

[10] Adolph Loos, "Die kranken Ohren Beethovens," in Nuria Nono-Schoenberg, *Arnold Schoenberg, 1874–1951: Lebensgeschichte in Begegnungen* (Klagenfurt: Ritter, 1992), 120. Loos dedicated the article to Schoenberg.

[11] That Schoenberg no longer played chamber music in his middle to later years is clear from a poignant letter to Oskar Adler written on 2 July 1949, when he was seventy-five: "I have heard that you still play in quartets a lot, which I haven't done any more for a long time now..." (*Letters*, no. 242).

as the dominant of the dominant (f♯–a♯–c♯) which can almost be construed as the dominant itself." He then continues, with characteristic pride: "Since then, there are good classical models, I do not have to be ashamed of producing something of this sort myself."[12] Whereupon Schoenberg cites his own use of fluctuating tonality in such early works as the orchestral song op. 8, no. 5, "Voll jener Süße," which, he says, wavers principally between D♭ and B major; and the song op. 6, no. 7, "Lockung," which expresses E♭ major without ever presenting an E♭ major triad as tonic. The whole of the *Harmonielehre* is permeated with Schoenberg's defense of artistic originality, and even the revolutionary, as he anchors both in a disciplined knowledge of the past. He writes, "Artists, those who submit to such necessities [the search for true originality] and cherish them, are accused of all possible crimes that can be culled from the rubbish of the political vocabulary." What is truly new is always nourished by tradition assimilated at a deeper level than the public can usually comprehend; as Schoenberg puts it, "No one loves his predecessors more deeply, more fervently, more respectfully, than the artist who gives us something truly new; for respect is awareness of one's station and love is a sense of community."[13]

To keep this discussion to a reasonable length I will certainly not list or describe Schoenberg's many citations of the Beethoven quartets but will focus instead on a few revealing passages. In the posthumously published treatise *Der musikalische Gedanke*, Schoenberg again returns to Beethoven's Opus 18, no. 4, for examples of melodic formation and elaboration.[14] Elsewhere, discussing the role of an introduction in establishing the basic material of a movement or a composition, he first invokes "La Malinconia," the mysterious introduction to the finale of Beethoven's Opus 18, no. 6; then he turns to the harmonic fluctuations of the opening of Opus 59, no. 3; and his final example comes from the opening slow introduction to the "Harp" Quartet, op. 74. Let us look briefly at his analysis of Opus 74.

This introduction is famous for its harmonic ambiguity at the very beginning. Starting with the tonic chord of E♭ major in root position, it immediately

[12] Arnold Schoenberg, *Theory of Harmony*, trans. D. W. Adams (New York: Philosophical Library, 1948), 383.
[13] Ibid., 401.
[14] Schoenberg, *Der musikalische Gedanke* (*The Musical Idea*), with both original German text and English translation, ed. and trans. Patricia Carpenter and Severine Neff (New York: Columbia University Press, 1995), 188ff.

Example 1

Poco Adagio
Violin I
Violin II
Viola
Violoncello
soto voce
soto voce
soto voce
soto voce
6
cresc.
cresc.
cresc.
cresc.
11
espr.
espr.
p
f
16
p
f

Example 1 (continued)

Example 2

deviates to the subdominant by introducing the flat seventh, D♭, first in the cello and then in the first violin, suggesting the subdominant A♭ major as an immediate goal. Now Schoenberg writes:

> the third measure begins with an E♭-triad that lacks the seventh, as if a previously unresolved D♭ had not been left hanging! Measure 7 (viola) and measure 8 (cello) bring forth the opening motive under a continuing upper voice, thereby shaping the two-bar unit into a quasi-one-bar (resolution!). For the rest, the preparatory function is completely clear (see Exx. 1 and 2).[15]

With remarkable subtlety Schoenberg follows the initial harmonic conflict between the opening E♭ major tonic chord and the destabilizing D♭ that pulls the harmony toward the subdominant; then he traces the consequences of this struggle for the rest of the introduction and the Allegro that follows. Measure 3 of the phrase repeats measure 1 and the first violin moves again to D♭, but now the harmonic tension moves up a significant notch by virtue of the diminished seventh harmony under that D♭ (m. 4), introducing chromatic motion and suggesting further ramifications that will be picked up later in the movement. The D♭ in the first violin moves chromatically up to D♮ at m. 5 while other chromatic tones hold the pressure. Schoenberg then focuses on mm. 7–8, where the viola and cello present slightly altered versions of the opening motif from m. 1, showing that what had been a two-bar phrase is now reduced to one bar. His music example then demonstrates how mm. 11–13 further carry out the implications of the earlier situation, dramatically refocusing on the D♭ in m. 13 when it suddenly erupts in an unexpected forte chord on the third beat. Schoenberg sees at m. 13 a retrograde form of the opening motif (witness his two arrows). And in the rest of the example he shows how the eighth-note theme of the opening of the Allegro (Violin II, mm. 26–29) flows directly from the *espressivo* motif of mm. 11 and 12, while he also suggests a similar derivation for the bracketed motifs in Violin I, mm. 28–29.

The same kinds of insights abound in his discussions of Beethoven's F minor Quartet, op. 95, and especially the late F major Quartet, op. 135. In the first movement of Opus 135, which he discusses in various parts of the treatise, Schoenberg uses close motivic analysis to discern germ ideas that will have far-reaching consequences. As Patricia Carpenter and Severine Neff observe, "What mattered ultimately was not so much the discovery of a relationship as the comprehension of how that relationship was revealed during the course of the work."[16]

[15] Ibid., 187–189 (Opus 18, no. 4), 283 (Opus 18, no. 6; Opus 59, no. 3; and Opus 74).
[16] Ibid., 39. The discussions of Opus 135 are at pp. 39–43, 154–155, and 244–245.

In the essays collected in *Style and Idea*, Schoenberg picked up the same issues. Opus 59, no. 2, and Opus 95 again figure prominently; their striking uses of initial semitone relationships and strongly pointed tonal contrasts rose immediately in Schoenberg's memory as he looked for examples that prefigured his own procedures. The late quartets were of course rich sources of material for him, in view of their stress on linear and contrapuntal relationships, their obscure formal structures that deviate in countless ways from the abstract norms, and their use of dissonance and harmonic mixtures. The A minor Quartet, op. 132, comes up several times, as does the *Große Fuge*. But the place of honor is again reserved for Opus 135, a central example in his seminal essay "Composition with Twelve Tones" of 1941. In this important elucidation and defense of the twelve-tone "method," Schoenberg finds in Beethoven a major father figure. Turning to the finale of Opus 135, he shows how the heading for the movement first presents its initial three-note figure and is at once transformed into the twice-stated motif with the enigmatic motto "Muss es sein? Es muss sein!" (Exx. 3 and 4). He then goes on to show its main uses in the Allegro, first as principal subject and then in its continuation figure (mm. 5–6, 7–8). To quote the essay, "The original form, *a*, 'Muss es sein', appears in *b* inverted and in the major; *e* shows the retrograde form of this inversion, which, now reinverted in *d* and filled out with passing notes in *e*, results in the second phrase of the main theme."[17]

It is no accident that in the same essay Schoenberg juxtaposes the Opus 135 finale with his own Chamber Symphony, op. 9, written in 1905, long before his arrival at the twelve-tone method. Here he grapples head on with the question that he knew many would raise about the Beethoven example, namely, could Beethoven really have been aware of such relationships? From his own experience he writes that at first he worried about the possible absence of connection between the two principal themes of his Chamber Symphony:

> Directed only by my sense of form and the stream of ideas, I had not asked such questions while composing; but as usual with me, doubts arose as soon as I had finished. They went so far that I had already raised the sword for the kill, taken the red pencil of the censor to cross out the theme b. Fortunately I stood by my inspiration and ignored these mental tortures. About twenty years later I saw the true relationship.[18]

[17] Schoenberg, "Composition with Twelve Tones," in *Style and Idea: Selected Writings of Arnold Schoenberg*, ed. Leonard Stein, trans. Leo Black (Berkeley and Los Angeles: University of California Press, 1984), 221f.
[18] Ibid., 222f.

Example 3

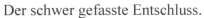

Der schwer gefasste Entschluss.

Example 3 (continued)

Example 4

Beethoven, String Quartet, Op. 135, 4th movement

Example 4 (continued)

Kammersymphonie, Op. 9, E major

He goes on to show that theme *b*, despite its complexities, is in its principal tones an inversion of the principal tones of theme *a* (see Ex. 4).

His lifetime dialogue with Beethoven, begun in the bank, comes to fruition years later. This prescient self-awareness, this surrender to the stream of ideas and to the musical impulse combined with a longing for the strongest organic connections, is fully characteristic. It is probably also true that, when Schoenberg looked at his favorite Beethoven works for models akin to his own ways of thinking, he would certainly have been aware of the emergence of the earliest serious scholarship on the Beethoven sketches, drafts, and autographs, which had first appeared in the later nineteenth century as he himself was coming of age. Schoenberg knew the publications of Gustav Nottebohm, the pioneering scholar of the Beethoven sketchbooks, and he was probably aware that Nottebohm, who died in 1882, had belonged to the circle around Brahms, himself a famous collector of Beethoven manuscripts. We can be sure of this because Schoenberg's library contained the 1924 reprint of Nottebohm's two long essays on single sources: the "Kessler" sketchbook of 1801–1802 and the "Eroica" sketchbook of 1803–1804. The latter sketchbook is the main source for our knowledge of the genesis of the *Eroica* Symphony, not only a major lifetime model for Schoenberg but one of the explicit antecedents for Schoenberg's own First Quartet, as he himself later declared.[19]

Schoenberg's indebtedness to the Beethoven quartets is of course most powerfully represented in his own string quartets. But because the four quartets and the String Trio extend over a vast span of his development, from early to late, I limit the discussion here primarily to one work: the First Quartet, op. 7, in D minor, composed in 1904. It was Schoenberg's later view that the First Quartet embodied a break with the programmatic late Romantic styles of *Verklärte Nacht* and *Pelleas und Melisande* and moved his work decisively in the direction he felt he could follow. He said of the first quartet that

[19] The bibliography of Schoenberg's music library shows the entry for the Nottebohm reprint. See *Arnold Schoenberg Institute Archives: Preliminary Catalog*, sec. 3, 170. I am indebted to Karen Painter, who examined Schoenberg's copy for me. Schoenberg also owned various editions of the Beethoven letters, as well as the short biography by Ludwig Nohl, *Beethoven* (Leipzig: Reclam, 190-) [date as given in the catalog]. In the Nohl book Schoenberg's underlinings, as indicated by the catalog, consist only of references on pp. 16–17 to Mannheim performance styles and the exact observation of fortes and pianos. His reference to the *Eroica* Symphony as one of the sources for the First Quartet is found in the essay "Bemerkungen zu den vier Streichquartetten," in *Stil und Gedanke. Aufsätze zur Musik*, ed. Ivan Vojtech, vol. 1 of *Gesammelte Schriften* (Frankfurt am Main: S. Fischer, 1976), 410.

in this work "I combined all the achievements of my time...the building of extremely large forms; very extended melodies connected to a richly moving harmonic language and new sound-progressions; and a contrapuntal technique which solved the problem that resulted from the interwoven layering of independent voices that moved in a very free tonal scheme and often encountered one another in wandering harmonies."[20] All of these ideas—freely moving voice-leading, contrapuntal techniques, and advanced harmonic language—define essential features of the late Beethoven quartets, and it is therefore no surprise to learn that another of the basic models for Opus 7 was Beethoven's C♯ minor Quartet, op. 131.

In what ways and within what limits does this relationship obtain? First, in scope and connection of movements: both works consist of a series of interconnected movements that have no formal breaks from start to finish. Opus 131 is unique even among the last quartets in its apparent seven-movement scheme. I say "apparent" because the numbering of movements has its own paradoxes. One movement, no. 3, is a short transition of only eleven bars, and another, no. 6, is best understood as a twenty-eight-bar introduction to the Finale, even though it is in the dominant minor. Beethoven's deployment of the extended movements in a grand progressive tonal scheme is more idiosyncratic here than anywhere else in his output. This must have given Opus 131 a special appeal for Schoenberg, as for Wagner before him, as he sought to build on this model and formulate in his own language an even more unusual combinative formal structure. His solution to the problem of large-scale formal unity entails the simultaneous interplay of two large basic formal designs. One consists of a set of movements in the familiar classical four-movement plan: an Allegro first movement; a Scherzo; a slow movement; and a Rondo finale. Schoenberg binds all the movements together through thematic relationships and at the same time spreads a single enormous sonata-form structure over all four movements. Thus the first movement contains an exposition, first development, and a first recapitulation; the Scherzo reprise turns out to present a second development and a second recapitulation; and a final third recapitulation emerges between the slow movement and the Rondo finale. The formal components cohere in various ways when seen from various angles, not unlike the planes of a cubist painting. The work has a basic tonality of D minor, but its rich chromaticism and avoidance of cadential articulations brings it to the borders of traditional tonality.

[20] Schoenberg, "Bemerkungen," 410.

In Opus 131 the initial movement is a fugal Adagio, neither traditional nor strict in fugal structure but sharing with other late Beethoven fugal movements the gradual emergence of its dynamic formal plan from its contrapuntal content. The fugue develops in phases of harmonic direction that prefigure some of the basic harmonic goals of the whole quartet. As many analysts have noted, only this quartet in all Beethoven's works presents a succession of keys so remarkable: C♯ minor; D major; the short transition from B minor to E major; A major; E major for the Scherzo; G♯ minor for the introduction to the finale; and finally a return to the C♯ minor tonic, long delayed, in the Allegro finale. Furthermore, the close derivation of the basic thematic material from the initial subject of the opening fugue is a hallmark of this work, and thus it served Schoenberg as a Beethovenian model possessing tight thematic and motivic unity over a vast time span—a perfect exemplar of his own compositional ideals.[21] It is also possible that the movement plan of Schoenberg's First Quartet is a kind of free rearrangement of the movement plan of Opus 131, with a fugue now placed as the transition between the first movement's Group l and Group 2 themes. A similar fugal texture appears at the transition in recapitulation I (C35–49).

The dense content of the First Quartet has never been described more tellingly than by Alban Berg in his celebrated essay from 1924, "Why Is Schoenberg's Music So Hard to Understand?"[22] There Berg could bravely say about this work that its opening ten bars were "no longer considered impossible or difficult to comprehend," but the fact is that for many casual listeners even now its tonal language is not easy. Even Berg admitted that "if at a first hearing one wishes only to recognize the main voice and follow it through to the end of these ten bars, to feel the whole as a single melody, which is what it is and thus ought to be just as whistleable as the opening of a Beethoven quartet—if that is what the listener wants to do, I am afraid he will be faced

[21] On this complex topic, see first of all Schoenberg's own writings both theoretical and critical; for a good précis, see Patricia Carpenter and Severine Neff, "Schoenberg's Philosophy of Composition: Thoughts on the 'Musical Idea' and its Presentation," in Brand and Hailey (eds.), *Constructive Dissonance*, 146–162.

[22] Originally published on 13 September 1924 in *Musikblätter des Anbruch* for Schoenberg's fiftieth birthday; English translation in Willi Reich, *Alban Berg*, trans. Cornelius Cardew (New York: Harcourt, Brace & World, 1965). On the First Quartet and its indebtedness to Beethoven I profited from Margaret Notley, "With a Beethoven-Like Sublimity: Beethoven in the Works of Other Composers," forthcoming in *The Cambridge Companion to Beethoven*, ed. Glenn Stanley (Cambridge, 1999); I am grateful to Dr. Notley for providing me with this essay prior to publication.

with problems of comprehension as early as the third bar." Berg noted the characteristic asymmetry of the phrase structure—the avoidance of simpler symmetrical two- and four-bar subphrases—to which he ascribed any difficulties listeners might have with the quartet. Later in the essay Berg rewrites the opening in a simpler style as a sample of what Schoenberg could have done if he had been willing to pander to popular taste. The result is a travesty, as Berg intended.

As to the later quartets, from the new landscape of the Second Quartet of 1908 with its vocal finale, to the Third Quartet of 1927, the Fourth of 1936, and the String Trio of 1946, their relationship to Beethovenian models is inevitably buried much further below the surface than is the case with the First Quartet, but one can at least observe that in matters of large-scale formal planning along classicist lines and in their integration of thematic material, they continue to bear witness to Schoenberg's deep and continued study of the late Beethoven quartets.

In this essay I have very partially framed a vast topic: Schoenberg's assimilation of the Beethoven quartets as a body of work that informs his thinking at every stage of his complex musical development. Christopher Hailey comments, "Few composers have been so shaped by their identification with a canon—which for Schoenberg served as both his own artistic frame of reference and the source of those criteria by which he insisted that others judge the meaning and value of his works."[23] As Oskar Kokoschka put it in a letter to him, "Your cradle was Beethoven's *Große Fuge*."[24] It is no accident that the Beethoven quartets, especially the late quartets, were basic elements in the repertoire of the Kolisch Quartet, who regularly programmed them together with Schoenberg's quartets; nor is it surprising that the Kolisch tradition of preferring the *Große Fuge* as the finale of Opus 130 was associated with Schoenberg's views. The persistent presence of the Beethoven quartets in Schoenberg's lectures and writings, from Vienna to Berlin to Los Angeles, along with his recognition of their fundamental status as monumental antecedents and counterparts to his own works, only confirms the impression that these works influenced Schoenberg's heart and brain right to the end.

[23] Christopher Hailey, "Schoenberg and the Canon," in Brand and Hailey (eds.), *Constructive Dissonance*, 164.
[24] Quoted by Leon Botstein, "Music and the Critique of Culture," ibid., 3.

Appendix

Beethoven, String Quartet in C# Minor, Op. 131 Movement —plan

1.	Adagio man non troppo	C# minor	[Freely organized fugue]	121 mm.
2.	Allegro	D major		198 mm.
3.	Allegro moderato	b---E	[Transition]	11 mm.
4.	Andante ma non troppo e molto cantabile	A major	[Slow mvt: Variations]	277 mm.
5.	Presto	E major	[Scherzo]	498 mm.
6.	Adagio quasi un poco abdabte	G# minor	[Introduction to Finale]	28 mm.
7.	Allegro	C# minor	[Finale]	388 mm.

[The absence of full stops at the ends of movements assures the continuity of the whole work; although Beethoven numbered the movements in the corrected copy he sent to his publisher, it seems clear that "No. 3" is a short transition, and the "No. 6" can be construed as an extended introduction to the Finale; thanks to the work of Robert Winter on the sketches for the work we know that its planning entailed as many as five different movement-plans, and that the essential components of the formal conception were the opening fugue, the variations slow movement, the scherzo, and the finale. That the subject of the opening fugue furnishes the intervallic content of all subsequent principal themes is a long accepted truth about the work which also underlies its basic organization as one gigantic formal structure subdivided into contrasting movements.]

Schoenberg, String Quartet in D Minor, Op. 7 **Movement —plan**

The work is organized in two concurrent cycles; 1) in the traditional four-movement form of first Allegro movement; Scherzo; slow movement; rondo finale; and 2) as a single enormous sonata-form structure spread out over these four "movements." The close intervallic relationships of all later movements to the basic thematic content of the first movement underlies and lends unity to the whole, very much in the manner of Beethoven's Op. 131 although with indebtedness as well to such works as Liszt's B minor Piano Sonata.

The following overview is indebted to Walter Frisch, "Thematic Form and the Genesis of Schoenberg's D-Minor Quarter, Op. 7," JAMS, XLI (1988), p. 292.

	Four-mvt. form	Sonata Form	Rehearsal Letters in Score
1.	[Allegro] Nicht zu rasch	*Exposition*	
		Group 1	
		Transition [fugato]	A 1
		Group 2 themes	A 56
		Development I	B 1
		Recapitulation I	
		Group 1	C 1
		Transition	C 35
		Group 2	C 49
2.	[Scherzo] Kräftig		
	Scherzo		E 1
	Trio		F 44
	Scherzo reprise	*Development 2*	G 34
		[Groups 1 and 2]	H 1
		Recapitulation 2	I 38
		[Group 1]	
3.	[Slow mvt.] Mäßig		
	A section		K 1
	B section		K 52
	A′ section		L 1
		Recapitulation 3	L52
		[Group 2]	
4.	[Rondo finale] Mäßig		
	A section		M 1
	B section		M 26
	A′ section		M 48
	C section		N 1
	A′′ section		N 68
		Coda	O 1

Perspectives on the Works:
Six Studies

MICHAEL CHERLIN

Motive and Memory in Schoenberg's First String Quartet

As would be true of any enduring piece of music, there are multiple ways to think about what matters most in Schoenberg's First Quartet: the genesis of the work's themes as the quartet unfolds and the ways they form familial relations as well as the conflicts and contrarieties that any family must have; the work's prodigious use of counterpoint, and the concomitant technical and expressive solutions to problems that lesser composers dare not even attempt; the complex and elusive sense of harmony and voice leading, an aspect of early Schoenberg that after nearly a century still confounds theorists; the question or questions about the work's relations to a larger tradition of string quartet composition; the many different voices that emerge out of Schoenberg's unifying voice—shadows of Beethoven, Schumann, Liszt, Wagner, Brahms, Mahler, Reger, and probably others that I haven't yet recognized; the place and force of this work in Schoenberg's creative evolution. All of these questions, and more, provide substantial and fertile ways to focus on Schoenberg's Opus 7. Although this essay will touch on some of these topics, its primary focus is on the work's musical form. Or perhaps I should say, its musical *forms*, for Opus 7 is not a static, singular object; its formal unfolding is full of wonder and surprise, and surprise precludes and undermines the kind of stasis that the singular "form" seems to indicate.

To state the obvious, Schoenberg's music is grounded, from beginning to end, in the craft and many of the assumptions of his precursors. In particular, the embedding of multiple movements in a single movement form is a problem that is inherited from Beethoven, Liszt, and others. It is the formal problem that Schoenberg sets for himself in every one of his early large-scale compositions, and a problem that he returns to at end of his life in the String

Trio and the Phantasy for violin and piano. An interrelated set of problems that Schoenberg also inherits from the nineteenth century might be characterized as the problematics of *memory.* Concerns with the nature and impact of memory are particularly significant among the multiple changes in perspective and focus that distinguish the Romantic worldview from that of the Enlightenment. This is true of Romantic poetry as it is of music, as it is of historical narratives. Even more forcefully, it can be argued that Romantic music, especially in Germany and Austria, is an encoding of memory and consciousness itself. The forms of Romantic music mimic the processes of coming to know, the processes of anticipation and recollection that form consciousness, or self-consciousness. It's no wonder that Schopenhauer thought that music was a direct representation of the "Will." The problematics of memory are inherited from the Romantics by the generation that fills the first half of the twentieth century. In a sense, *all* of the writings of Sigmund Freud are about the problematics of memory. In literature, the play of memory is central for James Joyce, Marcel Proust, and Thomas Mann. And the music of Schoenberg, and his students, as well as that of Stravinsky and his students, each in its own very different way, uses new forms and processes that find new ways to play on our sense of musical memory, both within works and as those works participate in larger traditions. Of course, the perception of musical form, *any* musical form, is bound up with the problematics of musical memory. Schoenberg recognizes this in his essay "Brahms the Progressive": "*Form in Music* serves to bring about comprehensibility through memorability."[1] Musical themes and their generative constituents, musical motives, are the primary means through which musical memory is forged.

The title of this essay is a pun on the title of a book by the philosopher Henri Bergson, in its English translation: *Matter and Memory.*[2] Bergson, who had his heyday in the early part of the twentieth century, was a philosopher well known to the Second Viennese; yet although Schoenberg had the German edition of *Matter and Memory* as well as four other books by Bergson in his library, the fact that not all of the pages in his copy of *Matter and Memory* are cut seems to indicate that the book was not exactly at the top of his reading list.[3] And so, I am not about to present a Bergsonian reading of

[1] Arnold Schoenberg, "Brahms the Progressive," in *Style and Idea*, ed. Leonard Stein, trans. Leo Black (Berkeley and Los Angeles: University of California Press, 1984), 399.

[2] Henri Bergson, *Matter and Memory*, trans. N. M. Paul and W. S. Palmer (New York: Zone Books, 1991).

[3] My thanks to Therese Muxeneder, archivist for the Arnold Schönberg Center in Vienna, for this information.

Schoenberg. Nonetheless, I do think that a distinction that Bergson makes about two types of memory is useful in coming to terms with the form of Opus 7. Bergson's categories are useful because they are inherently musical, not because Schoenberg was a Bergsonian.

At one point in *Matter and Memory* Bergson describes the process of memorizing a passage.[4] The student reads the material over the course of several occasions, and at the end has committed the passage to memory. The final "knowing by memory" is the result of a cumulative effect. To recall the passage, the student need not explicitly recall the several study sessions that led to the passage being memorized. Nevertheless, there *are* the memories of having studied the passage, the specific memories of having come to know it. The one type of memory is the accumulation of the past that informs the present as it is oriented toward the future. The other type of memory self-consciously and selectively reflects back on the past, and brings it into the context of the present, sometimes to anticipate a future. The second type of memory brings a particular kind of focus to information presumably available but not consciously recollected in the first.

In the temporal unfolding of a musical composition, there is generally a sense that the ongoing present is informed and motivated by the cumulative past. This is like Bergson's first type of memory (and this is an attitude implicit in David Lewin's development of his "interval function").[5] In addition, music also has the ability to make us recollect specific passages within the work. In doing so we remember their original place and impact, and self-consciously relate what *is* happening to what *has* happened. This is like Bergson's second type of memory. It is through the variables of projecting an ongoing, cumulative past, which in turn stimulates selective recollections of that past, both recent and remote, that composers create our sense of musical form. I find the play of these two types of memory to be particularly apposite in understanding the form of Schoenberg's Opus 7.

For Bergson, time and space are radically different kinds of things. His title *Matter and Memory* is meant to suggest a disjunction, rather than a conjunction, of the two. He claimed that our understanding of time is sullied by conceptualizing time spatially, as something extended. In contrast, Schoenberg's discussions of form and function in music are often spatial in their orientation; his concept of tonal regions and his discussions of phrase shapes provide clear examples. And though he writes about memory, here

[4] Bergson, *Matter and Memory*, 79–83.

[5] See David Lewin, *Generalized Musical Intervals and Transformations* (New Haven: Yale University Press, 1987), especially 88–104.

and there, for example in the passage from "Brahms the Progressive" that I have already cited, the role of memory is not particularly well addressed in Schoenberg's pedagogy.

In the course of this essay, my approach will try to mediate between spatial and temporal aspects of musical form. To insist that music unfolds in time, not space, is like insisting that bachelors are unmarried men. It doesn't tell me much. In fact we do experience the time of music as suggesting musical spaces; aspects of our common parlance, such as references to thematic areas, or even to pitch as high or low, indicate as much. On the other hand, composition can contain thematic or motivic references that leap over established musical spaces and that function to evoke recollective memories that cut across boundaries of time and space. In sum, I will suggest that the perception of musical form, and the form of Opus 7 in particular, is based on the interaction of memories that define musical spaces, on the one hand, and memories that challenge and in some sense redefine those spaces, on the other.

Schoenberg's program notes of 1906 and their revision in 1936 are a good place to start. The program notes provide an overview of the work's formal design and a catalogue of its principal themes. Table 1 outlines Schoenberg's presentation, omitting musical examples and adding measure numbers.[6] Schoenberg begins his 1906 analysis with a caveat:

> The following analysis distinguishes between four parts; they are not, however, four separate movements, but rather connected sections which blend into one another. To be sure, the thematic types are those of the traditional four movements, but their intricate structure is an attempt to create a single unified, uninterrupted movement.[7]

The paragraph stands in opposition to the rest of the essay as a warning that the formal overview that Schoenberg will be able to provide cannot sufficiently address the most central aspect of the work's formal design, the integration of multiple movements into a single movement form. Nonetheless, the program notes are useful in getting a general orientation toward the piece.

Schoenberg's outline divides the work into four principal sections. In sum these correspond to the movements that might have constituted a string quartet by Haydn or Mozart: sonata, scherzo, adagio, and rondo. While the

[6] The program notes are included in Ursula Rauchhaupt, ed., *Schoenberg, Berg, Webern: The String Quartets, A Documentary Study* (Hamburg: Deutsche Grammophon Gesellschaft, 1971), 11–13, 35–42.

[7] Ibid., 11.

Table 1

Analytic Outline of the First Quartet
Based on Schoenberg's Notes of 1936 [and 1906]

Part One: Sonata

I. Principal theme group
- a. opening bars
- b. mm. 14ff.
- c. mm. 24ff.

Transitional
- Rehearsal A ff.

II. Subsidiary Themes (2d Theme Group)
- a. 57 after A…
- b. 71 after A…
- c. reformulations of IIa at 82 after A and at B

Development and Transition
- Rehearsal B to E

Part Two: Scherzo

Scherzo: Rehearsal E
Trio: Rehearsal F
Concluding Section: Rehearsal G
Development: 34 after G to 38 after I
Recapitulation of the Principal Theme Group: 38 after I

Part Three: Adagio

Main Theme: Rehearsal K
Middle Section: 52 after K
Repetition of First Adagio Theme [actually a contrapuntal combination of both themes, which functions as a development —M.C.]: Rehearsal L
Transition: 24 after L
Recapitulation of the Subsidiary Theme Group and Transition: 52 after L, 78 after L

Part Four: Rondo Finale [Description from 1906 Analysis]

Reformulation of First Adagio Theme: Rehearsal M
Reformulation of Second Adagio Theme: 26 after M
Reformulation of Principal Scherzo Theme: Rehearsal N
Small Development of Rondo Themes: 35 after N
Closing Group
- Using the Opening Theme Its Companions and the Scherzo Theme: Rehearsal O to the End

division of the whole into four parts is central to Schoenberg's formal overview, even in this bare-bones outline there are aspects that modify or even disrupt what might have been a more typical four-movement design. Most noticeably, the Sonata movement does not recapitulate its principal and subordinate theme groups after its development section. Instead, Schoenberg places the recapitulation of the Sonata's principal theme group at the end of the Scherzo, and the recapitulation of the Sonata's subordinate group at the end of the Adagio. In this respect, primary articulators of musical form are displaced so that they interpenetrate the embedded movements. Moreover, even a cursory examination of Schoenberg's themes reveals that the first theme of the Scherzo is introduced in the transition between the two theme groups of the Sonata and that the Rondo derives its themes from the Adagio and then goes on to include the principal Scherzo theme, finally closing with material derived from the opening of the Sonata.

In short, even the basic thematic catalogue of Schoenberg's program notes can give us some indication of the ways in which the composer has associated the quasi-independent movements to create a larger dramatic and structural design. Nonetheless, the most salient aspect of Schoenberg's outline remains the division of the whole into four parts, and the division of those parts into thematic areas that correspond with traditional forms. Part 1 contains the two opposed thematic areas of a sonata. Part 2 is a scherzo including a trio section and a modified *da capo*. Part 3, the Adagio, is constructed as an ABA form. And Part 4 is a concluding Rondo.

Figure 1 is a schematic of the form extrapolated from Schoenberg's program notes, purposely disregarding the important interpenetration of thematic content that we have already noted. As Schoenberg's warning predicted, the schematic does not capture the formal complexity or the formal unity of the whole.

The dotted lines between the principal sections are a clumsy attempt to show that the sections "blend into one another." Assuming that this blending is done through transitional material—and we shall subsequently see that this assumption is quite inadequate to the form—the figure shows the four movements connected like box cars in a freight train, with only their couplers to keep them from drifting apart. Figure 1 clearly fails as a model for the kind of form that Schoenberg has achieved.

Figure 1

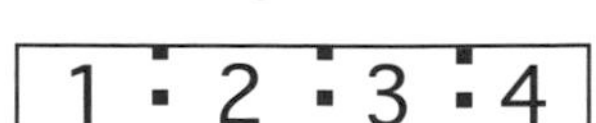

In contrast to Schoenberg's notes, Anton Webern's program notes of 1912 make a concerted effort to describe the single-movement form.[8] An outline based on Webern's notes is shown in Table 2. It is a fair assumption that

Table 2

Analytic Outline of the First Quartet Based on Webern's Notes of 1912

Two sections Precede the Big Development [G34 to I38]:

A main sonata movement [Schoenberg's Part 1], with a long fugato [A to A56] separating the Principal and Subsidiary themes
[Webern does not mention the development section of Reh B to E in this context but assumes this first development later in his analysis]
The Scherzo and Trio [E to G34]

Following the Development:

Recapitulation of Principal Theme [I38 to I80]
Adagio [K to L38]
Recapitulation of the Subsidiary Theme [L52]

And at end:

Rondo Finale [M to end]

Webern had noticed that the unity of the single-movement form was not well addressed in Schoenberg's notes. His comments on this crucial aspect of the piece are particularly interesting:

> At bottom the form of the Quartet is that of a single enormous sonata movement. The Scherzo and the big development are interpolated between the first development [B to E] and the recapitulation, while the recapitulation itself is extended by the Adagio between the Principal and Secondary Themes. In this scheme the Rondo-Finale can be considered as a greatly expanded Coda.

In order to characterize the entire work as a large-scale sonata movement, Webern's analysis highlights the recapitulations of the Sonata's Principal and then Subordinate theme groups, which we have noted as being embedded respectively in Schoenberg's Scherzo and Adagio, giving them a structural

[8] Ibid., 16.

emphasis that is not explicit in Schoenberg's thematic catalogue. Then, in order to make sense of all the intervening and subsequent material, Webern characterizes the Scherzo as an interpolation, the Adagio as a cadential extension, and the Rondo as coda. Figure 2 reduces Webern's view to a schematic drawing.

Figure 2

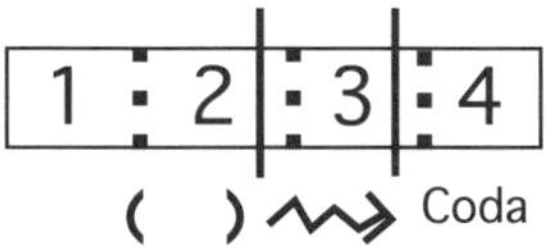

While Figure 2 addresses aspects of a single-movement form not well addressed in the schematic of Figure 1, for most listeners it is at the cost of intuitive plausibility. The Scherzo, Adagio, and Rondo simply comprise too much musical matter to be relegated to the status of parenthesis, cadential extension, and coda. Nevertheless, Webern was on to something. The work does have the unity that Schoenberg claimed for it. And, moreover, that unity *is* based on principles that Schoenberg had learned from studying the dynamics of sonata form.

Early in the nineteenth century the premier expositor of sonata form, Adolph Bernhard Marx, had viewed the form as a dialectical unfolding wherein the Principal and Subordinate themes were conceptualized as the basis for opposition as well as higher unity.[9] I would suggest that principles not so very different from the ones described by Marx underlie the dynamics of form in Schoenberg's Opus 7. But Schoenberg's basic opposition is not between the Principal and Subordinate themes of the sonata; it is between the work's two halves. A schematic of this opposition and higher unity is given in Figure 3, which in turn is stimulated by David Lewin's work on transformational networks.[10]

[9] Marx's dialectical description of a musical period is originally found in *Die Lehre von der musicalischen Komposition*, vol. 1 (Leipzig: Breitkopf & Härtel, 1841). In English translation, the passage is found in *Theory and Practice of Musical Composition*, trans. and ed. Herrman S. Saron (from the third German edition) (New York: Mason Brothers, 1860), 88. Marx's description of sonata form is found in *Die Lehre von der musicalischen Komposition*, vol. 3 (Leipzig: Breitkopf & Härtel, 1845), 217–218.

[10] Lewin, *Generalized Musical Intervals and Transformations*, 157–244.

Figure 3

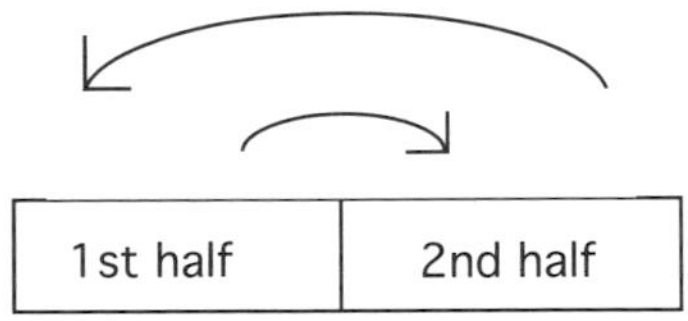

In conceptualizing Figure 3, I reduce musical functions in the work into two broad categories, each of which contains two opposed forces. The first category of functions is spatially oriented; it opposes functions that lead to individuation and closure versus those that assert the interconnectedness of the parts and the unity of the whole. While the comparison with Bergson's two memory types is inexact, we might say that space forming corresponds most closely with Bergson's cumulative memory. Within Figure 3, functions that lead to individuation are shown by the vertical lines that create boundaries. Functions that create unity are shown by the horizontal lines. A second category of functions is concerned with leaping over boundaries, and with an explicit orientation toward time. Within this category, one set of functions is engendering and anticipatory; it is denoted by the arrow moving left to right. An opposed set of functions is recollective and integrative; it is denoted by the arrow moving right to left. Both arrows reflect aspects of Bergson's recollective memory.

We can begin to fill in the schematic with content by considering the ways that Schoenberg articulates the formal divisions of the quartet. Toward these ends, I find three principal techniques. First, unity is created through thematic continuity and formal disjunction by thematic differentiation. Second, various levels of closure within the work are articulated by the varying size and force of motivic liquidations of the kind that Schoenberg describes in his pedagogy. Third, despite the harmonic ambiguity and instability that dominates this work, Schoenberg uses clear and strong points of harmonic arrival as major structural downbeats.

By all of these criteria, the strongest articulation internal to the piece is the arrival of the Adagio at Rehearsal K. As we have already noted, the first two movements are thematically bound together by the anticipation of the principal Scherzo theme within the sonata's transition. We have also noted that the Rondo derives its main themes from the Adagio. Here we can add that the Adagio themes, in mood as well as intervallic and rhythmic structure, are the single greatest departure from the opening material within the work. On thematic grounds alone, the quartet divides most basically into two halves. Moreover, the liquidation at the end of the Scherzo, just before the Adagio begins, is the largest liquidation of the piece, both in terms of sheer size and in terms of dramatic impact as the ensemble grinds its way down to the repeated Ds and then to the sustained cello solo that gives way to the Adagio. Finally, the beginning of the Adagio articulates A minor, the minor dominant for the piece, distinctively, if fleetingly, in a way that sets it apart from previous points of arrival.

On the other hand, the need to go on at the end of the first half is signaled by several principal means. There is the incompleteness of the initial sonata, as emphasized in Webern's analysis. There is no sense of harmonic closure. Moreover, given a sonata followed by a scherzo, Schoenberg trusts, I assume, that we will have the expectation of a slow movement and finale. The boundary of the first half necessitates the second half. The recollective memory that leaps over the boundary of the first half into the second is largely based on our knowledge of tonal forms, the forms used by Schoenberg's precursors. The single anticipatory and engendering arrow of Figure 3 indicates the need to go on at the juncture between the two halves. In dialectical terms, Schoenberg has engendered a first that needs a second.

At the end of the work, the final statement of the opening theme, radically transformed but instantly recognizable, has a recollective and integrative function. This, depicted by our right-to-left arrow, is the primary means through which the articulated or divided sections are brought back together into a larger unity. The recollective and integrative function embodied in the final statement sums up and in a sense remembers all of the recollective functions throughout the work. These functions operate in two basic forms. First, a series of recapitulations of the opening theme (and other themes as well) reflect back on successively larger and larger spans of unfolding formal design, perceived through cumulative musical memory. Second, Schoenberg intertwines contrapuntal reminiscences of earlier themes within the ongoing exposition or development of subsequent musical themes. Thus, concurrent and concomitant with the opening of new thematic space, Schoenberg is able to reach back into the work's past, integrating that past into the music's present. The remembering of the first theme at the very end is the last in a series of restatements, the passages Schoenberg characterized as recapitulations included. Each of these functions to recollect, through the perspectives of all that has happened in between, the entire work's unfolding, up until that point. The sublimity of the final recapitulation, at Rehearsal O, owes much of its power to the perception of the huge gulf of time and experience that separates it from the original statement. It carries the weight of the most fundamental recollective and integrative function in the piece; it gets its force from all that has happened remembered through it.

In sum, I believe that Webern was right to recognize sonata principles at work in the larger form of Opus 7, but he misses the call in thinking that the primary opposition lies between the Principal and Subordinate groups of Schoenberg's first-movement sonata. The synoptic opposition is between the two halves, and the most far reaching recapitulation is achieved in the stability of D major only at the very end of the work. In this sense, the work as a whole can be viewed as a larger sonata form.

Figure 4

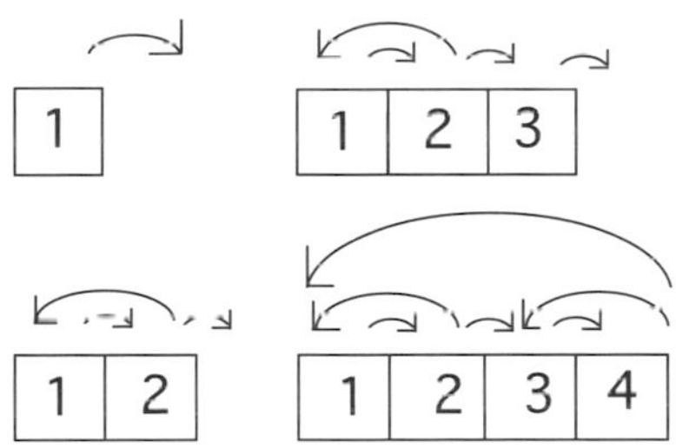

Figure 4, constructed along the lines of Figure 2, depicts the work in four different stages corresponding to Schoenberg's four parts. The first stage is from the perspective at the end of the Sonata. Although there are recollective and integrative functions within the movement, the schematic shows only the most basic engendering and anticipatory arrow, pointing into the space that will be filled by the Scherzo. This left-to-right arrow is the result of several combined forces: the recapitulation of the Sonata is incomplete, the Scherzo theme has been anticipated but has not yet been given thematic status, and the liquidation of the Sonata, at Rehearsal C to C30, is without harmonic closure.

The second stage of Figure 4 is located at the end of the Scherzo. The principal constituent of the recollective and integrative arrow, right to left, is the recapitulation of the Principal theme group of the sonata at I38. Like the final statement of the opening theme at the very end of the work, this recapitulation reflects back on the source of all that we have experienced within the piece up until this time. Reaching back through the Scherzo to the beginning of the Sonata, this arrow creates the larger unity of the first two quarters. In addition, stage two includes the anticipatory and engendering arrow that is carried over from the first stage as well as the arrow anticipating the second half, as in Figure 3.

The third stage of Figure 4 is located at the end of the Adagio. The figure omits the reflective and integrative arrow that is suggested by the recapitulation of the Sonata's Subordinate theme group, as well as other recollective functions within the Adagio, and instead emphasizes the most basic function of the Adagio as engendering and anticipating the Rondo.

The fourth stage reintroduces the overarching arrow, right to left, that we have already seen in Figure 3. In addition, a new recollective arrow connects the Rondo to the Adagio. This function is expressed generally through the relatedness of the Rondo themes to those in the Adagio, and more specifically through the double recapitulation of the Adagio/Rondo themes at N68, just before the final restatement of the work's opening theme at its close. The final stage of Figure 4 shows that the two halves are isomorphic with each other, as well as with the most fundamental dialectic, as shown in Figure 3.

The combination of spatial and temporal aspects in Figures 3 and 4 is suggestive of two approaches toward an understanding of musical form. The arrows, anticipatory and recollective, suggest a phenomenological account of the piece. This is from the vantage of traveling within the form and experiencing its various perspectives through a succession of now-times. On the other hand, the boxes, which denote the work's four parts, suggest an overview of the work, perceived in spatial terms, as an object outside of time or at least aside from its temporal unfolding. Whereas the formal overview tends toward the fixed and hierarchical, a phenomenological account will be based on changing perspectives of boundaries, both anticipated and recollected.[11]

The kind of contrast between the fixed and hierarchical versus the unfixed and changing nicely corresponds with distinctions between two kinds of space, conceptual and literal, that were defined by the philosopher Gilles Deleuze. In the formulation found in his book *Difference and Repetition*, Deleuze names his spaces *agrarian* and *nomadic* and associates the two spaces respectively with the ancient Greek ideas of *logos* and *nomos*, logos denoting fixity and order in the cosmos, and nomos, associated with the Greek word *nemo* (to pasture), denoting unfixed boundaries.

> A distribution of this type [i.e., agrarian space] proceeds by fixed and proportional determinations which may be assimilated to "properties" or limited territories within representation. The agrarian question may well have been

[11] See David Lewin, "Music Theory, Phenomenology, and Modes of Perception," *Music Perception* 3/4 (1986): 327–392.

> very important for this organization of judgement as the faculty which distinguishes parts ("on the one hand and on the other hand"). Even among the gods, each has his domain, his category, his attributes, and all distribute limits and lots to mortals in accordance with destiny. Then there is a completely other distribution which must be called nomadic, a nomad *nomos*, without property, enclosure or measure. Here, there is no longer a division of that which is distributed but rather a division among those who distribute *themselves* in an open space—a space which is unlimited, or at least without precise limits.... To fill a space, to be distributed within it, is very different from distributing the space. It is an errant and even "delirious" distribution, in which things are deployed across the entire extensity of a univocal and undistributed Being. It is not a matter of being which is distributed according to the requirements of representation, but of all things being divided up within being in the univocity of simple presence (the One—All). Such a distribution is demonic rather than divine, since it is a peculiarity of demons to operate in the intervals between the gods' fields of action, as it is to leap over the barriers or the enclosures, thereby confounding the boundaries between properties.[12]

While the two kinds of space can be used to distinguish among composers—for example, Bruckner strikes me as "agrarian," while Mahler's forms are more "nomadic" in tendency—for our present purposes I am interested in thinking of the perception of musical form as a dialectic between the two kinds of space.

Figure 5, in the form of a branching diagram, provides an "agrarian" overview of the entire work. A phenomenological orientation will subsequently provide a complementary and antithetical "nomadic" perspective. The Key to Figure 5 provides the reader with content for each branch. My discussion here will concentrate only on the most fundamental and far-reaching aspects of the diagram. The trunk in Figure 5 bifurcates into the work's two halves, and then again into its four movements. Each of these trifurcates into a three-part form, and the process of trifurcation occurs again for all branches of the Sonata and Scherzo, as well as for the leftmost branches of the Adagio and Rondo. At the lowest level, the leftmost branch of the Sonata trifurcates once again.

[12] Gilles Deleuze, *Difference and Repetition*, trans. Paul Patton (New York: Columbia University Press, 1994), 36–37. Deleuze and Félix Guattari rename and further develop "nomadic" and "agrarian" space as "smooth" and "striated" space in their book *A Thousand Plateaus: Capitalism and Schizophrenia*, trans. Brian Massumi (Minneapolis: University of Minnesota Press, 1987), 474–550 and passim. In this context the authors specifically associate their discussion with music and with ideas derived from Pierre Boulez, *Boulez on Music Today*, trans. Susan Bradshaw and Richard Bennett (Cambridge, Mass.: Harvard University Press, 1971). I find the earlier opposition of "nomadic/agrarian" more suggestive than the formal pair "smooth/striated" and use the earlier source for that reason.

Figure 5

OPUS 7 OVERVIEW

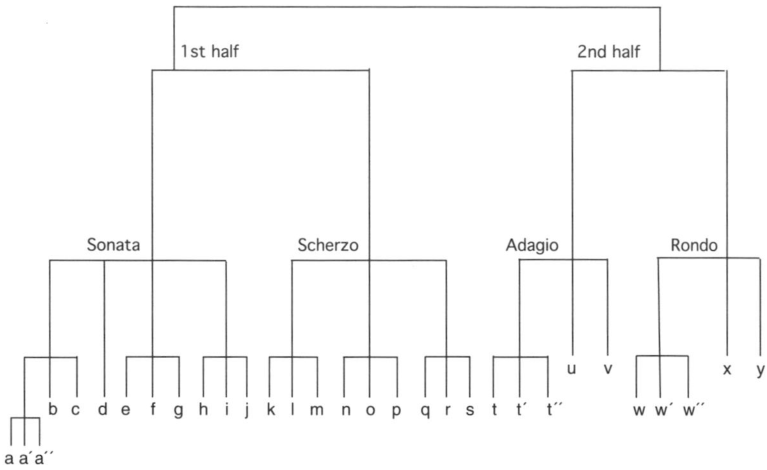

Key to Figure 5

Branch, Measures	**Formal Function**	**Salient Features**
a, 1–13	first Principal theme, "liquidation theme"	establishes d minor tonic
a′, 14–23	Second Principal theme	b♭ minor
a′′, 24–29	close of Principal group	V/e♭
b, 30–64	development of P	tonicize e♭ and c♯
c, 65–Rehearsal A	recap and liquidation of P	return to d minor
d, A–A55	transition to Subordinate theme group	anticipates Scherzo as well as first Subordinate theme
e, A56–A70	first Subordinate theme	begins in E♭
f, A71–A81	second Subordinate theme	begins in F, ends in A♭
g, A82–A103	close of S group	modulatory, cadences on A♭ and E♭
h, Rehearsal B	1st part of Development	waltz in e, based on S1
i, C–C30	2d part of Development	restate P1 in C♯
j, C30–E	end Development and transition to Scherzo	cadences on E♭ and D, includes transformations of P and S

k, E–E50	main Scherzo theme	in G♭
l, E50–E105	lyric Scherzo theme	unstable, homage to Brahms
m, E106–E133	close of Scherzo	to G♭
n, F–F79	first section of Trio	unstable
o, F80–F141	lyric Trio theme	to E, includes transformations of P2
p, G–G33	transition based on Scherzo theme	unstable, includes cadences on E and c♯
q, G34–G111	development of Scherzo	begins in c♯
r, H–I37	2d part of Scherzo development, liquidation of Scherzo	unstable, includes transformations of P1
s, I38–I80	recap of P and liquidation of the first half	return of d minor tonic
t, K–K51	first Adagio theme	a minor, includes transformations of S
t′, K52–K79	second Adagio theme	E major, include transformations of P1
t′′, L–L23	combine Adagio themes	f minor
u, L24–L51	transition of recap of S	unstable to V/B♭, includes transformations of P1
v, L52–L91	recap S group, transition to Rondo	unstable
w, M–M25	first Rondo theme	A major, transforms 1st Adagio; includes transformations of P1
w′, M26–M47	second Rondo theme	unstable, transforms 2d Adagio; includes transformations of P1
w′′, M48–M59	return of first Rondo theme	A major, return of 1st Adagio
x, N1–N89	development and liquidation of Rondo	F major, A major; includes transformations of Scherzo theme
y, O1–O51	close of entire quartet	D major, transforms P1

The patterns of branching—bifurcation at the highest levels and trifurcation at lower levels of structure—suggest nested symmetries, smaller forms embedded within the larger forms. In discussing Figures 3 and 4, we have already considered some aspects of the primary bifurcations. The trifurcation of the leftmost branch within each of the four movements is particularly salient; in each case the result is a miniature version of the larger three-part form.

The lowest three branches at the bottom left, labeled a through a´´, form a miniature sonata exposition, where branch a is the first theme (mm. 1–13), branch a´ the contrasting lyric theme (mm. 14–23), and a´´ the closing theme (mm. 24–29). A larger sonata form comprises branches a through c. Here, branches a through a´´ constitute the exposition, branch b is the development, and branch c is the recapitulation. At the next higher level of structure, branches a through c make up the Principal Theme Group, branches e through g are the Subordinate Group, and branches h through j represent the Sonata's development.

Similar kinds of nesting take place within the other movements as well. The leftmost branches of the Scherzo, k through m, form a miniature Scherzo-Trio-Scherzo, and the leftmost branches of the Adagio and Rondo each compose a smaller ABA form in the context of the larger ABA that constitutes the movement. In sum, the overview of a branching diagram suggests an orderly disposition of nested forms. Figure 5 presents a stable, hierarchical, and geometric conception of formal design.

A phenomenological perspective will result in a very different account. Here a space that has been traversed or anticipated is reconsidered in the context of a subsequent and larger frame of reference so that old boundaries are eroded or given new meaning as the piece unfolds. This aspect of experiencing musical form is somewhat analogous to experiencing architectural space, not through the overview of a floor plan but through the changing perspectives that we experience as we inhabit or walk through that space. The result is something in between Deleuzian agrarian and nomadic spaces. Perception centers on defining and delimiting space, but the boundaries are not stable and secure.

Needless to say, this kind of spatial revision affects the details of phrase design as well as larger aspects of form. Here I will concentrate on large-scale revisions. We recall that the opening of the work creates the initial space of a miniature sonata form. The rapid unfolding of the miniature sonata exposition suggests the kind of condensation that we associate with Schoenberg's music beginning with his next major work, the *Kammersymphonie.* The entire initial exposition, comprising first theme, its liquidation and transition to the second theme, the second theme's liquidation, and then the closing theme, all takes place within twenty-nine bars—about a single minute's worth of music. Even adding the first development, and then the recapitulation of the first theme along with its liquidation, we still have heard less than 3 ½ minutes of music altogether.

The experience of the opening exposition suggests a highly compact musical form, and the condensed development and initial recapitulation does little, if anything, to alter that perception. To all of this, the music that functions in our overview as the transition to the Subordinate group—branch d of Figure 5—stands in stark contrast. We can consider this transition as the initial passage of formal aporia. As I enter its space, through a last-moment twist in the shape of the liquidation motive, I experience a sense of formal disorientation. This is the place at which I come to doubt the force of my initial perceptions of space and place. The transition unfolds at a more leisurely pace than all that preceded it—in fact, it is nearly twice as long as the initial exposition—yet the passage is perceived as a transition nonetheless, and as such it is our first indication of the larger dimensions of the work to come. What had the force of the main hall gradually comes into focus as an anteroom, a status that will be revised again and again as ramifications and recollections of the opening material embrace larger and larger spans as the piece unfolds.

The other left-branch nestings, at the outset of each larger movement, result in similar kinds of formal revision. For example, in traversing the leftmost branches of the Scherzo, the second branch has the force of a contrasting Trio. The subsequent space of the larger Trio, branches n through p, forces a perceptual revision that negates our initial perception of functions and boundaries by placing the nested form into a larger, more comprehensive space.

A technique with implications similar to those involving nested forms occurs at branch h, the beginning of the larger Sonata development. Here Schoenberg gives us eighty-six bars of an unmistakable waltz. Granted, its motivic materials evolve directly out of the Subordinate group. Nonetheless, it is as though we have leapt directly into the dance movement. When the restatement of the first theme of the Principal group occurs, in C♯ at Rehearsal C, it undercuts the status of the waltz and brings it convincingly back into the space of Sonata development. As with our initial perceptions of a condensed sonata form and of a condensed scherzo, the force of this initial waltz at first suggests a radical foreshortening of space, which is negated by subsequent perceptions.

In sum, while the nesting of forms in our overview is suggestive of symmetry, hierarchy, and stability, the phenomenological results are asymmetrical and destabilizing. Yet there is another aspect of form that is even more "nomadic" in its implications, and that aspect is far less recognized by the branchings of Figure 5. This aspect of form derives from the interpenetration of themes across the formal boundaries of the movements. An early example of this technique within the work is the anticipation of the Scherzo within the transition between theme groups in the Sonata.

The transition introduces two new themes, albeit in incipient forms: the first theme of the Subordinate group and, more emphatically, the principal theme of the Scherzo. Anticipating the Subordinate group in the context of a transition to that group is more in line with the Deleuzian concept of "agrarian" form. This aspect paves a smooth transition into the next section of the

Table 3

Thematic Recollections of Sonata themes outside of 'Sonata space'

Measures	*Place in Formal Overview*	*Themes Recollected*
C30–E	transition to Scherzo	$P_{1,2}$ and $S_{1,2}$ in counterpoint with anticipations of the Scherzo theme
F80–F141	middle section of Trio	P_2 in counterpoint with dolce theme
H–I37	2nd part of Scherzo development	$P_{1,2,3}$ in counterpoint with Scherzo material
I38–I81	recapitulation of Principal group	P_1
K–K51	first Adagio theme	$S_{1,2}$ in counterpoint with first Adagio theme
K52–K79	second Adagio theme	$P_{1,2}$ in counterpoint with second Adagio theme
L24–L51	transition to recapitulation of the Subordinate theme group (middle of the Adagio)	P_1 transformations fill L38-L51 to lead directly to the recapitulation of S
L52–L91	recapitulation of the Subordinate group	$S_{1,2}$ in counterpoint with second Adagio theme
M–M25	first Rondo theme	P_1 in counterpoint with first Rondo theme
M26–M46	second Rondo theme	P_1 in counterpoint with second Rondo theme
O	close of the work	P_1 transformations

larger Sonata. The incipient Scherzo theme, however, is more nomadic in its force. And although it has transitory reappearances during the development of the Subordinate group and in the transition to the Scherzo, it is only at the Scherzo proper that the transition's principal motive finally takes on the solidity of a true thematic statement. In anticipating its "realization" as the Scherzo theme, the Scherzo motive of the Sonata transition leaps over the boundaries that separate the two movements, and suggests the larger opposition and unity of the Sonata and Scherzo.

The most profound aspects of this kind of thematic displacement involve transformations and recapitulations of the Sonata themes outside of the "Sonata movement." The passages that involve this technique are summarized in Table 3. Recalling Bergson's two kinds of memory, cumulative versus self-consciously recollective, we can say that the placement of these Sonata references outside of the initial "Sonata space" allows and requires them to function as musical recollections. These are the functions that we began to study in Figures 3 and 4 through our left-to-right arrows. Here we can add that such recollections are particularly "nomadic" in their implications. They override and disregard the boundaries of formal subdivisions, and, especially in those passages where Sonata recollections intertwine with the unfolding of new thematic space, rather than dividing space in the agrarian manner, they range through the space of a unified whole that resists being divided into parcels.

We have already considered the most basic aspect of this technique in discussing the recollective and integrative arrow of Figure 3. I have characterized the successive restatements of the first principal theme as summations that take us back to the beginning of the piece to recollect all that has transpired in between; at end, the closing of the work is a sublime reaching-over of its entire span. For my own closing, I would like to turn to the related technique, where thematic recollections intertwine with the ongoing exposition of new thematic material.

The first set of recollections in Table 3, the transition to the Scherzo, allows that passage to reach forward, as transition to the Scherzo, and reflect back in a quasi-coda-like way on the Sonata just past. At Rehearsal D, the transformation of the first Principal theme, marked *langsam* and *ausdrucksvoll,* not only recollects the motives of the work's opening, but in temperament it also anticipates the final recollective statement at the end of the quartet. Like the final statement, we can consider this a *sublimation* of the opening. The same technique is used during the Trio and Scherzo development. In each instance, sublimated references to the opening reach back to the beginning and anticipate the close.

The order of recollections is particularly interesting during the Adagio. As the Adagio's first theme unfolds, the counterpoint recollects the Subordinate group of the Sonata. And then as the Adagio's second theme unfolds, the counterpoint reaches further back to the Principal group. In sum, as the Adagio goes on, the recollective memories within it reach further and further back to the works origin.

Toward the end of the Adagio, the passage just before the recapitulation of the Subordinate group remembers the first Principal theme. Once again, this recollection is a sublimation of the opening. In its immediate proximity to the recapitulation of the Subordinate group it enlarges the space of recollecting beyond that of the recapitulation proper.

Although it is not included in Table 3, the Rondo can be understood as a recollection of the Adagio. Like the recollections of the Sonata throughout the quartet, it is as though the Rondo sees the Adagio in a new light. In this case, the Rondo as a whole performs the traditional role of comic reconciliation. In counterpoint with its comic recollections of the Adagio, the Rondo continues the series of sublimated references to the Principal theme group of the Sonata. Finally, the close at Rehearsal O completes the series of sublimated recollections, as I have said, by reaching back over the entire work. Indeed, by achieving a tonal stability nowhere else achieved within the work, we may say that the end reaches back beyond the work's frame to a tonic stability that Schoenberg's world, like that of Brahms before him, could only imagine in nostalgia, through the recollections of sublimated memories.

JUDITH RYAN

"Ich fühle luft von anderem planeten": Schoenberg Reads George

Two books first set me thinking about the complex relationship between modernism and aestheticism. The most provocative of these was Peter Bürger's *Theory of the Avant-Garde*, which appeared in Germany in 1974 but was not translated into English until 1984.[1] The second was Albrecht Dümling's *The Alien Sounds of the Hanging Gardens*, subtitled "The Public Isolation of New Music as Exemplified by Arnold Schoenberg and Stefan George," which came out in German in 1981 and remains untranslated, as far as I know.[2] Both books deal, in different ways, with the extraordinary intercalation of aestheticism and modernism. But while Bürger's study concerns the relation between the art-for-art's sake movement and the radical experimentation of Dada and surrealism, Dümling explores the continuities and ruptures within what in German is known as "die Moderne," a period that

[1] Peter Bürger, *Theorie der Avantgarde* (Frankfurt: Suhrkamp, 1974); *Theory of the Avant-Garde*, trans. Michael Shaw, foreword by Jochen Schulte-Sasse (Minneapolis: University of Minnesota Press, 1984).

[2] Albrecht Dümling, *Die fremden Klänge der hängenden Gärten: Die öffentliche Einsamkeit der Neuen Musik am Beispiel von Arnold Schönberg und Stefan George* (Munich: Kindler, 1981).

encompasses both the aestheticism of the late nineteenth century and the innovations of the twentieth-century modernist movements.[3]

Dümling's book presents an extremely subtle analysis of the problem—to express it in its simplest form—why Schoenberg, poised on the threshold of experimental modernism, should turn to George's aestheticist poetry for textual inspiration. The problem becomes even more sharply profiled when we recall, as Reinhold Brinkmann has pointed out, that Schoenberg's interest in George's poetry is coterminous with his own period of atonality, and only with that period.[4] On the most basic of thematic levels, one might posit some kind of kinship between George's claim to have created a new mode of poetic expression and Schoenberg's claim to have developed a "new music"—the idea in both cases of a pathbreaking creative innovation.[5] But the two types of newness are not congruent. Rather, their most fundamental tendencies run counter to each other. Martin Stern has argued that Schoenberg needed George's firmly structured poems to anchor his new atonality: George's "rhythm, sentence- and line-lengths, rhymes and stanzas provided and supplemented the structural scaffold that Schoenberg had abandoned, gave it support and set limits for it."[6] Plausible as this argument may seem in the abstract, it does not at all conform to what Schoenberg actually does with George's rigid forms.

Schoenberg is believed to have first come to know George's poetry in 1904 at a meeting of a group run by Conrad Ansorge and known as the "Ansorge-Verein." Founded in 1900, the Ansorge group was dedicated to bringing music and poetry together; at its meetings, poems were both recited and performed in musical settings. Ansorge himself was simultaneously a devotee

[3] The terminologies used by these two German scholars are not easily transferable into English. Bürger's distinction between "die Moderne" and "die Avant-Garde" is closer to Matei Calinescu's distinction between "modernity" and "the avant-garde" in the first edition of his book *Faces of Modernity* (Bloomington: Indiana University Press, 1977) than to the distinction between "modernism" and "the avant-garde" that has come into recent use, perhaps via Andreas Huyssen's *After the Great Divide* (Bloomington: Indiana University Press, 1986). Schulte-Sasse, in his foreword to Bürger's book, uses the term "modernism" where Bürger uses "die Moderne." Dümling speaks throughout of "die Moderne," i.e., the modern movement that began in the late nineteenth century, as does Reinhold Brinkmann in his various articles on Schoenberg.

[4] Reinhold Brinkmann, "Schönbergs Lieder," in *Arnold Schönberg: Publikationen des Archivs der Akademie der Künste* (Berlin: Akademie der Künste, n.d.), 46.

[5] Ibid., 47

[6] Martin Stern, "'Poésie pure' und Atonalität in Österreich: Stefan Georges Wirkung auf das Junge Wien und Arnold Schönberg," *Modern Austrian Literature* 22 (1989): 134..

of the naturalist poet Richard Dehmel and of the aestheticist Stefan George, rivals and apparent opposites on the contemporary lyric scene. Ansorge's music and poetry group, with its unique combination of interests, eased Schoenberg's transition from Dehmel to George, as Dümling shows. Schoenberg's specific knowledge of the two texts by George that he sets in the Second Quartet, op. 10, "Litanei" (Litany) and "Entrückung" (Rapture) is due to his pupil Karl Horwitz, who sent him copies of the two poems.[7]

First published in 1904 in George's trend-setting poetry magazine, *Blätter für die Kunst*, "Entrückung" was included in George's volume *Der siebente Ring* (The seventh ring) three years later. "Entrückung" is the final poem in a sequence in this volume titled "Maximin": these were poems of mourning for George's young friend Maximilian Kronberger, who had become a kind of godlike figure for George and his circle after George had met him in Munich and who died a year later at the age of sixteen. George describes him as one who even as a child "had been filled with seething divinations of the beyond."[8] Maximin was not only a symbol of "sacred youth," but also an "embodiment of world-creating eros."[9] After a series of epiphanic experiences that George, using a word closely related to the language of his poem, terms his "days of rapture," Maximin "passed from a fevered dream into death."[10] The "fever-ridden frenzy" of the third tercet of "Entrückung" doubtless refers to Maximin's final illness.

"Litanei," the other poem from this volume that Schoenberg set in his Second Quartet, is drawn from a cluster of poems grouped under the heading "Traumdunkel" (dream darkness) in *The Seventh Ring*—a group of poems that follows the Maximin group but continues the process of mourning the strangely divine youth. "Litanei," to my mind a far less interesting poem than "Entrückung," is nonetheless intriguing because of its unrhymed form and passionate expressive quality, held in bounds only by complex alliterative structures and vowel alternations. It would be interesting to know whether Schoenberg was aware that, in placing "Litanei" before "Entrückung" in his quartet, he was reversing the order in which they appeared in *The Seventh Ring*. Schoenberg's placement, in any event, makes "Litanei" a prayer for divine intervention and "Entrückung" a form of response.

7 Dümling, *Die fremden Klänge*, 176.

8 Stefan George, "Maximin. Ein Gedenkbuch" (Berlin: *Blätter für die Kunst*, 1907), n.p. [= p. 4].

9 Cited in Klaus Landfried, *Stefan George. Politik des Unpolitischen* (Heidelberg: Lothar Stiehm, 1975), 112.

10 George, "Maximin. Ein Gedenkbuch," n.p. [= p. 5].

Schoenberg's own comments on his setting of "Entrückung" in the fourth movement of his Second Quartet suggest that he understood at least the introduction to this movement as a kind of program music:

> The fourth movement, "Entrückung," begins with an introduction that depicts a departure from the earth to another planet. The visionary poet has anticipated sensations here that will perhaps soon be confirmed. Emancipation from gravity—drifting up through clouds into ever thinner air, forgetting all the travail of earthly life—all this will be portrayed in this introduction.[11]

Given that Schoenberg regarded his own free atonality as an "emancipation from gravity," there is no reason to limit our interpretation of this passage to the idea of space travel in the literal sense. Still, the "liftoff" experience Schoenberg describes here—space travel in a more metaphorical and capacious sense—is not at all remote from George's views at the time he composed the poem.

The text can be located precisely toward the end-point of George's "cosmic phase." The "Kosmische Runde" or "Cosmic Circle" was a group of writers and thinkers who gathered in Munich between 1899 and 1904. The charismatic center of this group was Alfred Schuler,[12] an archaeologist devoted to Johann Jacob Bachofen's mystic beliefs in the Magna Mater or Great Goddess.[13] Contemporaries who took part in the meetings of the Cosmic Circle have given amusing depictions of the group's festivals and their attempts to usher in a revival of ancient heathen cult practices.[14] The Cosmic Circle put on masques and masquerades, held banquets in classical costume, performed bacchanalia accompanied by wine and incense (and possibly mind-expanding drugs as well).[15] George attended four of these

[11] Schoenberg, "Bemerkungen zu den vier Streichquartetten," quoted in Dümling, *Die fremden Klänge*, 188.

[12] Wolfgang Frommel writes of Schuler's "außerordentliche Ausstrahlung" ("Alfred Schuler. Spuren heidnischer Gnosis," *Castrum Peregrini* 34 [1985]: 5–23).

[13] Their point of departure was Bachofen's *Das Mutterrecht* (Stuttgart: Krais & Hoffman, 1861). After the dissolution of the "Kosmische Runde," Schuler continued lecturing on ancient mysticism and the Orphic cults; his lectures exerted an influence on the later work of Rilke.

[14] See Roderich Huch, "Erinnerungen an Kreise und Krisen der Jahrhundertwende in München-Schwabing," *Castrum Peregrini* 110 (1973): 5–49. See also Franziska zu Reventlow's comic novel about the Cosmic Circle, *Herrn Dames Aufzeichnungen oder Begebenheiten aus einem merkwürdigen Stadtteil* (Frankfurt: Ullstein, 1987).

[15] See Marita Keilson-Lauritz, "Stefan George, Alfred Schuler und die 'Kosmische Runde.' Zum Widmungsgedicht 'A.S.' im *Jahr der Seele*," *Castrum Peregrini* 34 (1985): 30. She points out here also that George had also tried hallucinatory drugs before his involvement with the Cosmic Circle.

occasions, in 1899, 1903, and 1904, and his poem "Maskenzug" (Procession in costume) toward the end of *The Seventh Ring* evokes one of these gatherings, in which the procession is led by a veiled figure at once "man and mother with the lamp." [16] Indeed, the final poem of the volume can be read as an address to members either of the Cosmic Circle or of his own George Circle: invoking the farewell toast and the warm handclasps of friends as they depart, the speaker declares: "how I feel myself light, today, as never before, immune to friend and foe, ready for any new journey." [17] One kind of "new journey" is depicted in the poem "Entrückung."

George finally broke with the Cosmic Circle for two reasons. One had to do with prejudices and rivalries among the members of the two groups.[18] The other was George's belief that the "hidden powers" capable of creating a new type of art and transforming modern culture were ultimately not to be found in dionysian impulses. While both the Cosmic Circle and George urged a return to antique ideals, George promulgated a Hellenic, and thus more male-oriented, model. In the youthful Maximilian Kronberger, renamed "Maximin," George saw a reincarnation of the divine and an image of the new human being that was to be ushered into existence by the new poetry.

The poem "Entrückung" is located on the border between gnostic belief in a mother cult and a new promotion of manly ideals. Bearing this ambivalence in mind will help us come closer to the poem as it appeared to its first readers in 1904 and 1907. We can now start looking at the poem itself. The poem and my English translation are included at the end of this chapter. "Entrückung" is one of the most untranslatable texts I have ever wrestled with; and although I have tried to recreate some sense of the poem's rhythms and evocative power, there are many formal features (notably the rhymes) that I have not even tried to reproduce, and many semantic compromises I have been forced to make. Those who know German will have preferred the greater accuracy of a prose gloss; but I would like non-German speakers to gain some sense of how it feels to read this poem in the original.

"Feel" is a crucial word: it occurs twice in the poem, once in the first line and again at the end of the second-to-last tercet. The German verb "fühlen" includes both outer sensation and inner emotion. The whole poem turns on this combination of meaning. When Martin Stern, in his article on Schoenberg's setting of the poem, repeatedly misquotes the opening words as "ich

[16] *Der Siebente Ring*, 5th ed. (Georg Bondi: Berlin, 1920), 211.

[17] Ibid., 213.

[18] Ludwig Klages had angrily demanded that George break with the Jewish scholar and writer Karl Wolfskehl; see Frank Weber, "Stefan George und die Kosmiker," *Neue Deutsche Hefte* 35 (1988): 274.

spüre luft," he not only recurs to more idiomatic German usage ("spüren" is the word one would expect in this context), he also reduces the semantic range of the poem's opening, in which the air from the other planet is both experienced as a tactile sensation on the skin and felt as an emotive response within the psyche. By the same token, the title of the poem, "Entrückung," suggests both ecstasy and physical displacement. "Rapture" is a good equivalent, but "transport" would also have been possible. Although the speaker of the poem is about to take off for an alien realm, the poem's opening line implies not that the speaker is entering the airspace of another planet but rather that the air of the other planet is moving toward him from outer space. This ambivalence allows us to understand the experience as happening simultaneously in the outer world and in the world of the imagination.

George's precious turn of phrase, "von anderem planeten," where the definite article is omitted, suggests the radical otherness of the alien planet. As the speaker leaves the earth, or imagines he is leaving the earth, friendly faces and familiar landscapes pale away as the "bright beloved shadow" comes more clearly into focus. I should really have translated "Schatten" as "shade," since it refers to a dead person—specifically, Maximin—but the German formulation also turns upon the oxymoron "lichter...Schatten," "bright shadow." A similar paradox is at work in the third tercet, where the shade or shadow is said to be completely "extinguished" in "deeper radiance." The word for radiance, like the verb to feel, is also polysemic: it means both incandescence—the shining that emanates from light sources, including heavenly bodies—and ardor, the glow within the passionate human heart.

The beloved shade is called, at the end of the second tercet, "the summoner of my torments." Yet the transfigured dead loved one, at once "extinguished" and sublated into "deeper radiance," also summons the speaker on the journey that brings him close to the atmosphere (or aura, to use a more specifically art-oriented term) of the alien planet. The "frommer Schauder" or "pious shudder" registers this paradoxicality but at the same time transmutes it into something more conventional.

Following this transfiguration of the loved one, the speaking subject is himself dissolved into musical tones, circling or orbiting like a planet or the "harmony of the spheres," but also "weaving" like Goethe's Earth Spirit or Pater's perpetually fugitive self, "that continual vanishing away, that strange, perpetual weaving and unweaving of ourselves."[19] While Pater's formulation

[19] "Conclusion" to *The Renaissance*, in *Selected Writings of Walter Pater*, ed. Harold Bloom (New York: Columbia University Press, 1974), 60.

describes the self in its accustomed state, George uses similar imagery to depict the dissolution of the speaking subject and its fusion with a vaster, transcendental realm.[20] Pater's notion that, in the constantly shifting nature of reality as we know it, "all melts under our feet"[21] is transposed in George's poem to become a description of a sphere beyond everyday reality in which, as the penultimate tercet has it, "the ground is trembling white and soft as whey." In submitting to the "mighty breath," the speaker of George's poem not only comes under the influence of the "air" from the "other planet," but also suggests that this air is identical with divine inspiration (also usually figured as "breath"). Dissolution of subjectivity and emergence of creativity are here placed in tandem.

The "gusts" that now traverse the speaker are a more tumultuous manifestation of this divine breath. No wonder women fall down in prayer as the speaker undergoes this experience. The lifting mists and mountain passes[22] in the following tercet invoke even more clearly the notion of natural phenomena opening up to make way for an emerging illumination. Indeed, the subject, after clambering over monstrous chasms, now feels himself swimming through a sea that is at once a kind of amniotic fluid and the receiving light of another world. Again, the verb "fühlen" suggests both physical and mental feeling, sensation and emotion. "Swimming" (or floating, which "schwimmen" can also mean) is simultaneously a mode of bodily progress and a sense of intellectual disorientation. Images of clear lightness and shimmering whiteness suggest both clarity (the sun-filled space) and insecurity (the whey-like earth). The crystal brilliance through which the self "swims" is at once a solid and a fluid medium, water, as it were, in two states simultaneously. The poem concludes with a dual observation in which the subject sees itself as both light and sound, visual and acoustic splinters of the divine being itself. Yet the "holy fire" and "holy voice" are not just those of the godhead—they are also those of the "bright beloved shadow" and "summoner of my torments," now transfigured into aspects of the transcendent.

[20] I do not agree with Walter Frisch's view that the self "dissolves his identity into music's collectivity" ("The Refractory Masterpiece: Toward an Interpretation of Schoenberg's Chamber Symphony, op. 9," in *Constructive Dissonance: Arnold Schoenberg and the Transformations of Twentieth-Century Culture*, ed. Juliane Brand and Christopher Hailey [Berkeley and Los Angeles: University of California Press, 1997], 96).

[21] Ibid., 60.

[22] The meaning here, "schmaler weg zum durchschlüpfen für das Wild" (small path for wild animals to get through), is given in Jacob and Wilhelm Grimm, *Wörterbuch*, vol. 9 (Leipzig: Hirzel, 1899), 841, col. 1.

Read in this way, the poem is clearly situated on the border between the Cosmic Circle's belief in a cult of the dead and the notion of a great earth-mother,[23] on the one hand, and a more masculine concept of renewal through the spirit of a godlike youth who had died before his time, on the other. The erotic energies in the poem cross the boundaries between what was seen, in the early twentieth century, as "feminine" and "masculine" paradigms. Receiving the sacred touch or "breath" of the universe, the speaker surrenders unquestioningly and permits himself to dissolve into the cosmic harmony. Nature, too, engages in erotic interplay, as the sun-filled clearing "embraces" the distant mountains, and the ground beneath the speaker's feet trembles and gives way. At the end of the poem, fusion with the cosmos is complete.

If we turn again to the question of how Schoenberg "read" George, we can see how much more complicated it has become. Dümling is right in observing that, far from using George's rigid formal principles to shore up his own atonality, Schoenberg "destroys" the "strict structure of George's poems."[24] But Schoenberg also selected—knowingly or unknowingly—a poem that itself undermines much of what George overtly claimed as the guiding principle of art: the repression or control of chaotic psychological impulses by imposing upon them the straitjacket of form. "Entrückung" enacts a simultaneous tightening of form—mainly through rhyme and meter—and loosening of form—mainly through enjambement and semantic ambiguity. It is at once future-oriented and atavistic, self-centered and self-abandoning. The "other planet" is thoroughly alien, but also the place where a dead loved one undergoes transfiguration and summons the self to share that experience. The poem depends on dramatic oppositions, but also on hidden correspondences without which rapture or transport could not occur at all.

Rather than seeing Schoenberg simply as undermining George's strict forms, I see him also as uncovering George's suppressed impulse toward loss of control. Schoenberg foregrounds, as it were, the underlying dionysiac strand in George's verse. George's unequivocal rhymes (there are no half-rhymes or eye-rhymes), one of the major sources of his formal control, tend to be occluded or at least somewhat veiled in Schoenberg's setting. George's almost invariable iambic meter undergoes unexpected expansions and contractions in Schoenberg's version. The equal lengths Schoenberg accords to the first three syllables of the poem ("ich fühle") throw the emphasis on the fourth syllable ("luft"), thus resisting the impulse to indicate the poem's

[23] See Wolfgang Frommel, "Alfred Schuler. Spuren heidnischer Gnosis," *Castrum Peregrini* 34 (1985): 20.

[24] Dümling, *Die fremden Klänge*, 198.

iambic meter from the very outset, and choosing instead to highlight the rhythm of the phrase as a whole (mm. 21–23).[25] Schoenberg sets the opening of the last two lines of the poem in a similar fashion (mm. 100–101). This rhythmic pattern is anticipated, in Schoenberg's introduction to the fourth movement of the quartet, by a motif with alternating pitches and the same device of three upbeats followed by a downbeat (for example, mm. 7–8). This more melodic version of the rhythmic pattern occurs only in the instrumental sections, never in the voice part. The voice, moving more slowly as if dazed or overwhelmed, echoes the rhythm, but not the melody that emanates from the universe and summons the singer to participate in the cosmic experience.

In his chromatic use of tones throughout his composition, Schoenberg frequently reminds us of speech melodies, without actually imitating them; the "two musics,"[26] that of poetry and that of traditional song, are held in constant tension, with both of them dissolving or on the point of dissolution, in Schoenberg's composition.[27] And in the poem's final tercet, Schoenberg diverges from George's metrics by dramatically expanding the length of the words "heilig" (mm. 110–113), "feuer" (mm. 104–105) and "stimme" (mm. 114–116). These last two lines, marked in George's poem by strict syntactic parallelism and caesuras that cut each line symmetrically in two, are reconfigured by Schoenberg's insistence on expressive emphasis, giving the highly charged adjective "heilig" (holy) much greater prominence than in George's verses. The C♯-major chord that concludes Schoenberg's piece suggests a radiant union of subject and cosmos beyond the sphere of human speech.

At the opening of the poem, Schoenberg disregards George's use of *terza rima* by isolating the first line dramatically from the rest of its tercet. In contrast, Schoenberg increases George's enjambement effects by treating the second and third tercets as if they belonged in an almost unbroken sequence with the last lines of the first tercet.

Schoenberg largely ignores, in other words, the tight control that George saw as heralding a new, more masculine poetic mode. Instead, he brings out

[25] I follow here, with some adaptations, the observations made by Reinhold Brinkmann about Schoenberg's setting of "Sprich nicht immer" in his article "Schönberg und George. Interpretation eines Liedes," *Archiv für Musikwissenschaft* 26 (1969): 1–28.

[26] See Wolfgang Osthoff, *Stefan George und "Les deux Musiques": Tönende und vertonte Dichtung im Einklang und Widerstreit* (Stuttgart: Franz Steiner Verlag Wiesbaden, 1989), 271. Osthoff shows how the problem of the "two musics," that of poetry and that of song, became more acute around the turn of the century.

[27] Osthoff, ibid., 43–45, shows how Schoenberg diverges from the intonation patterns of poetic speech in his setting of "Saget mir, auf welchem Pfade" from George's *Buch der hängenden Gärten*.

two tendencies that are at cross-purposes to the controlled style, but that nonetheless form hidden undertows in George's poetry: first, the continuation of a turn-of-the-century self-dissolution that was precisely what George's masterful metrics attempted to prevent; and second, the emergence of an expressive style that links George's poems on the emotional level with an as yet incipient expressionist manner.[28]

Reinhold Brinkmann points to the figure of a "Durchbruch" or "breakthrough" that was in common use during this period to describe the way in which the "inner world" of a creative person bursts forth into externalized expression. Kafka, writing of his 1912 short story "Das Urteil" (The judgment), called it his "Durchbruchserzählung," a representation of his "dreamlike inner world."[29] The "breakthrough" figure is particularly evident in George's "Entrückung," as the tormented psyche of the mourning poet first breaks forth but then reverses itself dialectically into a "breakthrough" of a very different sort: the recognition of a divine unity in which the deceased Maximin and the God of the universe are understood as part of a single phenomenon. This cognition is presented as breaking through and shining forth (as phenomena do) in the imagery of lifting mists and opening chasms. What breaks through here is not just George's private emotional turmoil after the death of Maximin, but also his suppressed attraction to the dionysian ecstasies of the Cosmic Circle.

In emphasizing this submerged current in "Entrückung," Schoenberg also "rereads" the persona uttering the words of the poem. To be sure, George was drawing on a long tradition of the lyric subject as penetrated by divine inspiration. Submission to rape—or rapture—by the divine was not understood in this essentially Romantic tradition as emasculating the poet. But Schoenberg transforms the speaker into a soprano voice. From a heterosexual point of view this might be motivated by the fact that the "bright beloved shadow" or "shade" is masculine—but the grammatical gender of "Schatten" is masculine and would have to remain so even if the dead beloved were a woman. From the text of the poem alone, there is no compelling reason for assigning

[28] Could the expressionist Johannes R. Becher have been thinking of Schoenberg's setting of "Entrückung" when he wrote his poem "Klänge aus Utopia," with its echoes of George's vocabulary, its allusion to cellos, and its remarkable final words, "Lang dröhnender Akkord"? (*Menschheitsdämmerung. Ein Dokument des Expressionismus*, ed. Kurth Pinthus [1920; reprint Berlin: Rowohlt Taschenbuch Verlag, 1959], 268.)

[29] In August 1914, Franz Kafka noted in his diary the central importance for his narrative method of "die Darstellung meines traumhaften innern Lebens" (*Tagebücher 1910–1923*, ed. Max Brod [Frankfurt: Fischer, 1951], 420).

one gender rather than another to the poem's speaker. Most scholars see Schoenberg as selecting George's "Litanei" and "Entrückung" at this point in his life because these texts seemed to express his own agony over his wife's unfaithfulness. In that case, why did he not set the poems for a male voice? I would like to propose that Schoenberg here once again deconstructs the apollonian ethos and the strongly shaped or "masculine" poetry that George had worked so hard to create.[30]

George's ambition to turn his esoteric and intensely elitist cult into the foundation of a new incarnation of Hellenism in Germany, a desire that was to reach its full expression in his 1928 volume of poetry *Das neue Reich*, led to co-optation of George's work after 1933 by the National Socialists. George declined the presidency of the Nazis' new Academy of Poets and somewhat humblingly went into exile in Switzerland. All the same, George's aestheticizing "will to power" can justifiably be seen as a form of proto-fascism that is not uncommon in high modernist art.[31] What Schoenberg saw, in 1907–1908, in a poem like George's "Entrückung" was clearly not this excessively controlling side of George's poetry. Rather, Schoenberg revealed in George a suppressed yearning for self-abandonment in the sense of the vanishing subject of 1890s "modernity," coupled with an impulse to project emotion outward in a way that was soon to become the hallmark of the new German movement, expressionism. Thanks to Schoenberg's setting, we can see, at least in this one example, how aestheticism paved the way for more radical forms of modernism.

[30] David Lewin gives a different—and less literal-minded—interpretation of Schoenberg's use of the soprano voice in op. 10, reading it as a "gender-free" representation of the transcendent voice that ultimately soars above the instrumental ensemble; see "Women's Voices and the Fundamental Bass," *Journal of Musicology* 10 (1992): 464–482, esp. 468–469.

[31] See, for example, Martin A. Simoneit, *Politische Interpretationen von Stefan Georges Dichtung. Eine Untersuchung verschiedener Interpretationen der politischen Aspekte von Stefan Georges Dichtung im Zusammenhang mit den Ereignissen von 1933* (Frankfurt: Peter Lang, 1978). Michael Petrow argues for a more impartial approach to George's poetry in *Der Dichter als Führer? Zur Wirkung Stefan Georges im "Dritten Reich"* (Marburg: Tectum Verlag, 1995).

Entrückung

Ich fühle luft von anderem planeten.
Mir blassen durch das dunkel die gesichter
Die freundlich eben noch sich zu mir drehten.

Und bäum und wege die ich liebte fahlen
Dass ich sie kaum mehr kenne und du lichter
Geliebter schatten—rufer meiner qualen—

Bist nun erloschen ganz in tiefern gluten
Um nach dem taumel streitenden getobes
Mit einem frommen schauer anzumuten.

Ich löse mich in tönen · kreisend · webend ·
Ungründigen danks und unbenamten lobes
Dem grossen atem wunschlos mich ergebend.

Mich überfährt ein ungestümes wehen
Im rausch der weihe wo inbrünstige schreie
In staub geworfner beterinnen flehen:

Dann seh ich wie sich duftige nebel lüpfen
In einer sonnerfüllten klaren freie
Die nur umfängt auf fernsten bergesschlüpfen.

Der boden schüttert weiss und weich wie molke..
Ich steige über schluchten ungeheuer ·
Ich fühle wie ich über lezter wolke

In einem meer kristallnen glanzes schwimme—
Ich bin ein funke nur vom heiligen feuer
Ich bin ein dröhnen nur der heiligen stimme.

Rapture

I feel air streaming from another planet.
Paling through the gloom behind are faces
That turned to me as friends a while ago.

And trees and pathways that I loved turn sallow
So that I hardly know them and you bright
Beloved shadow—summoner of my torments –

Are now extinguished in a deeper radiance
Wracked no more by fever-ridden frenzy
But with a pious shudder shining forth.

I dissolve in musical notes, I orbit, weave,
With thanks unfathomable and praise unnamed
Surrendering wishless to the mighty breath.

Suddenly turbulent gusts traverse my being
In rapturous consecration where fervent cries
Of women worshippers flung to the dust implore.

Then I notice gauzy mists start lifting
In a sun-filled limpid open space
Embracing just the farthest mountain passes.

The ground is trembling white and soft as whey..
I clamber over chasms monstrous, ghastly,
I feel myself, above the topmost cloud

And in a sea of crystal brilliance, swimming—
I am a light-spark only from the holy fire
I am a rumbling only of the holy voice.

Translated by Judith Ryan

JEFF NICHOLS

Metric Conflict as an Agent of Formal Design in the First Movement of Schoenberg's Quartet Opus 30

In comparison with the vast analytical literature on pitch structures in Schoenberg's music, relatively little has been published on its rhythm. What has been written has largely focused on works from Schoenberg's "atonal" period (1908–1923), works that change meters and subdivisions of the beat far more frequently than either his earlier tonal or later twelve-tone works and that therefore are regarded as rhythmically more complex. The twelve-tone works in particular have not only been comparatively neglected, but they have been criticized in some quarters (particularly by the postwar European serialists) for a conservative treatment of rhythm, texture, and form "incompatible" with the new pitch techniques of the twelve-tone method.[1]

The first movement of the Third Quartet can be taken as emblematic of the neoclassical stylistic features that offended the European serialists. It is in sonata form, has only one meter signature, and frequently makes use of theme-and-accompaniment textures. The assumption that such features are

[1] See Pierre Boulez, "Schoenberg Is Dead," *The Score* 6 (1952): 20: "The pre-classical and classical forms ruling most of [Schoenberg's twelve-tone] compositions were in no way historically connected with the twelve-tone discovery; the result is that a contradiction arises between the forms dictated by tonality and a language of which the laws of organization are still only dimly perceived.... The two worlds are incompatible, and he has tried to justify one by the other. This can hardly be called a valid procedure." This article is reprinted (and retranslated) in *Stocktakings from an Apprenticeship*, ed. Paule Thevenin, trans. Stephen Walsh (Oxford: Clarendon Press, 1991).

fundamentally at odds with Schoenberg's pitch language has been shown by many scholars to be misguided. Martha Hyde, for example, has published important studies showing how Schoenberg's twelve-tone music uses "metrical relations between harmonic and rhythmical structures analogous to those of tonal music."[2] Joseph Straus has shown how Schoenberg reinterprets the sonata as an arch form based on inversional symmetry in the Third Quartet's first movement.[3] By exploring the deep interconnections between metric and formal structures in Schoenberg's twelve-tone music, on the one hand, and its pitch structures, on the other, these authors have laid to rest the criticism that in these works the "new wine" of atonal harmony is poured into the "old wineskins" of tonal rhythms and forms. However, neither author directly addresses the question of whether Schoenberg's practice in the twelve-tone works does in fact represent a return to conventional common-practice rhythmic and metric structures after the experiments of the atonal period.

That the rhythms of the Third Quartet do not straightforwardly invoke classical norms becomes apparent with the most cursory attempt to scan the meter. Rhythmic motives are so ambiguous, and subject to such constant variation, that there are rarely four bars in succession that can be heard as clearly expressing a single meter. This metric complexity is facilitated—paradoxically—by the ostensibly neoclassical device of maintaining a continuous eighth-note accompanimental texture virtually throughout the movement. The constant stream of eighth notes can be regrouped in new metric configurations at will, providing a reference point in passages that are polymetric.[4] The ebb and flow of metric clarity, and the temporary ascendency of

[2] Martha M. Hyde, "A Theory of Twelve-Tone Meter," *Music Theory Spectrum* 6 (1984): 14. See also Martha Hyde, *Schoenberg's Twelve-Tone Harmony: The Suite Op. 29 and the Compositional Sketches*, ed. George Buelow (Ann Arbor: UMI Research Press, 1982).

[3] Joseph N. Straus, *Remaking the Past: Musical Modernism and the Influence of the Tonal Tradition* (Cambridge, Mass.: Harvard University Press, 1990), 121–132, 161–168. Although Straus sees this quartet as evoking "the textures, timbres, phrasing, and the forms of a nineteenth-century string quartet" and proposes Schubert's String Quartet in A Minor, op. 29, as a model for Schoenberg's, he argues that "Schoenberg's quartet misreads Schubert's, reinterpreting both...phrase structure and...large-scale harmonic organization....Beneath this surface [evocation of the sonata form] Schoenberg brings about a profound structural shift, through the revisionary strategy of symmetricization. The form becomes retrograde-symmetrical....Inversional balance pervades every level of the musical structure. Individual phrases combine series forms that balance about a musically articulated axis. Larger sections cohere through focus on a succession of axes. The movement as a whole balances entire sections in a similar manner" (130–131).

[4] This process is the inverse of the one John Roeder describes in his article "Interacting Pulse Streams in Schoenberg's Atonal Polyphony," *Music Theory Spectrum* 16, no. 2 (1994):

duple or triple groupings of pulses,[5] become primary determinants both of moment-to-moment rhythmic rhetoric and of our perception of the work's form. These aspects of its rhythmic design can be understood in dialectical terms—appropriately, for a work in sonata form. I assume that any listener will try to hear successions of regular pulses metrically, and that alternative ways of grouping those pulses will be heard as opposed to each other, particularly if other dimensions of the music reinforce such a hearing. By focusing on this metric aspect instead of myriad other motivic processes in the work's rhythm, I am singling out a process that I think has particularly far-reaching organizational potential. The basic question of whether the complex accentual patterns of the rhythmic surface ultimately express duple or triple meters becomes in my view a motivating structural tension in the movement as a whole.[6]

I shall not for the most part attempt to integrate my observations in this essay with analyses of the work's pitch structure. The rhythmic processes discussed here function in tandem with the melodic and harmonic processes described by Straus, Hyde, and others.[7] It is not necessary, however, to know the twelve-tone derivation of the intervallic and contour relations to which I shall occasionally refer to follow the present discussion.

231–249. Roeder's theory "analyzes an irregular surface as the sum of several concurrent regular continuities, much as a Fourier transform analyzes a complexly aperiodic sound as the sum of periodic sine waves." My discussion of the Third Quartet, by contrast, derives higher-level complex groupings of attacks from a single unvarying pulse stream always present on the surface of the music.

[5] In this essay I shall refer to "groupings of pulses" any time the pulses in a stream fall into a regular pattern of accentuation, however fleetingly. I shall reserve the term "meter" for more extended and for more hierarchically elaborate regular groupings. The distinction is one of degree rather than kind, and it allows me for example to refer to a passage in 6/8 meter as an instance of "triple grouping of pulses," when it is *not* an instance of triple meter.

[6] For a discussion of a related concept applied to much shorter works from the atonal period, see Charles D. Morrison, "Syncopation as Motive in Schoenberg's Op. 19, Nos. 2, 3 and 4," *Music Analysis* 11, no. 1 (1992): 75–93. Although Morrison feels that "it is hard to imagine a foreground syncopation controlling forward motion throughout an entire piece, or a formal section of even moderate scope," he acknowledges a structural potential in extended metric tension: "The repetition of unresolved dissonant patterns [i.e., *metrically* dissonant] in the short pieces discussed here means that syncopation affects progression and recession, cadential openness and closure, and overall formal design" (75–76).

[7] For example, elaborations of the semitone motive of the melody in m. 5 throughout the movement play a crucial role in my discussion of triple pulse-groupings, and also appear as the fulcra about which inversionally related set forms pivot in passages such as mm. 19ff.; see Straus, *Remaking the Past,* 124–125.

Although the movement's formal outlines are very clear,[8] the chief landmarks in its metric structure do not correspond to predictable junctures in the sonata form. The movement's climax, for example—the moment of highest tension between duple and triple meters—occurs not in the development section but at the end of the recapitulation. The primary expositions of triple rhythms occur in the development section, and the movement's metric "resolutions"—those passages most unambiguously hearable in single meters—are deferred to the coda. In the remainder of this essay I shall discuss each of these parts of the work in turn, showing the gradual sharpening of the underlying conflict between duple and triple meters. That conflict provides a long-range rhetorical trajectory unifying the complex accentual patterns and rhythmic motives of the surface. It functions independently of the conventional dramatic functions of sonata form, although its principal landmarks correspond to major articulations in the traditional formal outline.[9]

Because so much of the rhythmic surface of this movement is metrically ambiguous, I shall begin by discussing a passage in which duple and triple

[8] I follow the outline Straus gives in *Remaking the* Past, 122, which is essentially identical to the outline in the published score: Exposition: First Theme, 1–32; Transition, 33–61; Second Theme, 62–94; Development: 95–173; Recapitulation: Second Theme, 174–206; Transition, 207–238; First Theme, 239–277; Coda: 278–341.

[9] The question of the nature of sonata form in this movement is a complex one that I cannot fully address in this essay. In "Neoclassic and Anachronistic Impulses in Twentieth-Century Music," *Music Theory Spectrum* 18, no. 2 (1996): 220–235, Martha Hyde elaborates on Straus's analysis of this work. She argues that the Schubert A Minor Quartet (which Schoenberg uses as a model) *itself* treats sonata form unconventionally. She agrees with Straus that Schoenberg uses the neoclassic dialogue with the past as a springboard to innovation: "Schoenberg's imitation of Schubert does not lead us backward into deepening engagement with a past classic. It leads forward into new territory and asks its audience to follow" (235). In her view, the neoclassic aspect of this work is not revealed in the general revival of tonal forms, but in the relation of a new and highly integrated language to the unique structural properties of a particular model. "In Schoenberg's recreation, Schubert's abandonment of thematic contrast [between the first and second themes—a characteristic shared by the Schoenberg quartet] seems to evolve into a deeper structural principal....Schoenberg makes the unconventional stylistic similarities among Schubert's principal themes a structural feature of the row that generates his twelve-tone sonata form....Schoenberg's imitation of Schubert...[also] challenges the harmonic structure of classical sonata form, an even more basic premise of tonal form than contrasting themes," by basing the harmonic progressions of the work on principals of inversional symmetry and balance.

I shall argue in this essay that the superficial evocation of regular meter and theme-and-accompaniment textures in this quartet masks a no less radical revision of classical practice in these dimensions.

meters are presented with unusual clarity, at least in individual strata of the texture. Example 1a shows what I regard as the climax of the movement, mm. 268ff., notated without any beams or bar lines but otherwise identically to the published score.[10]

Clearly the ensemble as a whole is not governed by a single metric structure. As shown in Example 1b, the violin's repeated i13's[11] seem to project a compound duple meter of 6/4 onto the background stream of eighth-note pulses, and so do the cello and second violin when they start their long notes in imitation of the first violin's line. But since the attacks of the various instruments in this layer of the texture are staggered (each successive entry appearing on the third quarter-note pulse of the previous statement's second 6/4 "measure"—thus emphasizing the subdivision of the long notes into three quarter notes), they do not seem to project a single ensemble meter, either at the outset or when the violin reenters with the motive twice as fast (at letter X in the example). What is clear is that each attack within this layer of the texture groups the next-faster pulse (quarter notes at first, then eighth notes at X) into threes.

While this series of iterations of the long-note motive is going on, at any given moment two of the other instruments are playing another rhythmic motive, a series of seven eighth-note attacks followed by a rest of varying duration, one version of which is shown in Example 1c.[12] This rhythmic motive is also treated imitatively; each successive voice in this layer of the

[10] I refer to this passage as "the climax" because it has the longest stretch of forte and fortissimo dynamics before the coda, culminating in a sustained fortissimo six-note chord in m. 277 that is probably the loudest sonority in the movement before the eight-note final chord. There are certainly other climactic passages, notably mm. 222–234 in the development and the end of the coda, but they do not prevent my hearing the end of the recapitulation as the dramatic high point of the movement.

[11] In this essay I use the abbreviation "i" to mean interval; "ic" to mean interval class; and integers to refer to half-steps. Thus "i1" refers to a semitone, regardless of direction; "ic1" refers to all i1's, i11's, and their compounds; +2 and -6 refer to intervals of two ascending and six descending semitones, respectively.

[12] These eighth-note motives could of course also be read as *beginning* with the eighth rests that set them off, shifting their accentuation to correspond to the weak-to-strong metric orientation of the repeated notes in the original accompaniment figure. Several factors lead me to hear the orientation shown in Example 1c instead, primary among them the placement of the sforzandi on weak eighths in the two measures preceding the passage in the example (mm. 266–267), but also including the shifting orientations of repeated notes with respect to the notated meter that occur in the development section (see the discussion below), shifts that facilitate hearing repeated eighth notes as commencing on the quarter-note pulse.

Example 1

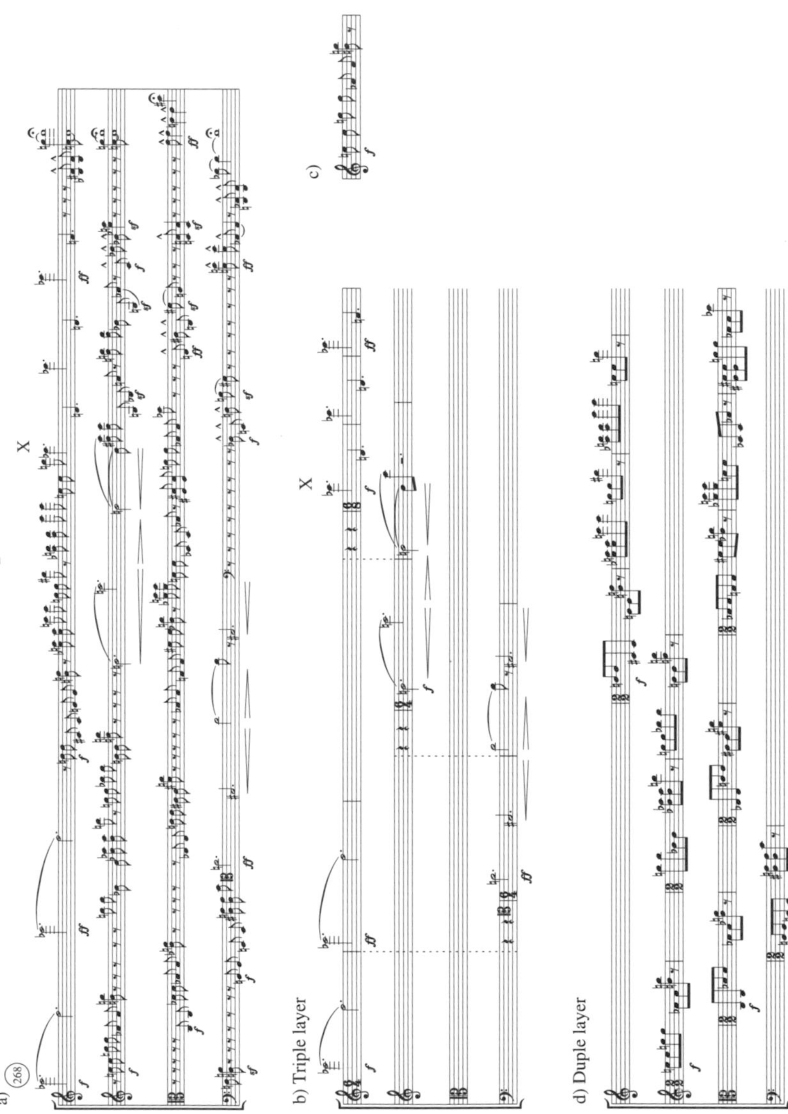

texture enters after four eighth notes, creating a metric effect of staggered 2/2 measures, as shown in Example 1d. The pitch content of this layer is more complex than that of the first layer, because two pitch successions along with their inversions, retrogrades, and retrograde-inversions are used. However, the similarities of rhythm and contour among the various versions of this motive make each entrance sound imitative nonetheless.

In the last third or so of the excerpt presented in Example 1a (from X on), the rhythmic layers begin to merge. They lose their internal metric consistency, while not yet projecting an ensemble meter (thus becoming ametric). The beginning of the passage, however, is irreducibly *poly*metric. At no point in the excerpt is there a clear ensemble meter.

So what orients us rhythmically in this passage? Clearly, the repeated motives provide perceptual reference points, but to what do they refer? I shall argue that in the context of the entire movement, we hear the rhythms of this passage at least partly as framed by a conflict between duple and triple groupings of pulses. At its outset neither metric orientation prevails and yet both are clearly manifest in separate layers of the texture. The stark contrast between those layers, each unyieldingly projecting its own grouping of underlying pulse streams, subsumes the complex accents of the surface rhythms not into an ensemble meter, but into an idea: duple and triple pulse-groupings struggling for priority. The culmination of the passage shown in Example 1a (corresponding to m. 277 in the score) does not resolve this conflict.[13]

To understand how this climax is prepared, we must return to earlier passages that adumbrate the tension between duple and triple meters, beginning with the opening bars of the quartet. At first glance the opening seems rhythmically rather square. Its textural strategy resembles countless familiar common-practice pieces, like the opening of Mozart's G Minor Symphony, K. 550—to name one written in the same meter as the Schoenberg and evincing a similar emphasis on repeated notes. Like the Mozart example, Opus 30 starts with an accompaniment pattern made up of a continuous eighth-note pulse, creating a rhythmic and harmonic context before the entrance of the theme. But the Schoenberg opening does not project a metric hierarchy as clearly as does the Mozart accompaniment. In the Schoenberg quartet, the whole-note pulse, corresponding to the bar line, is articulated by the alternation between the second violin and the viola and by the terraced dynamics.

[13] With the fermata at the end of m. 277, the fortissimo figure in the viola, G4-E4-E4-D#5, can be heard either in 2/2 as notated, or in 3/4 with downbeats on the initial G4 and the sustained D#. (For that matter, the desultory three-eighth-note groups that follow in mm. 278–281 remain metrically dislocated.)

The underlying stream of eighth-note pulses is equally unambiguous. But what about the pulses in between these values? In particular, how is the half-note pulse (the primary metric subdivision in 2/2) articulated? It is at these intermediate levels that Schoenberg's accompaniment figure diverges from classical models. Unlike the G Minor Symphony's accompaniment pattern, where continuous eighth notes combine as repeated-note pairs to articulate quarter notes, then in pairs of pairs to articulate half-notes, and finally in bar-length spans emphasized by the octave shifts in the celli and basses, in the Schoenberg quartet the repeated eighth notes are displaced throughout the bar. This obscures somewhat the quarter- and half-note levels in the metric hierarchy. Other factors being equal, a change of pitch will be perceived as an accent; in the Mozart example, repeated notes happen *within* the quarter-note pulses, so changes of pitch articulate the quarter-note pulses of the underlying metric hierarchy. In the Schoenberg quartet, repeated eighth notes happen *across* the quarter-note pulses, so changes of pitch articulate syncopated quarter-note spans. Example 2 shows the original accompaniment figure followed by several beat patterns that its repeated notes can be heard to imply, depending on how the quarter-note spans are grouped.

Example 2

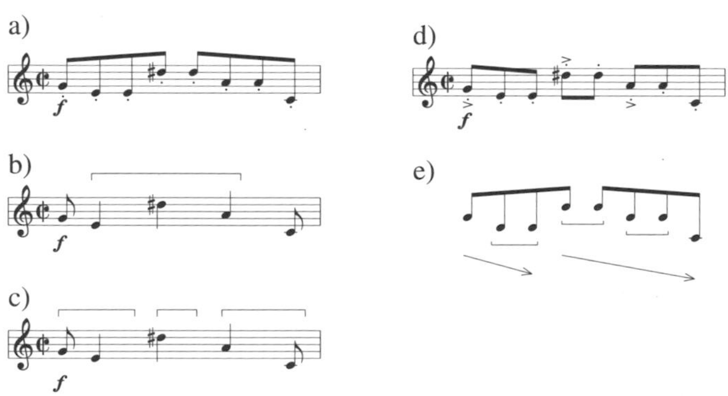

There are essentially two such patterns. One is the series of three quarter notes offset by an eighth note shown in Example 2b; the other, shown in Example 2c, groups adjacent long and short values to form slower pulses. The grouping in Example 2c could of course be brought out by accenting the original figure, as shown in Example 2d. Both Examples 2b and 2c imply triple groupings, either of three quarter notes or of three eighth notes, contradicting the normal duple hierarchy of the 2/2 meter. Even here ambiguity prevails, however; as Example 2d shows, in a 3+2+3 grouping of eighth notes the placement of the repeated notes in the two dotted-quarter spans differs (in the first the pattern is xyy, in the second xxy).[14]

Clearly Schoenberg is not consistently writing in a meter other than the notated cut time (say, 3+2+3/8).[15] Meters that combine irregular groupings of eighth notes were hardly unusual in music of the first half of the century, but that is not what is happening here. The entrance of the first theme in the first violin in m. 5 contradicts any of the possible irregular meters implied by the accompaniment's groupings of repeated notes. The violin enters with an accented syncopation at the quarter-note level; in that sense it does respond to the implied syncopations of the accompaniment. But because the violin enters on a *quarter* note in the notated metric scheme, it confirms the idea of syncopation only by analogy with what is going on at the eighth-note level; as an event occurring simultaneously with the accompaniment, it actually confirms the "normal" metric hierarchy of eighths subsumed within quarters, quashing any potential ensemble meter based on grouping the repeated eighth notes within dotted-quarter pulses. This contrasts strongly with common-practice rhythmic procedure, in which accompaniments generally prepare the metric orientation of the theme. Only in very extraordinary circumstances, and certainly almost never at the beginning of a piece, would the accompaniment be as metrically ambiguous as this one is or lay out a metric pattern that the entrance of the theme so thoroughly contradicts.[16]

As the first theme unfolds, each phrase of the melody realizes more clearly a triple grouping of quarter notes. Example 3a shows just the violin and cello parts (the melodic lines) of the first theme, with each triple grouping of quarter notes marked by a bracket. Although the beginning of the second phrase in the cello (m. 13) imitates the contour and rhythm of the first phrase in the violin, its bowing, accents, and durations are altered to fit much more clearly into a 3/4 meter, as shown in Example 3b.

[14] As the reader will infer from these examples, I think a good performance of the opening should articulate the staccato eighth notes of the accompaniment as evenly as possible, allowing the pitch content of the figure to intimate various potential metric groupings within the bar without tipping the balance in favor of one metric reading or another through dynamic accents.

[15] It is the lack of a consistent *alternative* reading that distinguishes this piece from such well-known common-practice instances of metric displacement as the beginning of the Brahms Horn Trio or the theme from the variations movement of Beethoven's quartet op. 74.

[16] It is a procedure with many precedents in Schoenberg's own music, however. For an extended discussion of metric disjunctions at the beginnings of vocal works in Schoenberg's atonal period, see David Lewin, "Vocal Meter in Schoenberg's Atonal Music, with a Note on a Serial Hauptstimme," *In Theory Only* 6, no. 4 (May 1982): 12–36.

Example 3

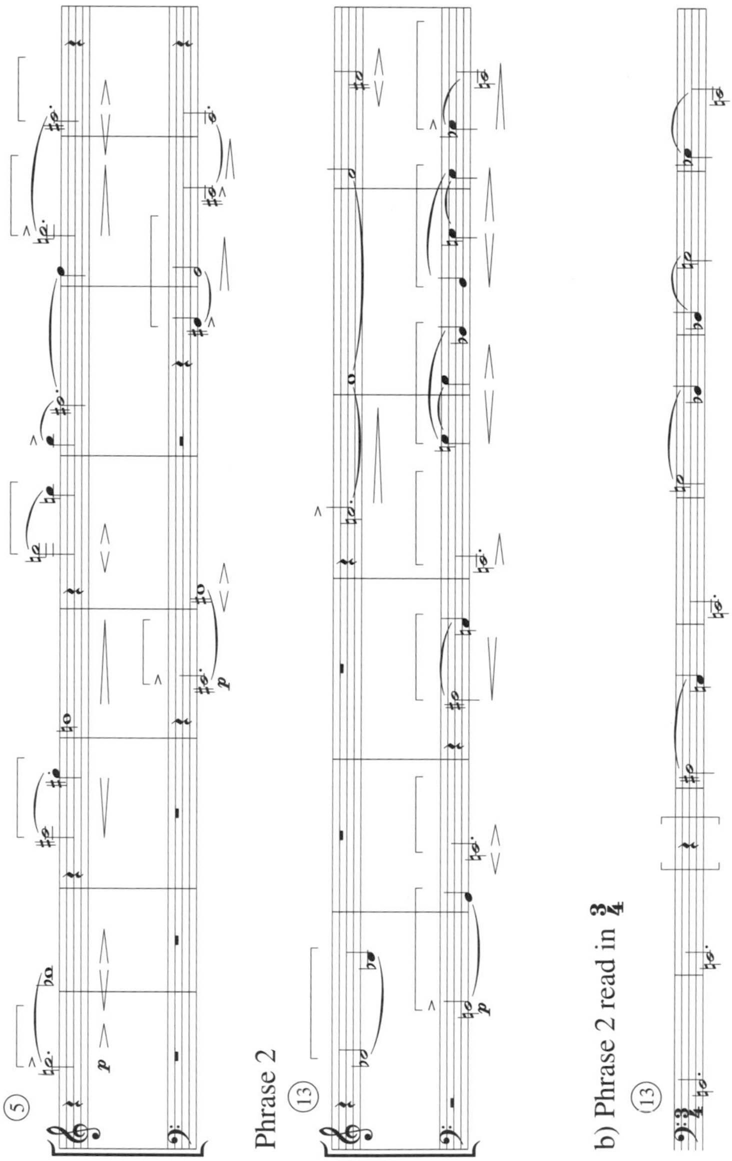

Throughout this passage the second violin and viola alternate accompanimental figures based on the rhythm and melodic contour shown in Example 2e. The opening of the quartet is thus characterized by increasing tension between the four-quarter-note spans articulated by the accompaniment and the increasingly clear three-quarter-note spans in the melodic lines. Put another way, over the course of the first theme, metric ambiguities implicit *within* the accompaniment figuration are gradually realized *between* the accompaniment and the melody.

The tension between duple and triple meters is not resolved in favor of one or the other in the course of the first theme (mm. 1–32). However, by m. 19 the implicit triple quarter-note groupings in the melodic lines begin to affect the previously unvarying accompaniment pattern, which in mm. 19–25 comes unmoored from the bar line. This does not mean the triple groupings in the melodic lines have taken over the whole ensemble; it just means that *both* melody and accompaniment become metrically fluid by this point. What had been an immutable reference point, the bar-length alternations of accompaniment figures, mutates. Yet one barely notices that this has occurred, because by the time the accompaniment actually shifts in m. 19, displaced accents in the other parts have already disoriented us sufficiently that the change is almost imperceptible. The reader can verify this effect by listening to the opening twenty-five or so bars of the quartet without referring to the score. What one notices is a gradual erosion of the sense of the bar line, not a sudden metric displacement in m. 19.

The path from the tenuous interplay between duple and triple groupings of pulses in the opening to the stark polymeters of the climax is anything but straightforward. I can do no more in this short essay than trace the outlines of an extremely intricate metric dialectic. I shall pass over the second theme group, which retains and enriches many rhythmic motives from the first while maintaining a prevalent state of metric ambiguity,[17] and move to the development section, where triple groupings are first clearly established as a dialectical antithesis to the notated duple meter.

[17] In "A Theory of Twelve-Tone Meter," 34–39, Martha Hyde analyzes the harmonic structure of the second theme as projecting an extremely slow-moving duple hypermeter, with highly irregular groupings of quarter-note pulses on the surface. (In other words, the second theme is virtually ametric at lower levels but still shows hypermetric organization.) It is worth noting in the light of the present discussion that the accompaniment of the second theme retains the repeated eighth notes characteristic of the first, but slurs them in such a way as to remove any implication of a syncopated quarter-note pulse. While the quarter-note pulse level is thus brought into alignment with the notated meter, the *whole-note* level—which had been perfectly clear in the first theme group—is now entirely

Triple groupings clearly emerge at several major junctures in the development section. The development section is divided into two parts. The first part begins by emphasizing three-quarter-note spans in mm. 95ff. and ends with a strong assertion of the written duple meter in mm. 134–137. The second part begins in m. 138 with a sudden shift of dynamics and texture and a return to emphasis on three-quarter-note spans (thus the center of the development section is marked by a strong contrast between duple and triple groupings of quarter notes). The second part continues to another high point in mm. 168–169 with gestures based on three-eighth-note spans, which are then liquidated in mm. 170–173 to close the development section. I shall now discuss each of these passages in turn, showing the specific transformations of basic motivic materials used to establish a triple antithesis to the movement's duple rhythms.

The development section begins in m. 95 with a series of altered versions of the first theme's accompaniment figure. The cello in m. 94 presents that figure with one note missing. That gap dissociates its end from its beginning, suggesting the possibility of lopping off the end of the figure—a suggestion that is followed in the next bar (Ex. 4a). The new, truncated version of the figure that appears in m. 95 spurs a quasi-imitative sequence rising from the cello through the viola to the second violin (Ex. 4b). Against this sequence yet another version of the opening figure is initiated by the cello playing pizzicato in m. 96. This figure stretches the truncated eighth-note version of the accompaniment into four quarter notes (Ex. 4c). The successive entries of the pizzicato figure overlap, however, so it still expresses a 3/4 meter (Ex. 4d). The 3/4 meter is strongly expressed by both sequences, but the two layers of the texture are staggered, so already by m. 96 the ensemble meter is ambiguous. In m. 97, the first sequential pattern starts again in the cello, and again it is staggered with respect to the preceding sequence. Example 4e shows the metric relationships among the overlapping sequences from m. 95 to m. 99.

In m. 99, the pizzicato notes disappear and in their stead a two-beat figure in the first violin joins the three-beat figure in the second violin (shown in parentheses in Example 4e). Heard at the culmination of the third 3/4 sequence, the entrance of the first violin's figure initially seems to reinforce that metric orientation. However, since it is missing its third beat, this figure does contain a slight hint of duple rhythm, which immediately spawns a new,

obscured by the irregularly placed quarter-note pauses in the accompaniment and the cross-accents of the second theme itself. In this way the exposition's status quo of metric ambiguity is maintained even though the locus of that ambiguity has shifted between levels in the metric hierarchy.

Example 4

a)

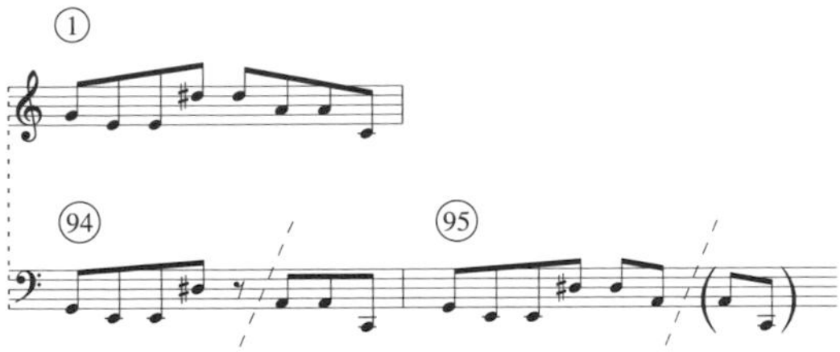

b)

c)

d)

e)

complex figure that subsumes the eighth and quarter notes, arco and pizzicato attacks, of the preceding measures into a duple meter (Ex. 5a). Beginning in m. 101 that figure also overlaps with itself (Ex. 5c), and in various fragmentations and recombinations (all tending to project overlapped duple meters) the two components of the motive, labeled x and y in Example 5b, become the basis for the following passage.

Example 5

a)

b)

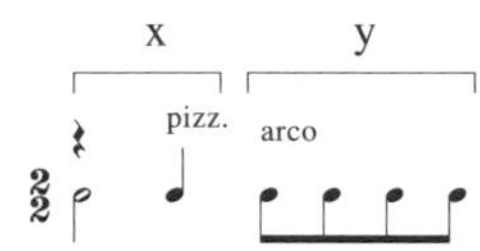

c)

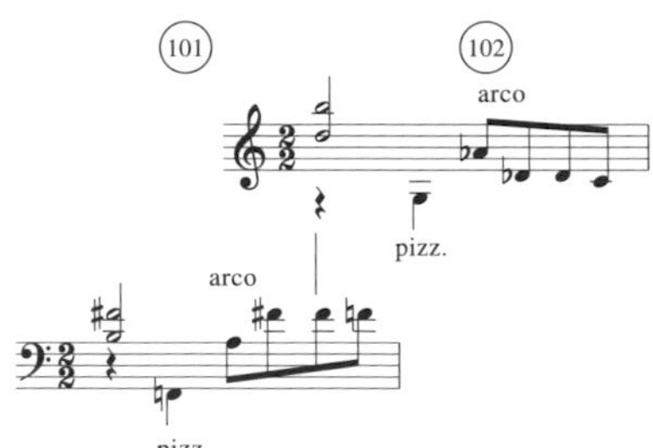

Notice the speed of transformation here. Each motive appears at most twice before disappearing, or being transformed into something else, or overlapping with itself in order to render metrically ambiguous what was threatening to become too stable. The transition from one sequence to another with a different metric orientation often pivots on a single gesture. Thus the missing eighth note in m. 94 prepares the 3/4 version of the accompaniment that dominates mm. 95–99; a further rhythmic truncation from three to two beats in the first violin in m. 99 leads to a new, duple basis for sequences and imitations in mm. 100ff. The extreme concision of this passage's motivic transformations is, as Alban Berg pointed out long ago,[18] typical of Schoenberg's writing from the beginning. For this reason, I do not hear this

[18] Alban Berg, "Warum ist Schönbergs Musik so schwer verständlich?" *Musikblätter des Anbruch,* 1924, 329–341. English translation in Willi Reich, *Alban Berg*, (London: Thames and Hudson, 1965), 189–204.

movement as Boulez did, as a revival of tonal meters. Rather, it seems to be building on atonal-period rhythmic techniques. As David Lewin has remarked of the opening of another twelve-tone work using classical forms, the Fourth Quartet: "Just as Schoenberg considered his extraordinary pitch networks to be 'pan-tonal' rather than 'atonal,' so can we consider his extraordinary rhythmic networks to arise from the abundant profusion of various metric and other rhythmic structures, rather than from the absence of such structures."[19] By comparing the "rhythmic networks" in Schoenberg's twelve-tone music to pantonality, Lewin implies that this music transcends traditional metric structures—if not by denying them, then by placing them in new, relativistic contexts.

In m. 138 the opening semitone gesture of the first theme (from mm. 5–6 in the first violin) is presented in stretto. In mm. 138–144, each voice in the texture can be scanned evenly in 3/4 for as long as six "measures" at a stretch, as indicated by the rebarring and brackets in Example 6. As in the opening of the development section in mm. 95ff., however, these 3/4 layers are overlapped at irregular intervals, preventing the formation of any consistent ensemble meter. At the end of Example 6, corresponding to m. 144 in the score, a figure derived from the first theme's *second* gesture (from mm. 7–8 in the first violin) appears in the cello; this figure initiates a similar stretto-like elaboration. The passage as a whole presents the first theme extended in this manner, each gesture developed in turn with its triple metric aspect emphasized.

Example 6

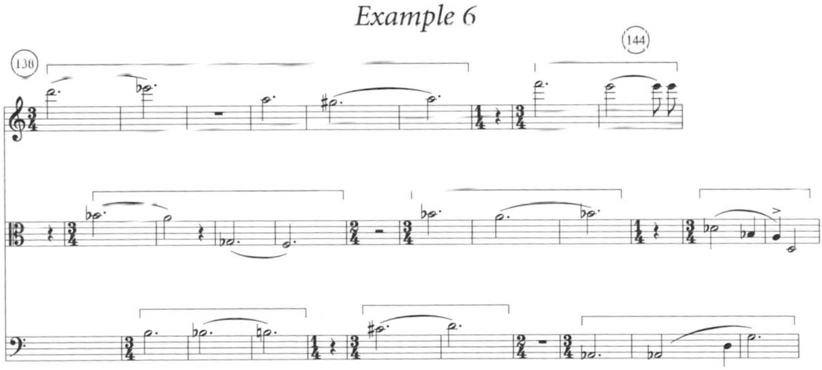

The accompanimental voices in this passage (mm. 138ff.) are characterized by the repeated eighth notes that have been a constant presence in the movement to this point, always taking the form of a pair of notes beginning

[19] David Lewin, "Vocal Meter in Schoenberg's Atonal Music," 34–36.

on a weak eighth.[20] Over the course of the ensuing passage, however, the repeated eighth notes gradually come to be treated explicitly and for extended periods in groups of threes—sometimes three repeated eighth notes, sometimes patterns of 1+2 or 2+1 eighth notes. This process starts very subtly in m. 145; here the beaming in the first violin suggests articulations of triple groups of eighths separated by a single eighth. The sense that the eighth notes are being reoriented metrically is enhanced by the extension of repeated eighths to more than two. Here it is only the beaming, and not melodic contour or any other notated accents, that raises the possibility of triple eighth-note groups. Beginning in m. 153, however, groups of three repeated eighth notes are marked with downbeat and upbeat symbols to create short passages explicitly in compound meter, at first in only one instrument at a time. This process culminates in a brief passage around m. 169, where a perceived 6/8 meter emerges in the cello and briefly subsumes the ensemble, as shown in Example 7.

Example 7

Although there may be common-practice antecedents for any one of the metric-motivic transitions I have discussed in the development section, their multilayered presentation here results in a nonhierarchical, at times polymetric and at times ametric rhythmic texture that is distinctively modernist. The recasting of first-theme materials into triple pulse-groupings of various sorts

[20] The only passage previous to this one in which eighth notes are explicitly accented in groups of three is in the transition to the second theme, mm. 52–61. However, even there repeated eighth notes come only in pairs—with the sole exception of the very last such grouping in the viola in m. 61. This transition foreshadows the second part of the

bears no similarity to such common-practice devices as transforming duple rhythms into triple rhythms at the end of a piece or movement to signal a coda or finale.[21] The basic motives of this work are ambiguous at the outset and therefore require transformation to assume a clear *duple* orientation as well; moreover, when they are presented in triple-meter versions, they are usually overlapped so that the rhetorical effect is one of heightened tension rather than relaxing into a dance rhythm. At no point do duple rhythms cede to triple ones for long (or vice versa). For all these reasons I hear duple and triple orientations of basic motives as participating in an oppositional structure without precedent in common-practice music.

Up to this point I have discussed primarily passages in which subtle metric implications of the opening measures have led to the emergence of triple groupings of pulses. These groupings have been my focus because they contradict the written meter and hence are somewhat less apparent than duple groupings. I hear their gradual emergence as the instantiation of a dialectical antithesis to the notated duple meter and the four-quarter-note spans articulated by the accompaniment at the outset of the movement. A comparable survey of duple groupings would be possible, and would show the same constant development and recontextualization of basic motives. In the interests of concision, however, I shall forgo a parallel discussion of the evolution of duple rhythms and proceed to the question of when in the movement its typically polymetric or ametric textures "resolve" into clear ensemble meters. Such moments contribute to the emergence of a metrical synthesis at the conclusion of the movement, but not in the manner one might expect, with one meter finally emerging as the primary metric context for all the movement's basic motives.

Although the exposition and development sections include brief passages in which an ensemble meter can be discerned (mm. 134–137 and 168–169, for example), it is not until the coda that the listener has a sense that all instruments project a single meter for more than three or four consecutive measures without constant cross-accents tugging at the metric fabric.

development section. Locally, however, its hints of triple-eighth-note groupings are abruptly contradicted by the accompaniment to the second theme, which again features repeated eighth notes displaced from the quarter-note pulse but slurred to remove any sense of syncopation and of the latent triple groupings one can hear in the first theme's accompaniment.

[21] See for example Mozart's Variations on "Ah, vous dirai-je, maman" or the last movement of Beethoven's String Quartet op. 127, which retains a duple meter but introduces two subsidiary levels of triple pulse–groupings when the coda moves from a 2/2 meter to 6/8 with triplet sixteenth notes.

Example 8 shows the beginning of a passage from m. 311 to m. 320 in which all four instruments articulate triple groupings of pulses, here transcribed into a 3/8 meter. At the outset it synthesizes melodic and accompanimental elements to form the violin lines. The legato articulation of the gestures marked Y in the example until now has only characterized slower-moving melodic lines made up of mixed note values (like the first and second themes; before this passage there are no slurred successions of eighth notes or quarter notes). The repeated notes marked as X in the example have been a constant—and exclusive—feature of accompanying voices, and have never before appeared with rhythmic values greater than eighth notes.[22] Thus melodic and accompanimental motives are no longer stratified into quarter- and eighth-note pulse streams, but are synthesized in the intermediate value of the triplet quarter note.[23]

Example 8

[22] Note that these triplet quarter notes should be somewhat slower than the prevailing eighth note in the movement, despite the dotted whole = whole notation at m. 311 (which normally would imply that these pulses are slightly faster than eighth notes). This is a result of the *Etwas langsamer*, *calando*, *sehr ruhig*, and *calando* indications in mm. 278, 282, 292, and 305 respectively. The *accelerando* that begins in m. 317 brings the triplet-quarter pulses *up* via the eighth notes in mm. 320–323 to the level of the eighth notes of *Tempo I* in m. 324. (Not all modern performances observe this relation, but it is very clearly observed in the composer-supervised Kolisch Quartet recording of 1936 [on the Archiphon label, arc-103/4.])

[23] The very end of the movement is not the only place such synthetic moments occur, any more than developmental processes cease the moment the recapitulation begins. (I have already noted that the climactic moment of conflict occurs in fact not in the development section but at the end of the recapitulation.) For example, the merging of melodic and accompanimental figures in mm. 311ff. is adumbrated in mm. 216–320, a passage that is part of a developmental retransition to the first theme in the recapitulation. In this passage

In the passage that starts in m. 321, the original eighth-note pulse is restored, and more explicit (but still quite condensed) remnants of the first theme and its accompaniment now fall into an ensemble-wide expression of the written duple meter. By virtue of the accelerando starting in m. 318, the triplet quarter notes of mm. 311–320 modulate into the eighth notes of mm. 320ff., so what changes here is not so much the underlying pulse as that pulse's metric orientation.[24] While the eighth notes (the erstwhile triplet quarter notes) still occur in groups of three, they feel like upbeats to the accented half notes. The repeated eighth notes do not create a feeling of cross-metric syncopation here as they did in the opening, because the rests that precede them and the strong accents in other voices on quarter- and half-note pulses clearly subsume the eighth notes into superior hierarchical levels of a clear 2/2 meter.[25] In the meantime, the first-theme motive also conforms to the written meter. It begins in the first violin in m. 324, syncopated on a weak quarter pulse as in m. 5. However, here its semitone shift happens one beat earlier, and is extended another semitone to an accented downbeat, so the nascent threat to the notated meter felt in m. 5 is neutralized. Unlike the opening of the quartet, where the accompaniment's repeated notes and the melody's displaced entrances both tended to obscure the basic half-note pulses of the 2/2 meter, here the vestigial syncopations of each layer of the texture function clearly as upbeats to accented half notes.

The placement of these two most extended expressions of clear ensemble meters so near the end of the movement suggests that the process of metric clarification is at the heart of its formal design. Neither duple nor triple metric groupings are primary; rather, *both* groupings are implicit but ambiguous at the opening, and are gradually disambiguated as the movement unfolds. This process has a double culmination. One is the

the opening half-step motive of the first theme and the first half of the basic accompaniment figure are joined in an unambiguous duple-meter motive (presented in overlapping imitations, like the 3/4 motives at the beginning of the development section).

24 This accelerando thus blurs the distinction between the eighth- and quarter-note pulses that stratify melody and accompaniment throughout the movement proper, just after characteristic elements of those previously distinct textural layers have been combined in the single pulse stream of triplet quarter notes.

25 I do not mean to imply that such syntheses happen all at once in this passage. A fuller dialectical analysis of these aspects of the movement would include passages like mm. 216–230, part of a developmental retransition to the first theme in the recapitulation. In that passage the opening half-step of the first theme and the first half of the basic accompaniment figure are joined in an unambiguous duple-meter motive, overlapped with itself. Over the course of the entire movement I hear a rough statistical parity between duple and triple groupings of pulses, mediated by the great majority of figures that hover between the two.

superposition of duple and triple pulse-groupings at the climax in mm. 268–277. The other occurs when these pulse-groupings are presented in *succession* in the coda. Both moments realize latent metric structures of the movement's opening, one in a way that generates tension, the other in a way that diffuses it.

Thus it would be misleading to speak of "the" meter of this movement. Its metric structure hinges on the shifting balance between duple and triple groupings of pulses. We might regard this as analogous to the emphasis on inversional balance in the work's pitch structure as elaborated in Straus's analysis. The piece starts with an orientation of its basic pitch materials that we label their "prime" form; those forms have a certain referential priority in the movement (for example, at the movement's climax in m. 277, the viola plays an exact repetition, rather than an inversion, of the opening pitches), but from a synoptic viewpoint the pitch structure is balanced between prime and inversional forms in such a way that the *axes of inversion*, rather than one spatial orientation or the other, become the basis of its large-scale harmonic design. Similarly, the notated 2/2 meter of this movement has a certain priority, both because of the notation and because the first few measures of the piece are more easily heard in that meter than any other. That priority, however, is challenged by alternative triple meters so early in the piece and so pervasively that by the end of the movement we stop trying to hear one or the other metric orientation as primary, and instead focus on the various ways they are pitted against each other, transformed into each other—in short, placed into dialectic relationships with each other.

This view of the piece accounts for what otherwise seems a curiously inconclusive ending. If one were to adopt a tonal analogy for the work's rhythmic structure, one might expect the sorts of metric conflicts I have described to end with a decisive "resolution" to the "tonic" meter, 2/2. The triple groupings that challenge the primacy of the 2/2 meter could be taken as a metric "dominant." In fact, mm. 311–330 seem to provide just such a resolution, when the "dominant" triple groupings of pulses progress to the "tonic" duple ones. However, the movement does not end with this reassertion of the 2/2 meter, but with a re-evocation of the metric conflict of the climax. From the end of m. 334 through m. 337, while first-theme-derived i1 motives articulate shifting four-quarter-note spans in the second violin and viola (each time joined by an ic5 in either the cello or the first violin), the accompaniment motive appears with triple-eighth-note groupings that realize the xyy and xxy repeated-note patterns first discussed in connection with Example 3d. The eighth notes alternate in groups of nine between the first violin and the cello, beamed to suggest a 9/8 meter. This passage echoes the metric superpositions of the climax, but reverses the motivic associations of the duple and triple pulse-groups.[26] The synthetic versions of the work's basic materials that have been presented in mm. 311–330 prepare this reversal and the idea it represents: the metric identities of the movement's basic materials become *interchangeable;* by the end of the movement—as emphasized by the metric reversals of the coda—each motive incorporates both duple and triple metric orientations as part of its identity. This, rather than the subsumption of one metric orientation into the other, represents the dialectical synthesis of the movement's rhythmic structure.[27]

Several aspects of this metric design distinguish the rhythmic syntax of this work from its common-practice antecedents. One is the inversion of the usual roles of metric clarity and ambiguity. There are plenty of instances of sophisticated metric play—and even the occasional experiment in polymeters—in works from *Don Giovanni* to the Brahms Horn Trio. But no entire common-practice movement is based on a state of metric suspension that is only occasionally resolved into any clear ensemble meter. Another remarkable feature of this work is the extent to which meter itself, or more precisely the metric orientation of the work's central motives, generates a dialectic process spanning an entire movement. The deployment of these rhythmic-rhetorical devices to articulate form is ultimately one of the most innovational aspects of Schoenberg's twelve-tone rhythmic practice. And perhaps it is here, rather than in the use of theme-and-accompaniment textures or sonata form, that the neoclassical aspect of this work is most apparent. The use of a dialectical opposition to sustain a large-scale structure,

[26] After the first-theme motive aligns itself with the notated meter in m. 337, the "9/8" stratum dissolves and the movement ends a few bars later on a downbeat. It is a curious feature of the eighth-note motive of mm. 334–337 that the shifting position of the repeated notes *within* the three-note groups has the effect of maintaining the prevalent weak-to-strong orientation of repeated eighth notes with respect to the notated meter. Schoenberg constructs the 9/8 figure differently each time for this to work. The first and third 9/8 "measures" (both in the first violin) orient the repeated notes this way: xxy, xyy, xxy; the second, however (in the cello), differs: xyy, xxy, xyy. This changing pattern of repeated notes is superimposed on a consistent interval pattern: -13, +14 (or 2), -11, +17 (or 5), -13 in prime and inversion. By maintaining the orientation of the repeated eighth notes with respect to the notated rather than the perceived meter, Schoenberg facilitates the dissolution of the 9/8 rhythms into 2/2 meter that transpires in mm. 338–341. (I use the word "dissolution" advisedly; the final three measures of the movement are hearable in 2/2 but are too brief and too complicated to constitute a final "resolution" of the movement's rhythms into a 2/2 meter.)

[27] Martha Hyde's view of the pitch functions of the coda is similar to my view of its rhythm. Her analysis of the relationship between the Schoenberg and Schubert quartets places

and the reduction of metric phenomena to their most primal elements—duple and triple groupings of pulses—to create that opposition, would have been seen by Schoenberg as new realizations of universal principles. From the vantage point of the late twentieth century, however, a return to binary oppositions after the more diffuse structures of Schoenberg's atonal music can be regarded as a return to the classical principle par excellence: polarity.[28]

I am not sure to what extent we can extrapolate from the example of this movement to say that Schoenberg's twelve-tone music typically incorporates metric dialectics into formal design. I am very cognizant of a point Milton Babbitt has often made, which is that the most astounding aspect of Schoenberg's genius is not that he was both one of the greatest post-Wagnerian Romantics and the inventor of the twelve-tone system, but that within each of his major periods from one work to the next, and sometimes from one movement to the next, he could radically transform the basic fabric of his musical language. It is true that many works contain idiosyncratic processes. At the very least, however, we can affirm that a close study of Schoenberg's rhythmic structures promises to immeasurably enrich our understanding of the means he used to recreate the musical forms of the past in his twelve-tone works. Schoenberg's neoclassicism has far less to do with the anachronistic atmospherics his critics impute to him than it does with the process Hyde describes: entering into a dialogue with the past in order to gain inspiration for the creation of new modes of musical expression.

special emphasis on the coda as a passage in which the work's essentially innovational features emerge most clearly. In "Neoclassic and Anachronistic Impulses," 234, she writes: "Instead of using the coda to reaffirm the movement's principal themes, as Schubert did, Schoenberg reasserts the movement's primary axis, with its symmetrical and inversional secondary axes." The coda reveals the essential twelve-tone harmonic structures that underlie this revisionary sonata form. Basic motives are liquidated as the work's structural foundations are laid bare, and in the process the piece places ever greater distance between itself and classical models. I hear a similar distancing in the coda's refusal to settle into a definitive metric framework.

[28] I am indebted to Anne Stone for this observation.

STEPHEN PELES

Schoenberg and the Tradition of Imitative Counterpoint: Remarks on the Third and Fourth Quartets and the Trio

I suppose it is possible that some readers, given the title of this essay, might be expecting me to talk about Schoenberg and the tradition of imitative counterpoint, and to offer some analytical remarks on the Third and Fourth Quartets and the Trio. Well, sort of. My concern, however, is as much historical as analytical. What I want to do is to suggest that Schoenberg understood that tradition somewhat differently than we understand it today and that the difference matters. In particular, I wish to suggest that the various procedures—canon, fugue, and the like—that we are apt to regard as exhausting the category (and which I fear some may have expected to be my main focus) were, for Schoenberg, merely its most prototypical members, the central elements in a "radial category," the other elements of which qualify for membership in virtue of the relations they enter into with the prototypical members, which relations are variable in both degree and kind, in consequence of which variability the boundaries of the category are apt to be in some measure indeterminate. It is that indeterminacy that enables traditions to expand and develop yet remain traditions.

If this story has merit, then it is clearly not the case that Schoenberg saw himself quite the way we see him. It is more or less conventional wisdom, for example, that Schoenberg happened upon his twelve-tone technique while exploring ways of rendering his motivic technique of the 1910s and early 1920s more coherent and comprehensible—a motivic technique, a contrapuntal technique, he later abandoned once he began to understand the unique potential of the twelve-tone system. While I think it is true that Schoenberg viewed the system (or "method," as he preferred) as contributing importantly to comprehensibility and coherence, I also rather doubt that he thought of himself as abandoning anything—I think he saw himself rather as breathing new life into the tradition of counterpoint as he understood it. To be sure, this suggests a particularly conservative cast of mind in some respects, but just as surely, to acknowledge it in no way diminishes his accomplishment, for, as David Lewin aptly observed in an article that will loom large in what follows, it is precisely when Schoenberg "is at his most conservative that he is at his most radical."[1]

If this is right, then it says something very basic about how Schoenberg thought about music; it entails assumptions *so* fundamental in that respect that I doubt he ever thought of them as assumptions. In this regard as in others the question is closely bound up with Schoenberg's largely unquestioning reliance on the inherited (and what we would regard as the grossly metaphorical) language of "organicism"—roughly, the claim that successful pieces are best understood as being successful because they in some sense emulate processes or morphologies most prototypically characteristic of living organisms. Indeed, that assumption was so foundational as to be more a cultural than a personal article of faith; like other Viennese of his generation, Schoenberg was inclined to assert it as if it were self-evident, at most adducing in its support examples from the Western canon that purportedly exemplified relevantly "organic" characteristics, a strategy of ostension that falls far short of what we would expect of a successful defense of what is ultimately, after all, a straightforwardly empirical proposition concerning human cognition. And it is against the cultural backdrop of such unquestioned assumptions that one needs to understand Schoenberg's conception of imitative counterpoint if one wants to understand why his conception differed from ours. To us, imitative counterpoint is a narrow category exhausted by familiar small-scale manipulations of motives (with "motive" itself defined quite narrowly as something like "a small fragment of a tune"). To Schoenberg these were merely the most straightforward manifestations of a more general sort of musical organization that we might call "pattern replication under transformation," which by definition plays itself out in a musical context that is inherently multidimensional. Less central members of the category differ largely in what counts as a pattern, as a transformation, as a relevant dimension, or some combination of these.

[1] David Lewin, "Inversional Balance as an Organizing Force in Schoenberg's Music and Thought," *Perspectives of New Music* 6, no. 2 (spring/summer 1968): 20.

I cannot argue my point simply by offering examples from Schoenberg's work, though there are lots of these to offer. Brief passages of such strict imitation can of course be found in many of the published twelve-tone works, and the numerous short canons—variously tonal, atonal, and twelve-tone—written to celebrate birthdays and other occasions of personal import bespeak a lifelong preoccupation with imitation in our narrow sense of the term. But as my main point is that Schoenberg regarded his less obviously "imitative" work nonetheless to lie within the same tradition—representing, as it were, just a comparatively advanced stage of its evolution—I shall begin instead with a document found among his papers after his death. It is as good an indication as anything I know that the Viennese—at least Viennese musicians of Schoenberg's generation who came of age in the first quarter of this century—were not like us.

The document in question is no doubt familiar to most readers: it is the one-page description of what Schoenberg called "Die Wunder-Reihe"—"The Miracle Set"—poignantly inscribed with a copyright notice dated 1950, not long before his death; a transcription of the set and one of its inversions as these appear in the document is provided in Example 1. The set in question is based on a [014589] hexachord (hereafter "type E" hexachord), though the accompanying text gives no indication that Schoenberg realized that most of the "miraculous" properties of the set stem from the content of its hexachords rather than the ordering of their constituents, or that he had used sets based on this hexachord in more than one of his works. Nevertheless, a number of these properties clearly excited Schoenberg. The symmetry of the set, for one thing: for example, transpose the second hexachord up two semitones and reverse it and you produce the first hexachord; transpose the first hexachord down two semitones and reverse it and you produce the second hexachord. More important, however, the set (like any E hexachord set) has three indices of inversion at which hexachordally combinatorial transforms are produced: thus, for example, the original set beginning on E♮ can be accompanied in this fashion by inversions beginning on A, F, or C♯. Schoenberg includes in this document a list of the *even* transpositions of the T0/T5I combination with which he begins (in the document each such combination is T10-related to its immediate predecessor on the page). Under that sequence of transpositions the disjoint hexachords either map entirely to themselves or entirely to each other, so what Schoenberg represents in the document are all and only those pairs of sets that fall into the same hexachordal region (or "area," as David Lewin has called it) and thus express the general partitioning notion that we might verbalize as "divide the collection of twelve pitch classes into the pair of disjoint hexachords {0,E,8,4,7,3} and

{1,5,2,6,9,T}, hexachords that are transformationally equivalent under various values of T and I, and accompany this succession of two hexachords with the same set of hexachords in reverse order" and represent it as I have in Figure 1a. That idea itself can be understood as a special case of a more general idea expressed in Figure 1b: two events, ordered with respect to one another in some dimension, appear subsequently (with respect to ordering in some other dimension), optionally transformed, and with the original ordering in the first dimension permuted. In Schoenbergian terms the tables and commentary in the "Wunder-Reihe" document express aspects of the "musical idea" represented in Figure 1.

Example 1

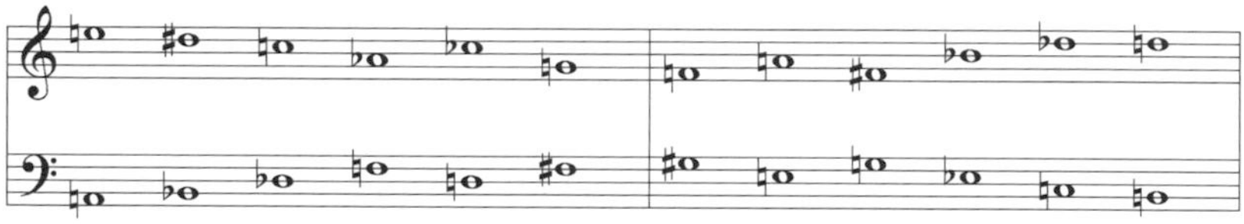

Die Wunder-Reihe (from Rufer *The Works of Arnold Schoenberg*)

Figure 1

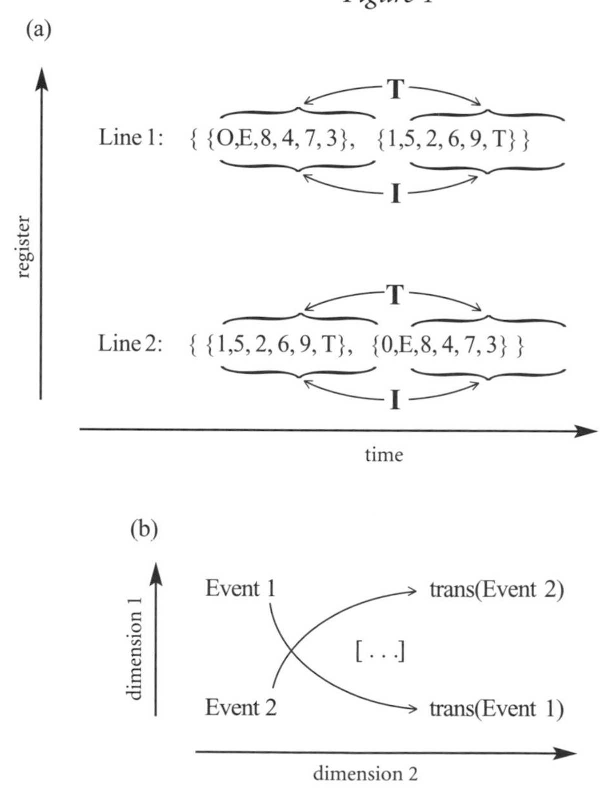

Given all this, however—given, that is, the set's remarkable potential in purely twelve-tone terms—it is Schoenberg's punch line that is most interesting. From his perspective, to what can this "miracle set" be best compared, given all the previous accomplishments of Western art music? (And few composers have felt the burden of the past as deeply as Schoenberg.)

> This offers a greater variety than double counterpoint of all sorts. Of course you have to invent your theme as ordinarily; but you have more possibilities of producing strongly related configurations, which in sound are essentially different.[2]

I trust that strikes readers as odd. If not, let me suggest the following *Gedankenexperiment.* Imagine a possible world identical to ours in all respects but one: imagine that we have not discovered the E hexachord yet. Imagine now that in the year 1999 a student composer, no doubt at Harvard, does so. With what previous benchmark, what prior historical high-water mark, would such a student choose to compare that discovery, so as best to convince the world of its importance? (It's worthy of a copyright, remember.) I would wager it would not be double counterpoint—modal, tonal, or any other flavor. I am frankly uncertain what a young composer these days would be apt to say an E hexachord is better than—except, perhaps, a C hexachord.

To make sense of Schoenberg's choice of double counterpoint as a standard of achievement we need to know more about how he viewed counterpoint as an organizing principle, as opposed to a technique in our narrow sense. Happily, he had a bit to say on that subject, though most of it remained unpublished until recently. Let me offer a few relevant quotations from *The Musical Idea and the Logic, Technique, and Art of Its Presentation*, a lengthy though unfinished manuscript dating mostly from the mid-1930s (though portions of it date from as early as 1923), published in an excellent translation by Patricia Carpenter and Severine Neff. As the title suggests, at issue is what Schoenberg called the "musical idea [*Gedanke*]"—which is not identical with the piece, but is presumed to be inferable from the piece by a properly qualified listener—and its relation to its "presentation" (*Darstellung*).[3]

[2] Josef Rufer, *The Works of Arnold Schoenberg: A Catalog of His Compositions, Writings, and Paintings*, trans. Dika Newlin (London: Faber & Faber, 1962), 151.

[3] There is no adequate English equivalent of *Darstellung;* certainly none that begin to capture the resonance the word had for Viennese intellectuals of Schoenberg's generation. "Representation" has become more or less standard, although in some contexts I think a case could be made for "interpretation." Some useful discussion can be found in Allan Janik and Stephen Toulmin's *Wittgenstein's Vienna* (New York: Touchstone Books, 1973).

> Science aims to present its ideas exhaustively so that no question remains unanswered. In contrast, art is content with a many-sided [presentation] from which the idea will emerge unambiguously but without having to be stated directly.[4]

> In counterpoint the issue is not so much the combination *per se* (i.e., it is not a goal in itself) as a many-sided presentation of the idea: the theme is so created that it holds within itself all these myriad *Gestalten* through which it [the many-sided presentation of the idea] will be made possible.[5]

> [A] contrapuntal idea has an *initial formulation* that permits shifting the position of the various constituents (themes, gestalten, voices) in a kaleidoscopic manner.[6]

Carpenter and Neff add some astute commentary. "In contrapuntal composition the idea is all the possibilities for combination that obtain among the given voices. . . . Notice that the combination contains all the *potential* combinations of the given voices. An actual fugue may use only a few of the possibilities, which can nevertheless be unambiguously reconstructed from the subject and countersubject. . . . Both the basic combination of contrapuntal composition and the basic set of the twelve-tone method contain all the possibilities they will subsequently unfold."[7]

By current standards this is a rather eccentric definition of "counterpoint" and uncomfortably Platonic to boot (though again, typically Viennese in its way): the *idea* of a piece encompasses things that need not actually happen *in* the piece—although, supposedly, they might have. In another context I might take the time to argue that there's a non-Platonic, psychological interpretation that could be put on that claim that renders it less implausible, and I might adduce in its support the difficulty any sufficiently acculturated Western listener is apt to have interpreting a pentatonic tune as anything other than a diatonic tune with elements of the diatonic collection missing. But since it is Schoenberg's psychology we are trying to understand, I want to consider how double counterpoint exemplifies the qualities Schoenberg stresses in the passages just quoted.

Remember what he said about how the "initial formulation" "holds within itself all the myriad gestalten" that follow (and presumably in most cases some that do not). That is one way, of course, of construing the initial

[4]Arnold Schoenberg, *The Musical Idea, and the Logic, Technique, and Art of Its Presentation*, ed. and trans. Patricia Carpenter and Severine Neff (New York: Columbia University Press, 1995), 18. This portion of the manuscript is dated 19 August 1923.

[5] Ibid., 19.

[6] Ibid., 111.

[7] Ibid., 18–19.

statement of the subject and countersubject in, say, a typical Bach fugue—a pair of voices almost invariably written in double counterpoint. That is, the subject, in conjunction with the syntactic constraints of the tonal system, has a finite number of possible countersubjects. Choose one that works in double counterpoint with the subject, and the possible inversions between the parts that might follow later in the fugue are further constrained—given a particular subject/countersubject pair, not every index of inversion will yield a syntactically well formed combination. Notice that in all cases it is not just the materials (if by that you mean only the notes) but rather the conjunction of the materials with the relevant principles of combination and succession that limits the size of the decision-space within which the composer works, and within which a competent listener will assume the composer works. Given this conjunction, not everything that *could* happen is equally likely; more important, perhaps, a properly qualified listener will be predisposed toward interpreting what *does* happen in light of its degree and kind of association with the presumed basic material of the piece and with known or inferred norms of combination, succession, and transformation. Put in those terms, "imitative counterpoint" describes a listening strategy as much as a compositional technique.

To summarize, I think double counterpoint (and imitative counterpoint more generally) was categorically central for Schoenberg because: (1) any such combination of two lines has potential implications for the subsequent unfolding of the piece, a fact that comported well with Schoenberg's organicist predisposition toward thinking of progression through a piece as a gradual realization of certain of the potentials of its materials (whatever else it might be in addition); (2) it's inherently multidimensional—at absolute minimum one needs, if one is thinking contrapuntally, to distinguish between intervals between notes in the same line and intervals between notes in different lines, for example; and (3) it's by definition imitative—events that occur in one line have the potential to reappear subsequently in another (so a notion of temporal succession is part and parcel of the concept), possibly under transformation (opening the door to conventional or novel techniques of variation and development).

This is starting to sound very much like twelve-tone composition as Schoenberg practiced it; at least the *Gedanke* of Schoenberg's twelve-tone method is one *Darstellung* of the idea. I am inclined to think that Schoenberg was being quite honest on the numerous occasions when he said in effect that he didn't regard himself as doing a different kind of thing than Bach or Brahms, and that his music differs from theirs not in the kinds of demands it places on listeners but in their *degree*—in the remoteness, for example, of the relations between events that Schoenberg expected a hypothetically qualified listener to be able to associate with one another. No doubt he was right about the demands. Some of the reasons are so well known that I shall merely acknowledge them without elaboration. One, of course, is the comparatively high degree of contextuality typical of these works: the tendency, that is, for certain principles of succession, combination, and transformation to be unique to the individual piece. Another has to do with the fundamental elements with which the twelve-tone system qua system is concerned. This one is so obvious that I am afraid to mention it, but so important that I'm afraid not to: viz., define your operations over pitch-*classes*, and pitch is suddenly free to do other things.

On Schoenberg's account, then, the demands arise not only from processes of the music but from the kinds of entities to which they are applied. What makes imitative counterpoint in the style of Bach more central to the category of thought I've been describing and makes Schoenberg's thinking less central rather than vice versa is that the components of Bach's counterpoint are closer to the centers of their respective subcategories. For example, both the subject and countersubject of a Bach fugue will straightforwardly exemplify the prototypical features of the category "line": roughly, a syntactically well formed temporally ordered sequence of single notes played by a single instrument in a register all its own. For purposes of the following discussion it will be useful to expand our concept of this category by generalizing from that prototype; henceforth, let us consider a "line" (or "voice" or "part") to be any temporally interpreted consecution of events that we have cause to regard as "going together."

As the opening of the Fourth Quartet is arguably the passage with which readers are likely to be most familiar, it seems an appropriate place to begin. Example 2 abstracts the passage in question; for reference I have also provided a twelve-by-twelve matrix of the twelve-tone set of the piece in Figure 2 and an informal chart of the passage in Figure 3. It is easy enough to hear the opening set statement in the first violin as a compound line composed of six underlying parts, each of which imitatively presents the same two-note motive, replicating—"answering" if you prefer—the pattern established by the first two notes of the tune; I have sketched these in Example 3.

Example 2

Example 3

Figure 2

	0	11	7	8	3	1	2	10	6	5	4	9
0	D	C♯	A	A♯	F	D♯	E	C	G♯	G	F♯	B
1	D♯	D	A♯	B	F♯	E	F	C♯	A	G♯	G	C
5	G	F♯	D	D♯	A♯	G♯	A	F	C♯	C	B	E
4	F♯	F	C♯	D	A	G	G♯	E	C	B	A♯	D♯
9	B	A♯	F♯	G	D	C	C♯	A	F	E	D♯	G♯
11	C♯	C	G♯	A	E	D	D♯	B	G	F♯	F	A♯
10	C	B	G	G♯	D♯	C♯	D	A♯	F♯	F	E	A
2	E	D♯	B	C	G	F	F♯	D	A♯	A	G♯	C♯
6	G♯	G	D♯	E	B	A	A♯	F♯	D	C♯	C	F
7	A	G♯	E	F	C	A♯	B	G	D♯	D	C♯	F♯
8	A♯	A	F	F♯	C♯	B	C	G♯	E	D♯	D	G
3	F	E	C	C♯	G♯	F♯	G	D♯	B	A♯	A	D

Trichords: W = D C♯ A; X = A♯ F D♯; Y = E C G♯; Z = G F♯ B

Figure 3

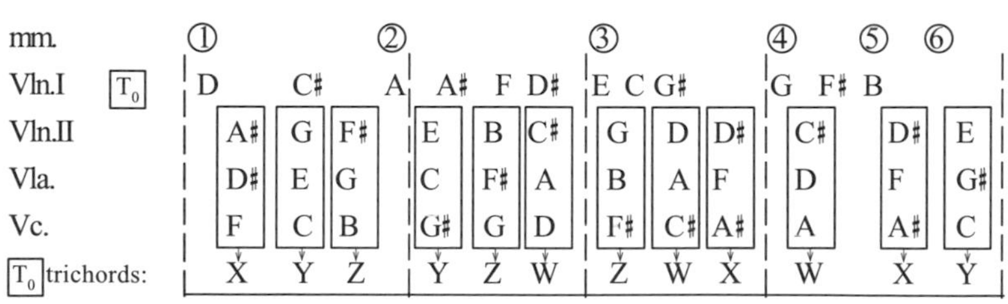

That is fairly straightforward, and we shall return to these lines in a moment, but Schoenberg's registral interpretation of this set has consequences greater in scope. As David Lewin noted in an early but seminal article, the last hexachord stands in a *pitch*-inversional relation to the first (that it stands in a pitch-*class* inversional relation, of course, is a matter of the set's ordering of pitch classes, and this is a typically Schoenbergian hexachordally combinatorial set in that respect), and it's at exactly the index of inversion that relates each hexachord of the set to its complement.[8] I find it easiest to hear this if I think of the set as ordered in two dimensions, time and register; I've represented the registral ordering in Example 4, along with an indication of the relevant inversional symmetry in that dimension—everything is balanced, so to speak, around the E and F immediately above middle C. As Lewin put it, this is an example of "Schoenberg registering his tune in a *pitch*-inversionally symmetrical way, so supporting the exposition of the basic pitch-*class* inversion."[9] The "basic pitch-class inversion" in question, of course, is the one between the set and its hexachordally combinatorial partner by inversion, which, notice, has not happened yet in the piece. But when it does—it is the next set form to be presented—its arrival is easily understood as realizing one of the potentials latent in the opening material.

Example 4

Lewin was absolutely right about this, and I would like to take a moment to pursue his observation further. One thing that does not happen for some time in this movement is a *simultaneous* statement of a set form with its combinatorial inversion. Instead, Schoenberg proceeds at a rather leisurely pace, presenting individually each of the four set forms that make up the initial hexachordal region. But the first sets to be presented simultaneously are, in fact, T0 and T5I. And as Lewin has argued—and the evidence of the music makes the point indisputable—the pairing of such sets constitutes a norm in Schoenberg's music as important as that of the set itself.

[8] Lewin, "Inversional Balance," 14–15.

[9] Ibid., 14.

Figure 4 illustrates what you get when you pair the first hexachords of these two set forms in a prototypical note-against-note fashion; I've labeled the resulting disjoint tetrachords Y, X, and Z for purposes of identification. Example 5 duplicates Example 4 with an added analytic notation intended to bring to your attention an important consequence of this choice of initial registration: the three resultant tetrachords shown in Figure 4—those that arise from the combination of T0 and T5I—are clearly projected in the registral ordering of the opening tune; they are what you get if you associate pitches pair-wise around the center of symmetry, each with its image under the relevant index of inversion. (Another way of putting this is that the two component dyads of each tetrachord are order number complements of each other to within the registral ordering of their respective hexachords.) And so the registration of the opening tune foreshadows not only the arrival of the set's combinatorial partner, but also the paradigmatic between-line collections that characterize their combination. It is perhaps worth emphasizing that this does *not* follow necessarily from the mere fact of pitch-inversional symmetry—there are numerous alternative ways of registering the opening set form that preserve its T5I symmetry around that particular E and F but that do *not* possess this contextually important property. To underscore the point I have provided one such counterexample in Example 6: its symmetries are identical to those in Schoenberg's version inasmuch as each pitch and its T5I partner are still balanced around the same center of symmetry, so I suppose it does as good a job of prefiguring the arrival of the next set form (we would have to get the viola to play it, of course), but unlike Schoenberg's version it fails completely when it comes to anticipating the *combination* of the second set form with the first (no doubt it is deficient in other respects as well).

Figure 4

T_0S:	D C♯	A A♯	F D♯
T_5IS:	G G♯	C B	E F♯
	Y	X	Z

Example 5

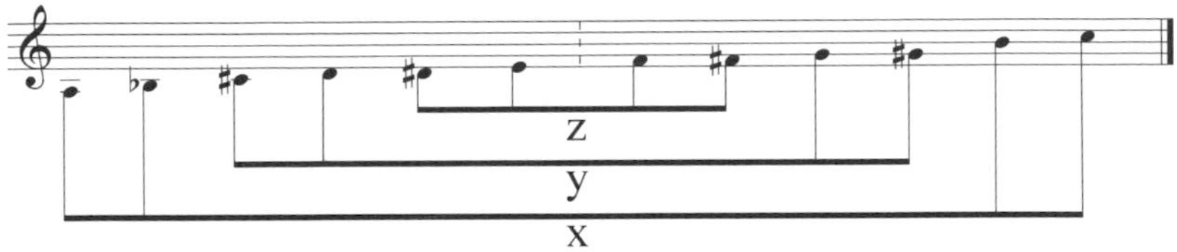

Example 6

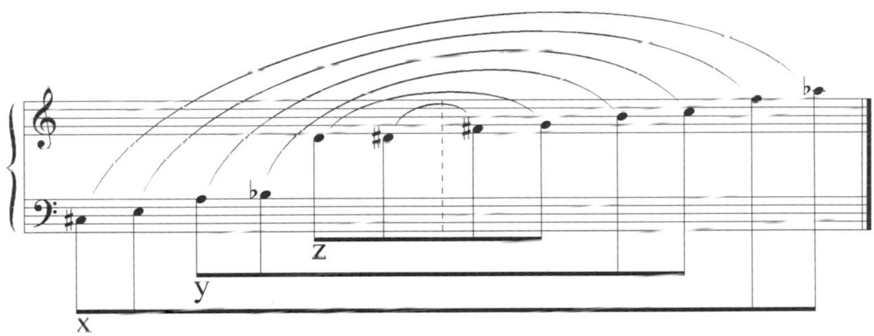

Thus far we have seen how one inferable pitch counterpoint underlying the opening tune anticipates collections typical of an *abstract*, paradigmatic T0/T5I combination. Schoenberg's tune also anticipates the first occurrence of that combination as it actually appears compositionally interpreted in the piece. Example 7 abstracts the spot in question, m. 27, another celebrated passage; the example shows the previous four measures as well. Measure 25 consists of a single statement of T0 shared by the second violin and viola; the next measure consists of a single statement of T5I in the same instrumentation. Measure 27 is where the sets are stated simultaneously (I have bracketed the first aggregate): T0 is shared by the two violins and T5I by the viola and cello; each instrumental pair induces a 3-plus-3 partition on each hexachord of its set form. In this case the trichords assigned to the instruments in the first aggregate are all of different types: [012] in the first violin, [015] in the second, [013] in the viola, and [014] in the cello. The [015] and [014] are not surprising as types or tokens: they are set segments. The first violin's [012] is not segmental here, but as a type it does occur as a segment in the set (in fact, the violin's D-C♯-D♯ occurs as an ordered segment in RT10); however, the viola's [013] is also nonsegmental, and you do not find a segmental [013] *anywhere* in the set. The particular partitioning scheme that has conjoined these non-consecutive elements of the set began in m. 25, of course, and the first hexachord of that T0 statement—about to become that set form's contribution to the first classical aggregate of the piece—reminds one a lot of the opening set statement.

Example 7

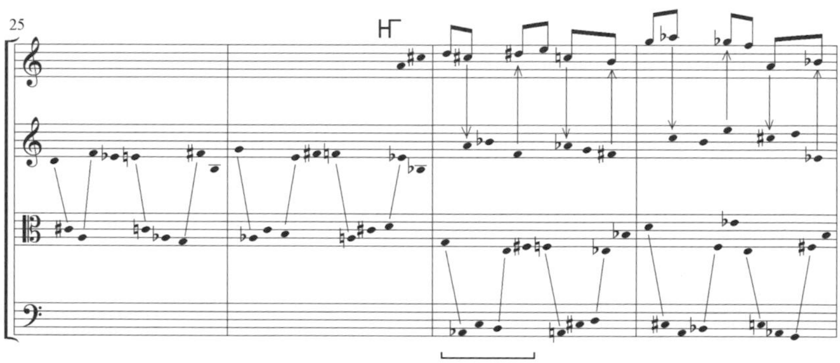

In fact, the instrumental partitioning of that first hexachord in m. 25 into a [013] trichord and a [014] trichord is almost redundant: it just reinforces the registral counterpoint that's at work here, which itself duplicates the counterpoint that underlies the opening tune—they are precisely the same pitches in both cases. Example 8 shows the registral ordering *within* the two temporally disjoint hexachords of that original tune. The counterpoint here is double counterpoint—invertible counterpoint—in several senses of the term. Example 9 clarifies, by portraying the registrally induced 2-partition of each hexachord: [013], the highest, and [014], the lowest in the first hexachord (the same order number partition as the one induced both registrally and *instrumentally* in the later passage), have their registral positions swapped—inverted—in the second temporal hexachord, a relation portrayed more abstractly in Figure 5. And the instrumental partitioning of the two hexachords that make up the aggregate in m. 27—one into a [012] trichord and a [015] trichord and the other into a [013] trichord and a [014] trichord—tells you something about what the hexachord of the set has in common with type-A hexachords, like the ones that now emerge in this passage in the two violins. Indeed, if you doubt that Schoenberg was trying to remind you of the opening of the piece here at the opening of this section, perhaps leading you to notice after-the-fact aspects of it that you might have missed originally, please glance at the first violin part—the *Hauptstimme*—in mm. 27 and 28. As is well known, it's a derived set, but consider what it's derived *from*: six [01] dyads, each registered as a minor second. And it's the *same* set of minor seconds (though not always in the original octave) with which we began this discussion, here temporally rather than registrally deployed—compare with Example 3. As Schoenberg might say, "Goethe would be proud."

Example 8

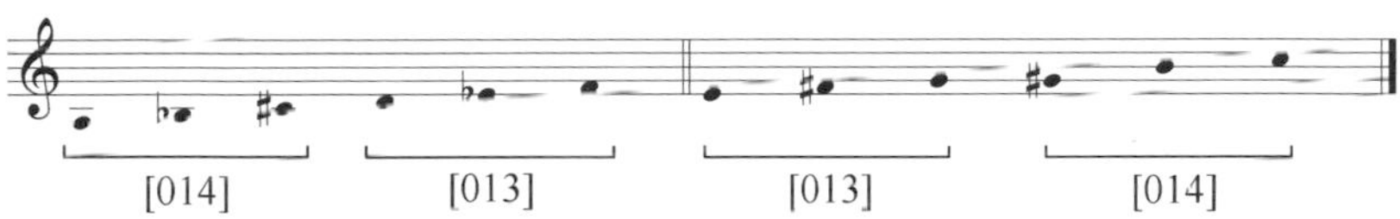

Example 9

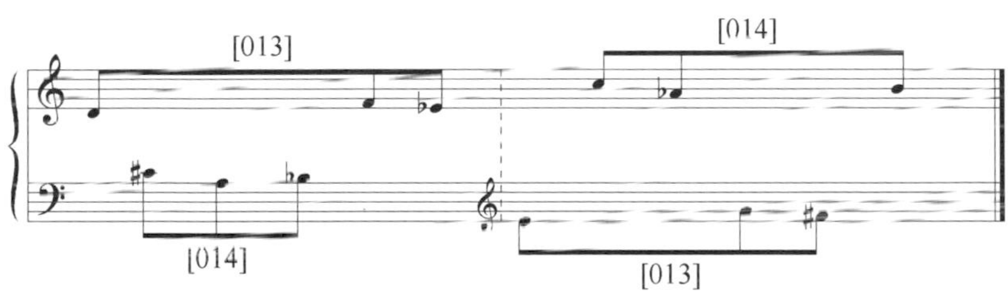

Figure 5

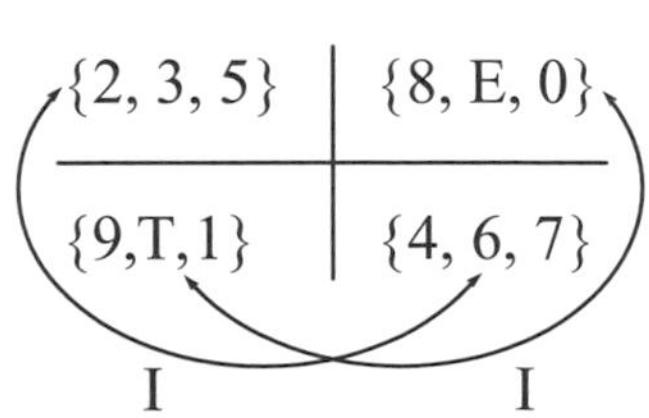

Had I the space there is much more that could be said about m. 27 and its relations to what precedes and follows it, but I shall have to be content with one final observation about the registration of the opening tune. Example 10 returns to the overall registral ordering, bracketing notes in such a way as to focus your attention on the intersecting segmental tetrachords exclusive of the middlemost dyad that defines the center of pitch symmetry; the [0123] tetrachord that includes that dyad will have to wait for another occasion. The example identifies the type of each, though that is not really my point (but I hope you can imagine how this could be redisplayed in such a fashion as to reveal another sort of double counterpoint); the point is in the transform labels I've applied to each to indicate, for example, that as a collection of pitch classes A, B♭, C♯, and D occur as a set segment in T0 and T7I. As indicated in the example, the four set forms thus associated with these collections are T0, T10, T5I, and T7I. As it happens, these are not inconsequential relations in the first movement, but I can do no more here than provide in Example 11 the opening of the slow movement with its celebrated unison statement of T10—it is the only movement to begin in a different hexachordal region—and leave it to the reader to make the comparison with Example 10, urging you to take register, rhythm, and metrical position into consideration when you do.

Example 10

Example 11

Notice that certain of the implications of the opening tune that we have observed are dependent—on my account at least—on the inversional symmetry involved, but some, in principle, are not (though I do not for a moment dispute the fundamental importance of the symmetry here and elsewhere). Thus, the recurrence of the combination of "lines" displayed in Example 3 as a succession of dyads in the first violin requires only that we reify them *as* lines to begin with, and the imitative relation between the first two violin notes—set apart from the rest in so many ways by Schoenberg's deployment of the set here—and the ten that follow makes that easy to do; indeed, I can think of this as one thing happening several times. But we have also done something rather more abstract that I want to acknowledge at this point: we have noted another *kind* of thing being replicated here that we might call a "partitioning motive." Here it takes the form of inducing an equal-size 2-partition on successions of pitches (we could easily describe this as an operation on order numbers); noticing a coherent relation that obtains by splitting the set six-plus-six in time emboldened us to do the same in register (as in Example 4) over the span of the entire set, as well as three-plus-three over the span of its temporal hexachords (as in Example 9).

A somewhat similar abstract partitioning scheme characterizes my next example. Space does not permit me an extensive consideration of the Third Quartet, and I admit to choosing the passage shown in Example 12, the opening of the slow movement, because of its personal appropriateness to this occasion: it was owing to a few remarks I made in print about it a number of years ago that I had my first contact with David Lewin, who wrote me a typically generous and quite alarmingly insightful letter about this passage and other matters from his desk at Yale. But the aspect of the passage that I want to touch upon here is musically pertinent to this discussion because it indicates one of the numerous ways Schoenberg extended the tradition. The imitation here is between different *kinds* of lines. Here the pitch-class content of a pair of *registral* lines is subsequently replicated in a pair of *instrumental* lines. The music in question is that of the two violins. They share a single set form—T0—in mm. 1–3, and another set form—RT5I—in mm. 6–9, in both cases stating the disjoint segmental dyads of the set as simultaneities. For reference I have written the relevant set forms beneath the example. Consider the registral lines through which the two violins move over the course of mm. 1–3; that they are hard to see is merely an artifact of our notational system, but they are reasonably easy to hear owing to the timbral homogeneity of the two instruments. The first part of Example 13 is a visual aid intended to encourage that hearing. It shows the ordering of that first set form in register; as was the case in the Fourth Quartet example, it is inversionally symmetrical, though that is not part of my story except insofar as the symmetry strongly suggests a hearing of this music in terms of equal-part 2-partitions. The lower part of Example 13 redisplays the instrumental lines of mm. 6–9 as they partition RT5I: as the example indicates, the pitch classes of the lower hexachord of the T0 statement are picked up by the first violin as its contribution to the RT5I statement, and the higher are picked up by the second violin.

Example 12

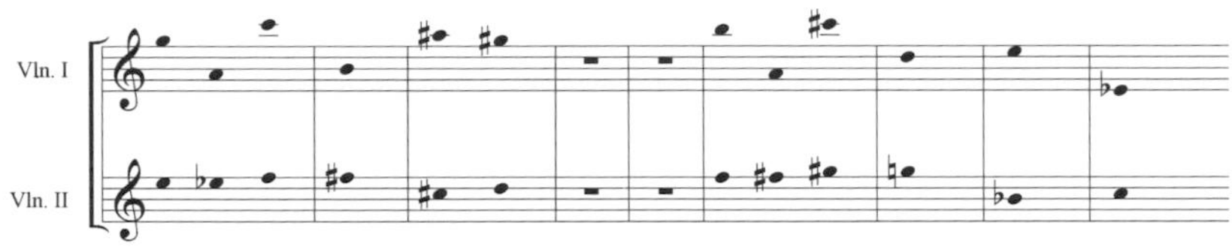

T_0:	G E	E♭ A	C F	F♯ B	A♯ C♯	G♯ D
RT_5I:	F B	F♯ A	G♯ C♯	D G	A♯ E	E♭ C

Example 13

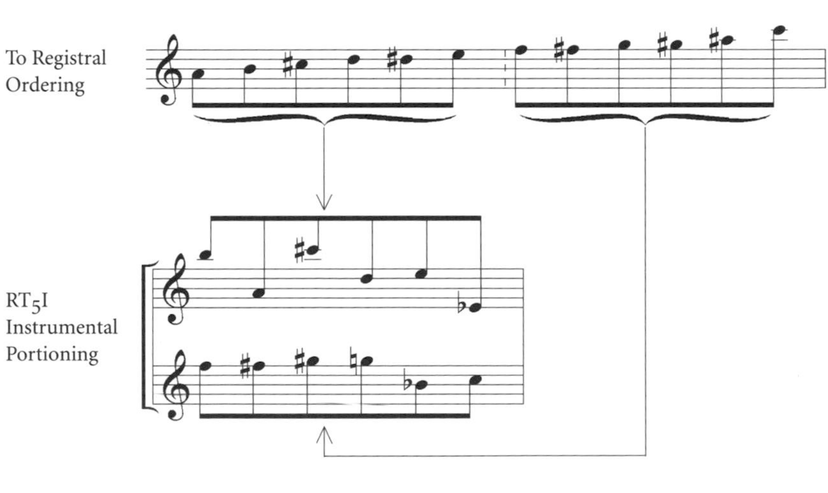

Example 14 is offered largely to discharge a contractual obligation incurred by the title of this paper; both Martin Boykan and Richard Kurth discuss the String Trio in detail elsewhere in this collection, so my own remarks will be brief. Example 14a abstracts the first measure of the piece, which is also the first aggregate. Example 14b shows the first measure of the second episode (the piece consists of five large sections: three ritornello-like "parts," with episodes separating them). Example 14c shows the ordering in register of the first aggregate, one pertinent property of which—just one, I would stress—is the occurrence in that ordering of two intersecting segmental hexachords equivalent in type to the hexachords of the set of the piece. It is hard not to hear this octachord as a well-defined grouping of pitches when it is first encountered at the opening of the piece: it consists of all (and only) those pitches assigned to the violin and viola; equivalently here, all (and only) those played as "quasi-trills." But it is the transposition levels of these registral hexachords that prompt this example. If you look at the lowermost of the two in Example 14c and glance back at the music at the beginning of Example 14b, you will see that it is the same collection of pitch-classes in both cases, though in each case arising through the interpretation of a different set form—"strongly related configurations, which in sound are quite different."

Example 14

(a) m.1

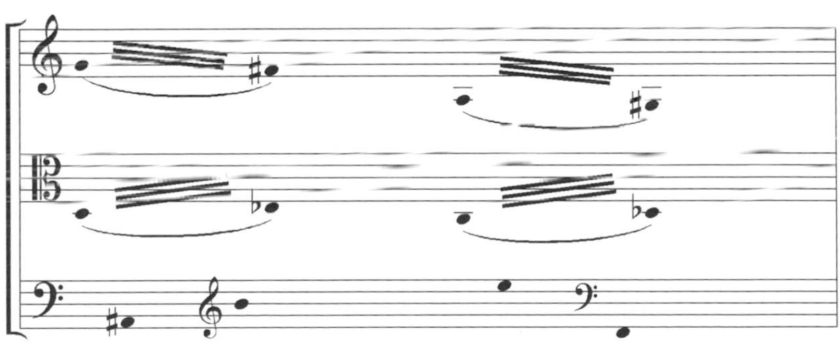

Example 14 (continued)

(b) m.180

(c) m.1: Registration of Aggregrate

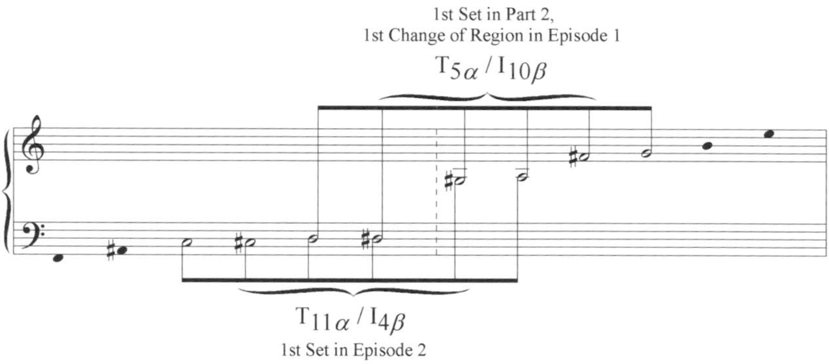

My last example is in some respects the most conventionally canonic that we have seen, but as is so often the case in Schoenberg's music its conventionality is deceptive. It is a case of imitation in service of permutation—a traditional technique employed for novel ends—and it occurs late in the String Trio. The passage in question begins with the cello line in the last measure of Example 15a—m. 188. It is a canon in even sixteenth notes at the time distance of an eighth note. Each instrument is playing the same 12-tone set, but it is not one of *the* sets, so to speak, of the piece. It has the same hexachordal content as those sets, but the ordering is different, and it is not related to any of them by any of the familiar interval-preserving operations. Crudely put, where does this come from?

Example 15

Vln.

T_8: B♭ G♭ C♭ F C A / D D♭ E G E♭ A♭

Vla.

To answer that question in the most local terms, it helps to notice where this ordering of the hexachord occurred earlier. You can see it, in inverted form, beginning on B♭ in m. 184, again in the cello. But where does *that* come from? The cello line is wholly dependent on the counterpoint between the two upper instruments, which, beginning in m. 184, share a single set form, T8. I have represented the partitioning of that set between the violin and viola in Figure 15c, and I will note in passing that that partitioning scheme is itself imitative, as Schoenberg's frequently are: it is a "cardinality canon," so to speak. Imagine a pair of read-only Turing machines sharing a single tape. The violin is the leader and the viola the follower. The violin takes one element, the viola takes one; the violin takes two elements, the viola takes two; the violin takes one element, the viola takes one; and so forth. At the end of the process each instrument has accrued six elements. And the cello line is in canon with *both,* alternately imitating the trichords of each, as summarized in Example 15b. But remember what has happened: the hexachord has been permuted, and not by any interval preserving operation. The result is a new set, and by m. 188 the imitative process that engendered it and the lines that were its ancestors have disappeared, and it has begun to live a life of its own.

I think it is fair to say that from Schoenberg's perspective his music wasn't any less imitative than his predecessors'—it was more so. He regarded himself as legitimate heir to the tradition in part *because* he expanded it, extending its principles and its influence in ways previously unimagined.

Of course this essay was inspired by the imaginative contributions of two people: Schoenberg, who did more than any composer in this century to change the way we think about music; and David Lewin, who has done more than anyone to change the way we think about Schoenberg—and much else. It's a pleasure, and a rare privilege, to be able to acknowledge, however inadequately, one's indebtedness to both of these remarkable musicians.

RICHARD KURTH

Moments of Closure: Thoughts on the Suspension of Tonality in Schoenberg's Fourth Quartet and Trio

But even standing where I do at the present time, I believe that to use the consonant chords, too, is not out of the question, as soon as someone has found a technical means of either satisfying or paralysing their formal claims.

– Arnold Schoenberg, "Opinion or Insight?" (1926)

I

At the end of the Fourth Quartet's first movement Schoenberg generates considerable harmonic tension, and I have often wondered what musical forces he is attempting to invoke and resolve there. In complete contrast, the String Trio does not so much end as dissipate; it seems to dismantle itself, but it also creates abiding and vivid expectancies by evoking latent musical forces at a moment of closure. These cadences, and others like them, stimulate the following observations about the suspension of tonality in Schoenberg's twelve-tone compositions.

Memory is one of the more general conditions for musical closure, and it operates in several dimensions. It engages elements within a specific composition to create musical forms; more broadly, it may also invoke materials of an earlier piece or compositional approach. Both of the works under scrutiny here use traditional formal techniques to recall earlier materials and create large-scale formal closure. (The systematic and exhaustive presentation of a circumscribed range of possibilities never became a form-generating principle in Schoenberg's music to the degree that it has, for instance, in Milton Babbitt's music.) Reprise plays a major role in the String Trio, but the episodic rhetoric and the intense developmental variation of motivic ideas create the impression of multiple modes and temporalities of recollection, each with altered emphases and degrees of ellipsis; the piece thereby acquires a quasi-narrative character in which reprise is a renewal and reenactment of narration, an act of reopening, rather than one of closure and resolution.[1] Reprise here lacks the full scope of large-scale resolution achieved by the more dialectical use of recapitulation, as a balancing and resolving force, that one finds in the Fourth Quartet. The first movement, for instance, presents a clear sonata-form recapitulation at m. 165, but the opening theme returns there transposed at the tritone. The original transpositional level does not return prominently until m. 239, and it takes on particularly compelling recapitulatory force only at m. 274 (*Tempo I*), so that the final eleven measures powerfully confirm what might be called a "tonic" harmonic level.

The word "tonic" in the last observation is at odds with the prevailing notion that Schoenberg's twelve-tone music completely abandons tonality in any relevant sense. What follows will explore how sonorities and continuities characteristic of Schoenberg's earlier tonal music *sometimes* surface in his twelve-tone works, especially at moments of closure. Such continuities, if rare in Schoenberg's twelve-tone compositions, are nonetheless significant for our understanding of his compositional thinking and its lifelong evolution.

[1] Some months after I wrote these remarks, a profound and elegant essay appeared in print which examines these notions in rich detail; see Michael Cherlin, "Memory and Rhetorical Trope in Schoenberg's String Trio," *Journal of the American Musicological Society* 51, no. 3 (1998): 559–602. The quasi-narrative character of the Trio may well reflect the extreme personal circumstances of its composition. Schoenberg composed the Trio between 20 August and 23 September 1946 while recuperating from a possible heart attack suffered on 2 August. The work reportedly represents in detail his memories of this event, which he later referred to as "mein Todesfall." For differing accounts, see Willi Reich, *Schoenberg: A Critical Biography*, trans. Leo Black (New York: Praeger, 1971), 219; and H. H. Stuckenschmidt, *Schoenberg: His Life, World, and Work*, trans. Humphrey Searle (London: Calder, 1977), 479. For summary and further argument, see Walter B. Bailey, *Programmatic Elements in the Works of Schoenberg*, Studies in Musicology 74 (Ann Arbor: UMI Research Press, 1984), 151–157. Cherlin, in the essay cited above, plumbs some deep connections between the experience and the composition.

The kind of hearing I shall discuss has had various proponents over the years.[2] Roger Sessions, for instance, neatly articulated the heart of the matter in 1951 (the year of Schoenberg's death):

> The twelve-tone technique, however, does not provide the answer to the question of how the ear perceives, co-ordinates, and synthesizes the relationships involved, nor does it attempt to do so. Its nature is essentially practical; and when it is used by composers of imagination who have really mastered it, the experienced listener will *inevitably be aware* of what may be called "tonal areas" or "tonal centers." But in no real sense are these matters definable in the older terms. For instance, in listening to the first movement of Schoenberg's *Fourth Quartet*...[the listener] will receive sensations which will suggest to him the key of D, even specifically of d minor; but if he tries to analyze these sensations in terms of this key in any known or knowable form,...he will find that he can adduce only the most fragmentary and hopelessly inadequate bits of evidence.[3]

Tonal sensations pose methodological and stylistic problems for the analysis of twelve-tone music, but Sessions asserts that we will "inevitably be aware" of them. I hope to indicate later—in effect by doubling Sessions's argument upon itself—why the evidence *must* be fragmentary, and also why D minor is not the only tonal sensation one might have at the end of the quartet's first movement.

We cannot deny that the reflexes of Schoenberg's own musical memory must have played a role in his acts of composition, even if we can never determine precisely what those reflexes were. Schoenberg's remarkably deft tonal thinking produced with amazing speed the extraordinary tonal structures of his early masterworks. Can such a mind completely suppress the multivalent tonal intuitions it acquired early on? When he goes about cadencing in his twelve-tone music, in the supposed absence of a tonic, how does he prevent momentary tonal implications from arising, especially at moments of

[2] Selected recent contributions on the topic of tonal evocations in Schoenberg's twelve-tone music include Cherlin, "Memory and Rhetorical Trope"; Silvina Milstein, *Arnold Schoenberg: Notes, Sets, Forms* (Cambridge: Cambridge University Press, 1992); and Hans Keller, "Schoenberg's Return to Tonality," *Journal of the Arnold Schoenberg Institute* 5, no. 1 (1981): 2–21. Also relevant to the present topic is Jonathan Dunsby, "Schoenberg on Cadence," *Journal of the Arnold Schoenberg Institute* 4, no. 1 (1980): 41–49.

[3] Roger Sessions, *Harmonic Practice* (New York: Harcourt, Brace, 1951), 406–407, emphasis added; see also 408 for relevant remarks. David Lewin quotes other remarks from the same pages in "Some Ideas about Voice-Leading between Pcsets," *Journal of Music Theory* 42, no. 1 (spring 1998): 25. I am grateful to Lewin for drawing my attention to Sessions's remarks, and for many, many other things as well.

closure, where they cannot be denied by what follows (and where his subconscious "sense of form" may well have exerted its strongest influence)? Late in life Schoenberg asked himself these same questions:

> In the last few years I have been questioned as to whether certain of my compositions are "pure" twelve-tone, or twelve-tone at all. The fact is that I do not know.... When I compose, I try to forget all theories and I continue composing only after having freed my mind of them.... Whether certain of my compositions fail to be "pure" because of the surprising appearance of some consonant harmonies—surprising even to me—I cannot, as I have said, decide. But I am sure that a mind trained in musical logic will not fail even if it is not conscious of everything it does.[4]

For Schoenberg, twelve-tone "purity" and theoretical or systematic matters are secondary to "musical logic," but we must not assume that this expression means "twelve-tone logic" as music theory understands it today. Training in musical logic, as Schoenberg conceives it, allows the musical mind to create and link coherent ideas spontaneously. If composition for Schoenberg involves a conscious forgetting (of theories) so that musical thinking and intuition can act productively and organically, then we are obliged to ponder seriously the possibility of submerged tonal reflexes in his later music. Conscious forgetting and subconscious remembering are very often woven into a single psychological knot.

I will therefore try to integrate Schoenberg's path from the remarkably sophisticated tonal masterpieces to the later twelve-tone compositions by drawing on the concepts of *schwebende* and *aufgehobene Tonalität* ("fluctuating" and "suspended" tonality) that he introduced in his 1911 *Harmonielehre*, to suggest that for him the twelve-tone method was perhaps not so much a way of abandoning tonality as a further means of "suspending" it.[5] The sporadic tonal compositions of the later years suggest that the abandonment of tonality may not have been an easy, or even desirable, matter for Schoenberg. As his compositional thinking evolved, he first extended tonality, then progressively emancipated it, then finally sublimated it within the twelve-tone system, where it makes its presence felt only in transitory moments of what I shall call tonal "potency" or "latency." These moments reveal that tonality is

[4] Arnold Schoenberg, "My Evolution" (1949), in *Style and Idea*, 91–92.

[5] On the concepts of *schwebende* and *aufgehobene Tonalität*, see Arnold Schoenberg, *Harmonielehre* (Vienna: Universal Edition, 1911), 430–431. For an English translation (based on the revised second edition of 1922), see Arnold Schoenberg, *Theory of Harmony*, trans. Roy E. Carter (Berkeley and Los Angeles: University of California Press, 1983), 383–384. See also Arnold Schoenberg, *Structural Functions of Harmony* (New York: Norton, 1969), 111.

not eradicated in his twelve-tone works, but is instead sublimated or *aufgehoben*, a condition that has significant implications for moments of closure in these compositions. After examining some excerpts from the works at hand, I shall draw on Schoenberg's prose writings to support this conjecture.

II

Example 1 sketches the first nine measures (to the downbeat of m. 623) from the Fourth Quartet's Largo third movement. This music is based on two row forms, here simply labeled P and I. Dashed bar lines on the example represent row-form boundaries: P is declaimed in unison at the outset; the retrograde of its combinatorial inversion (labeled RI on the example) begins with the cello A♭2 in m. 618; RP follows, beginning with the inner-voice A3 and E3 in m. 621.[6] The lozenge-shaped noteheads are analytical additions on my part, and will be discussed in due course.

Example 1

Reduction of Schoenberg, Fourth Quartet, III, mm. 614–623.

During the initial declamation of P, several factors create a sense of temporary tonal repose on the B♭3 in m. 616, and on the A3 in m. 618, one semitone lower. Both tones are points of cadential arrival, stressed by relatively long durations. The B♭3 seems consonant, stable, and root-like because of the D4 that precedes it (which is itself preceded by a repeating and increasingly agitated D♭ that sounds retrospectively as C♯, the raised second scale-degree of B♭); similarly, the descending fifth from E4 evokes a tonal cadence on the A3. Any sense of tonal organization, however, is at best of a *fluctuating* sort. (*Luftpausen* between the staffs on the example indicate the sense of fluctuation from one temporary close to the next.) Even so, a longer stepwise

6 See Lewin, "Some Ideas about Voice-Leading," 26–31, for an array of fascinating observations about the opening unison statement of P.

descent (beamed on the example) does link the initial C4 (sustained and prominent) to the medial B♭3 and the final A3. The C4-B♭3-A3 span suggests, if only somewhat abstractly, possible prolongational interpretations of the entire opening "soliloquy"; it *might*, for instance, be construed with reference to A minor tonality (with B♭ representing ♭II harmony, or a diminished fifth in an altered dominant harmony), or alternatively as a prolongation of dominant harmony in B♭ (with the closing G♭4, F4, and A3 strongly evoking dominant-function harmony). These two abstract prolongational alternatives, in combination, suggest that tonality is also *suspended* here by the simultaneous interaction of conflicting keys. B♭ and A are not the only relevant keys, however, and some other candidates will emerge shortly, to develop (and also reconfigure) those initial sensations.

The box on Example 1 (isolating the notes from the B♭3 to the A3) stages a thought experiment into the role of musical memory and its reflexes. The enclosed pitch sequence strongly evokes the opening of Wagner's *Tristan und Isolde*, transposed up one semitone. The leap from the sustained B♭3 to the G♭4 gives the initial memory-cue, and the motion from G♭4 to F4, set to agitated rhythms but repeated with increasingly definite metric orientation, acts out the process of an emerging memory-experience. The E4 would be the site of the memory-fulfilling "Tristan chord," which has been depicted here by lozenge noteheads.[7] The chord is not realized literally in Schoenberg's texture and must be imagined as a *Scheinakkord*, but the cadential A3 does reinforce an aural impression of the chord; arrows on the example indicate how the G♭5 and A3 can easily be adjusted in register to reinforce our aural imaging of the chord. C4 is the only chord member not in the immediate context of this imaginary event, but it was very prominent at the start in m. 614, and is easily recalled. It will also take on greater significance.

I shall not assert that Wagner is being quoted here. But the thought experiment does provoke us to listen differently than we might otherwise. The epiphanic *Scheinakkord* awakens musical memory, activates a sense of tonal function and possibility, and stimulates the interpretive process conveyed as Example 1 continues. Above the cello's A♭2, which begins RI, the pitches of the Tristan *Scheinakkord* have been retained as lozenges, to indicate how the A♭2 retrospectively transforms them into an altered dominant harmony in D♭ (with E4 as an augmented fifth, and A3 reinterpreted as the minor ninth B♭♭). The D♭2 that immediately follows in the cello succinctly resolves this altered dominant; the upper voices remain silent momentarily, and one can imagine

[7] For Schoenberg's comments on the "Tristan chord," see Schoenberg, *Harmonielehre*, 283; *Theory of Harmony*, 257–258; and *Structural Functions of Harmony*, 77.

the resolutions indicated by lozenge noteheads above the D♭ (which are among its overtones and correspond, in fact, to pitches heard earlier in the unison melody). The harmonic idiom, which is very characteristic of Schoenberg's earlier tonal works, emerges only because the chosen durations, rhythms, and registers allow it to; the composer could certainly have arranged those parameters so as to repress or obliterate it. Moreover, the progression "explains" the transition from row form P to RI quite differently than we normally would. It may also offer insight into the insistent repetition of D♭4 in m. 615, noted earlier.

Despite the momentary "resolution to D♭," the sense of tonality immediately fluctuates. A harmony inferable in m. 619, labeled X on the example, reconfigures the bass D♭2 as the diminished fifth of an altered dominant sonority, its root being the G3 sustained by the second violin. The viola, oscillating between C4 and B3 (the same two pitches that began the unison melody in m. 614), projects a conventional 7-6 suspension figure over the bass D♭, effectively defining C as a tonic and B as its leading tone. Near the end of m. 619 the first violin's D♯5 adds an augmented fifth to this dominant sonority.[8] Although the implied chord of resolution (C major) is not stated literally, the D♯5 does resolve as expected, to E5. The E5 is sustained solo for two full quarters, surely long enough for the listener to imagine vividly the implied C major harmony indicated by lozenge noteheads beneath the E5. It is particularly easy to imagine the cello's D♭2 moving down by semitone to C2; one observes likewise that the repeated D♭4 in m. 615 was just a semitone away from the initial sustained C4 in m. 614.

To be sure, the tonal progression just described ([V]-♭II-V-I in C) is hardly unequivocal. The harmonies in question either are functionally ambivalent "vagrant" chords, or they are represented by just a single tone. Lacking explicitness, they can at best convey tonal implication, potentiality, or latency. Those limited qualities, however, are desirable so far as the fluctuation and suspension tonality are concerned. The transitory C tonality that emerges here is plausibly conditioned by the opening C4, and sufficiently sustained over mm. 617–620, to merit our consideration.[9]

[8] The resulting dominant, {G, B, D♭, D♯}, involves both a raised and lowered fifth. Both alterations are characteristic of Schoenberg's thinking. See, for instance, *Theory of Harmony*, 392 (Exx. 321–323), where Schoenberg simultaneously raises and lowers the fifth of a dominant ninth chord to produce a whole-tone dominant.

[9] Silvina Milstein, in an analysis that belabors some very hypothetical connections between this movement and the F minor third movement of Beethoven's Quartet op. 59, no. 1, interprets the continuity up to m. 621 (and beyond) as projecting an F tonality. See Milstein, *Arnold Schoenberg*, 98–108.

In fact, some of the same potencies are reinforced over the ensuing measures. The same incipient "Tristan chord" emerges again in m. 621, incomplete but recognizable: it is signaled once more by G♭5 moving to F5 in the treble; that idea is then reversed in the bass, so that G♭2 sounds below the repeating inner-voice A3 and E3, and the exact intervallic structure of the Wagnerian chord is nearly replicated (except that the lozenge note C3 is missing). This time, the *Scheinakkord* resolves to D and B♭, echoing the earlier cadence on B♭ in m. 616. B♭ also represents the Wagnerian tonal context for our transposed "Tristan chord." Despite the sense of temporary repose on B♭ at the corresponding *Luftpause* on the example, the sense of an incipient C tonality is not lost. The first violin (solo) projects the dominant sonority X once more, with G and B especially prominent, and the opening C4 returns, metrically strong on the downbeat of m. 623, with a tonal potency that is almost too obvious. The accompaniment liquidates that impression in the nick of time, by initiating in m. 623 a new pair of combinatorial row forms that largely dissolve the sense of incipient C tonality (T9P and T9I). Even so, the cello's downbeat A2 in m. 623 briefly but palpably conveys the sense of a deceptive cadence in C, and its approach to C2 from C♯2 (= D♭2) in m. 624 also echoes similar approaches that were observed earlier.[10]

The *Luftpausen* on Example 1 serve to summarize temporary tonal evocations of B♭ (twice), A, D♭, and C (twice), which together produce a rather vivid sense of fluctuating (*schwebende*) tonality.[11] Tonality is also suspended (*aufgehoben*) here, because the tonal references are not explicit, and because the logic and coherence of the music does not depend on them in any case. The twelve-tone method emancipates tonality from its role as a long-range and continuous form-building procedure. Indeed, if we accept the hypothesis that the twelve-tone method realizes Schoenberg's concepts of fluctuating and suspended tonality systematically, a fairly equitable suspension of all twelve possible tonal centers should result, so that long-range coherence to a single tonic is no longer possible. Nor is it necessary, for the method guarantees other sorts of coherence, involving motivic variation, segmental invariance, and so forth.[12] Nevertheless, progressions recalling Schoenberg's earlier tonal style can still emerge on the surface, even if their tonal implications are

[10] The "deceptive cadence" at the downbeat of m. 623 is strikingly reminiscent, in many ways, of the deceptive cadence at m. 17 in the *Vorspiel* to *Tristan und Isolde*. That cadence, like the present one, also follows a sequence of fluctuating key references.

[11] It may be significant that the suggested keys involve two semitone pairs, separated by a minor third. Further commentary on that topic will appear in note 30.

[12] The classic discussion of the powerful twelve-tone structuring at work in this passage is Milton Babbitt, "Set Structure as a Compositional Determinant," *Journal of Music*

deflected, or left in suspense. We can understand such transitory tonal potencies in at least two ways, both of which I shall explore and endorse in what follows. We can approach the matter theoretically, and hear them as creating a temporary *imbalance* in an otherwise equitable (and carefully balanced) suspension of all tonalities. On the other hand, we can also hear them in a specific historical context, as traces of a deeper continuity in the evolution of Schoenberg's compositional idiom.

To reinforce the relevance of this second option, we shall turn briefly to an earlier, pre-twelve-tone composition. The Piano Piece, op. 19, no. 3 (composed in February 1911), predates by a few months the publication of the *Harmonielehre* and its introduction of the concept of *aufgehobene Tonalität*. This little piece, of nine measures cast in four phrases, suspends tonality in interesting ways, but fairly clear tonal organization does emerge at certain cadential moments. In particular, the second and last phrases both evoke cadential repose in B♭.

Example 2a extracts prominent events from the second phrase (mm. 3–4), to sketch how its cadence projects B♭ tonality at the midpoint of the piece. Answering the octave Fs that begin the phrase, the three most prominent right-hand tones are beamed on the example to convey how dominant-function harmony unfolds through the diatonic scale-segment A4-G4-F4; diagonal lines indicate the semitone voice leading that links the dyads {B♭3, D4} and {A3, D♭4}, suggesting a cadential six-four configuration (with the D♭4 understood as C♯4, an augmented fifth in the dominant harmony). Tonal focus on the concluding B♭ octaves accumulates as the phrase proceeds.

Example 2

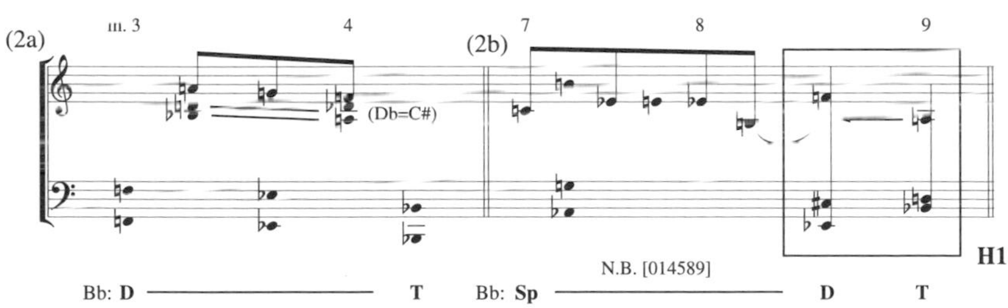

Selected features from Schoenberg, Piano Piece, op. 19, no. 2.

Theory 5, no. 1 (1961): 72–94. I am certainly not suggesting that tonal latencies override twelve-tone structures; I do think it is relevant, however, to view the former as meaningfully "complementary" or "supplementary" to the latter. I concur with David Lewin's reserved but open-minded attitude (regarding, in this case, a song from *Das Buch der*

Example 2b sketches how the cadence of the closing phrase (mm. 7–9) eventually corroborates this sensation of B♭ tonality. The three most prominent right-hand tones in mm. 7–8, beamed on the example, project subdominant-parallel function in B♭ (within a characteristically Schoenbergian [014589] hexachord!). The two closing trichords (through which the G3 is sustained) respond with dominant function (again with the augmented fifth, C♯) and tonic function respectively. (These two closing trichords together constitute a hexachord labeled H1 for future reference.) One notes, in fact, that the closing "tonic" trichord {B♭2, D3, A3} involves the same pitch classes and intervallic spacing as the first right-hand trichord in m. 3 (one octave higher), forging an aural bond between the two phrases and reinforcing their mutual inclination toward B♭ as a point of closure. An arrow on Example 2b also suggests how the A3 of the final trichord can be heard in two ways: as a belated leading tone whose scalar tendencies and dominant harmonic function imply a resolution to B♭, and simultaneously as a major seventh over the fundamental B♭, representing its own distant overtone.[13] Other events in the piece may obscure the impression, but it remains significant that the middle and final cadences both suggest B♭ as a tonal goal.

The tonal gravitation toward B♭ at the final cadence is kept partly in suspense by G3, which is sustained through the last two trichords with remarkable sympathetic reverberation on the piano. One can imagine Schoenberg wanting us to hear this tone as representing an overtone of the fundamentals of *both* the last two trichords, F and B♭. The scalar tendencies of the tones are vivid in this cadence, and one can easily imagine the G3 moving to an F3, and the A3 "resolving" up to a B♭3. But one can also imagine how the tones of the last trichord might also be related, *mutatis mutandis,* to the sustained G3 as a fundamental in its own right, with the implication of G minor closure. The cumulative result of these possibilities is quite unlike

Hängenden Gärten) that "in general, now, I feel that tonality functions in this work mainly as one means of clarifying, enriching and qualifying a basically contextual ('atonal') structure"; see Lewin, "Toward the Analysis of Schoenberg's Op. 15, No. XI," *Perspectives of New Music* 12, nos. 1–2 (1973): 74n.10. Lewin adds that "if one tried to push tonal analysis, however, beyond such considerations, I believe the results would be either too general…, or too speculative, or too mechanical and irrelevant." As will be seen, I will not be arguing that tonal latencies have any special analytic relevance, or that they play a large-scale structural role in the twelve-tone compositions, but that they do reveal a connection between the twelve-tone method and the concepts of *schwebende* and *aufgehobene Tonalität.*

[13] The latter idea corresponds well with Schoenberg's notion that dissonances are simply more distant overtones and differ from consonances only in degree. See, for instance, Schoenberg, *Harmonielehre*, 19; and *Theory of Harmony*, 21. See also Schoenberg, "Problems of Harmony," in *Style and Idea*, 271; this essay will be cited at length later.

conventional tonal closure. The music remains mobile in the imagination even after it has ceased to sound, and Schoenberg creates a remarkable mode of "closure" that is no longer final or static. He does so, nonetheless, by manipulating the relative gravitational power of several different fundamentals, and by generating a sense of mobility and resolution with respect to them. The result, tonally fluctuant even after it has ceased sounding, is the simultaneous confirmation and suspension of B♭ as a tonal center.

These observations are significant for the Fourth Quartet, because hexachord H1 plays an active role in the first movement. H1 is very strongly emphasized as the movement's final sonority, but unlike the quiet ending of the piano piece, the final effect of the quartet movement is summoned by sheer force. Why did Schoenberg find it necessary to invoke closure so violently?

As mentioned earlier, the last eleven measures of the first movement (mm. 274–84) recapitulate the original transpositional level. The accompaniment trichords at m. 274 clearly recall the movement's opening, while the first violin (with momentary help from the cello) declaims the row form mostly in half notes. After m. 280 the texture reduces to an antagonistic alternation, in *fortissimo*, of the row form's complementary hexachords (henceforth called H1 and H2), which appear in a variety of spacings, supporting the first violin's stubborn C♯6 (which belongs to H1). The alternation of H1 and H2 induces a strong sense of twelve-tone closure here, but H1 prevails at the end, and the last measures invoke certain properties of H1 that also color closure in specific ways.

Sessions described a sense of D minor in this movement, but closure in a *suspended* B♭ tonality is also a possibility here, as it was in the piano piece. The registration of the final chord (H1) is interesting in this regard. Examples 3a and 3b suggest two ways—among several—of hearing it as a superimposition of tonic and dominant functions in B♭. Example 3a portrays the chord as a superimposed tonic dyad (open noteheads) and dominant-seventh tetrachord with augmented fifth (filled noteheads). On Example 3b, tonic function involves a tetrachord with a major third in the bass and also a minor third (spelled as C♯) in the treble, while the superimposed dominant is represented here by {A, E♭}, the characteristic tritone of the key.[14] In a similar format, Examples 3c and 3d explore Sessions's assertion of D minor, sketching how the final hexachord can superimpose tonic and dominant functions

[14] H1 can also be partitioned into B♭ tonic- and dominant-function subsets in other ways, such as { {B♭, D, F}, {A, C♯, E♭} }, and { {B♭, C♯, D}, {F, A, E♭} }; another possibility, { {B♭}, {F, A, C♯, E♭, D} }, will be examined shortly.

in that key. The D minor tonal effect of Examples 3c and 3d is less compelling than the B♭ effect of Examples 3a and 3b, but the four examples together suggest one reason why the ending invokes such force, for H1, and the insistent C♯6 in particular, are sites of conflicting tendencies toward B♭ and D as tonal centers. The sensation of D minor that Sessions described is mitigated—and suspended—by equally powerful sensations of B♭ tonality.

Example 3

Selected features from Schoenberg, Fourth Quartet, I, mm. 274–284.

In fact, conflicting tendencies between D and B♭ are activated earlier in the passage. In mm. 274–275, the dyads D6-C♯6 (first violin) and A2-B♭2 (cello) are set in contrast and can be heard to invoke tonic and leading-tone scale degrees in the two respective keys. Within the accompanimental parts in mm. 277–278, one also observes a consistent pairing of dominant and tonic scale degrees in the two keys.[15] Example 3e extracts these dyads to show that they project harmonic function in B♭ more strongly than in D, because A and B♭ are consistently connected by semitone, to project a sense of dominant and tonic function in B♭.[16]

Several other factors confirm that B♭ is the stronger tonal force in the closing measures. The partition of H1 shown in Example 3a involves a unique property that is highlighted by Example 3f: its two subsets belong to different whole-tone fields, so that even-numbered interval classes can only be spanned *within* the tonic-function dyad or dominant-function tetrachord, while odd interval classes can only be spanned *between* them. In that specific sense, the superimposition of distinct tonic and dominant sonorities in B♭ is already an integral intervallic property of H1.

The registration of several H1 simultaneities in the final measures also supports a tonal focus on B♭. Example 3g depicts a long-range voice-leading "resolution" from the bass E♭2 in m. 280 to the bass D2 of the final chord; a strong impression of combined tonic and dominant function in B♭ can be heard by arpeggiating these two chords, the first one downward and the second upward. Example 3h observes that the H1 simultaneity in mm. 282–283, which is agogically accented, isolates B♭ in the bass and presents a more evenly spaced dominant-function pentachord above it.

While the alternating statements of H1 and H2 reiterate aggregate completion, their dialectic of alternation also recalls the V-I cadential reiterations heard in tonal compositions, only now the two harmonies take the aggregate as their measure, while tonic and dominant functions are to some degree integrated within H1 itself.[17] H1 dominates throughout this complementary dialogue; it is stressed in various ways, and it has the last word, so

[15] The second violin involves <F6, B♭5,...F4, B♭4,...D4, A3>; the viola projects <A5, D4,...>; and the cello involves <...A4, D4,...B♭3, F2>.

[16] The sense of dominant function of the {F, A} simultanieties is further heightened: they always sound with C♯, creating a vagrant V♯5 dominant that Example 3e suggests is more inclined toward B♭ than D.

[17] For relevant remarks on the dialectic of alternating complementary hexachords, see Carl Dahlhaus, "Tonality: Structure or Process?" in *Schoenberg and the New Music*, trans. Derrick Puffett and Alfred Clayton (Cambridge: Cambridge University Press, 1987), 69–70.

that it induces a supplementary mode of closure by creating (and suspending) tonal potencies that have overlapping implications.

The simultaneous invocation and suspension of tonal functions is itself a potent—and revealing—aspect of this moment of closure. In Derridean terms, closure in B♭ is held "under erasure" here, by tonal potency in D and by the twelve-tone technique and the aggregate at large. One could even suggest that tonal potency is the "supplement" of the twelve-tone method—at least as Schoenberg used it—since tonal potency is the feature that *reveals*, at rare moments, how the method suspends tonality.[18]

III

The problem of transitory tonal sensations in twelve-tone music can be related to arguments found in Schoenberg's essay "Problems of Harmony."[19] This essay, first presented as a lecture in 1927 and later revised for publication in 1934, falls solidly within Schoenberg's twelve-tone period.[20] Even so, the essay makes no explicit mention of the method. It focuses instead on a larger question: the role of tonality in general.

Schoenberg begins by demonstrating how all dissonances can be related to a tonal center via the overtone series; nonetheless, "tonality does not appear...of itself, but requires the application of...artistic means to achieve its end unequivocally and convincingly" (274). Nor, he argues, is tonality indispensable for musical coherence, because motivic repetition, variation, and development can also fulfill its unifying and articulating functions.[21] Schoenberg then examines the term "atonal," presenting the two examples shown in Example 4 to frame his argument (281–282). Example 4a, he claims, does *not* produce a coherent sense of tonality, even though it uses only triads and seventh chords and faithfully resolves their dissonances. Example 4b involves chords of more dissonant construction (connected intermittently to consonant triads), and neither prepares nor resolves many of their dissonances, but Schoenberg nevertheless claims that Example 4b creates the

[18] On Derrida's concept of the supplement, see Jacques Derrida, *Of Grammatology*, trans. Gayatri Chakravorty Spivak (Baltimore: Johns Hopkins University Press, 1976), 141 and passim; on the notion of erasure, see 60.

[19] Schoenberg, "Problems of Harmony," in *Style and Idea*, 268–287; citations for this essay henceforth appear in the text.

[20] On the dating of the essay, see *Style and Idea*, 524–525.

[21] See also Schoenberg, "Opinion or Insight?" (1926), in *Style and Idea*, ed. Leonard Stein, trans. Leo Black (Berkeley and Los Angeles: University of California Press, 1984), 258 and 261.

impression, a posteriori, that the final D minor chord is a tonic: "Strange to say, the ear accepts the final chord here just as it does a tonic and it might almost seem as if the preceding dissonances were really standing in legitimate relation to this tonic. The law mentioned before is again made manifest: 'The last prevails'" (282). (The same law also seems to be manifested by H1 at the end of the Fourth Quartet's first movement, even though H1 invokes more complex tonal potencies than does the D minor triad ending Example 4b.)

Example 4

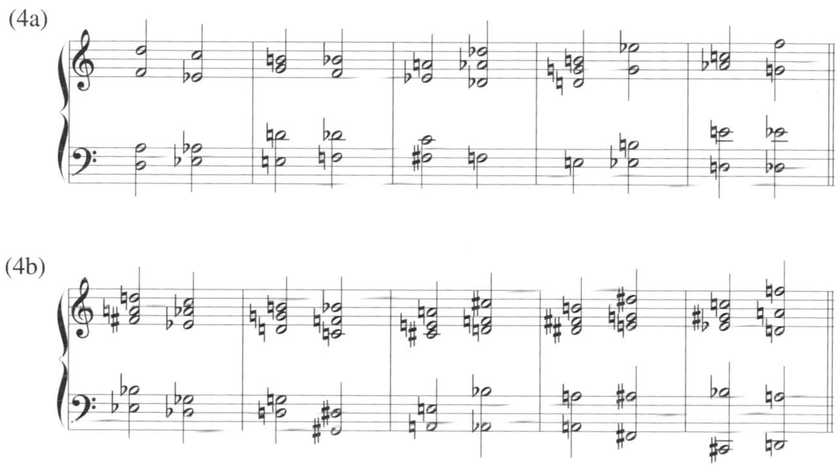

Two examples from Schoenberg, "Problems of Harmony" (pp. 281–282).

Schoenberg goes on to ask "Which of the two examples is tonal, which atonal?...Since the presence of complicated dissonances [in Example 4b] does not necessarily endanger tonality, and since on the other hand their absence [in Example 4a] does not guarantee it, we can ask now, what are the characteristics of that music which is today called 'atonal'?" (282–283). In response, he quotes the revised 1922 edition of his *Harmonielehre,* from which I now cite more extensively than he does:

> The word "atonal" could only signify something entirely inconsistent with the nature of tone.... A piece of music will always have to be tonal, at least in so far as a relation has to exist from tone to tone by virtue of which the tones, placed next to or above one another, yield a perceptible continuity. *The tonality* may then perhaps be neither perceptible nor provable; these relations may be obscure and difficult to comprehend, even incomprehensible.... Besides, there has been no investigation at all of the question whether the way these

> new sounds go together is not actually *the tonality* of a twelve-tone series. It is indeed probably just that, [and] hence would be a phenomenon paralleling the situation that led to the church modes, of which I say: "The effect of a fundamental tone was felt, but since no one knew which tone it was, all of them were tried." Here we do not yet even feel the fundamental; nevertheless it is therefore probably present.[22]

Several unexpected or paradoxical concepts are asserted here: the tonality of a twelve-tone series; the concept of a tonality that is neither perceptible nor provable; the notion that a fundamental must be present even though (because?) it is not felt; and so forth. These interesting paradoxes aside, it is evident that "tonality" and the presence of fundamentals remain relevant in Schoenberg's conception of twelve-tone composition. In "Problems of Harmony" he expresses his "hope that in a few decades audiences will recognize the *tonality* of this music today called *atonal*" (283). He asserts that the difference is only "a *gradual* one between the tonality of yesterday and the tonality of today," and advocates the term "pantonal":

> In my *Harmonielehre* I have recommended that we give the term "pantonal" to what is called atonal. By this we can signify: the relation of all tones to one another, regardless of occasional occurrences, assured by the circumstances, of a common origin. (283)

This definition implicitly equates "pantonality" with the twelve-tone method, since the "relation of all tones to one another" is a typical epithet for the twelve-tone method found elsewhere in Schoenberg's prose writings.[23] Here Schoenberg does not dismiss occasional sensations in twelve-tone music of a "common origin" (of an overtone series or fundamental, or of a related hierarchy among tones), nor does he view them as products of chance; on the contrary, they are "assured" by circumstances that presumably arise through the composer's agency and meet with his endorsement. Nonetheless, they make only occasional and probably local impressions, for pantonality would appear to be a way of ensuring the suspension of tonality, *by balancing all tonalities against one another*. Every individual tonality would be *aufgehoben*—kept in suspension and also raised to a new conceptual level called "pantonality"—by music that might temporarily evoke certain fundamentals or tonalities but that usually realizes no one of them in particular. Obviously, this situation alters certain conditions of closure. In conventional

[22] Schoenberg, *Theory of Harmony*, 432, emphasis added. The passage quoted in the penultimate sentence appears on p. 25 of the same volume. Roger Sessions judges the term "atonality" in similar ways; see *Harmonic Practice*, 408.

[23] See, for instance, Schoenberg, "Composition with Twelve Tones (1)," in *Style and Idea*, 218.

tonal music, closure typically involves resolution and balance with respect to a unique tonic. In contrast, the closing cadence from the Fourth Quartet's first movement suggests, quite remarkably, that closure of a supplementary kind sometimes results in Schoenberg's twelve-tone music, when a slight *imbalance* in the mutual suspension of tonalities by one another unveils a temporary sensation of some common origin (or origins).

I shall return to this concept later. For the present, let us note that Example 4a does not in fact lack tonal coherence to the degree Schoenberg would have us believe. In particular, its final whole-tone chord can project dominant function in several keys, including C major, and each individual voice (especially the bass) is chromatically coherent in that particular key. If one *imagines* a C major triad following the example, closure and tonal coherence both result, because every tone can be understood in a harmonic or a voice-leading relation to C as a "common origin." (Readers are encouraged to play the passage, appending a C major chord, to hear this effect.) Tonality is suspended in Example 4a, as written, only because the passage breaks off at an ambiguous dominant sonority that is left unresolved.[24] We shall now examine how a similar effect occurs in the final measures of the String Trio.[25]

Example 5a sketches the pitches of the closing measures of the String Trio (mm. 291–293), and identifies the relevant combinatorial hexachords with the labels H3 and H4. At the downbeat of m. 292, the parts converge on an A minor triad, and Example 5a explores how that unexpected sonority stimulates the perception of certain tonal latencies. The cello proceeds to G2, above which the viola presents the seventh F3 and then the tenth B3; the violin's E5 is easily heard as a so-called thirteenth, which in typical tonal practice would displace the fifth D5, and that tone does indeed appear a moment later. The expectations produced by this dominant sonority are largely satisfied: the cello moves to C2, and its overtone E5, just repeated and sustained in the violin, supports the C-rooted quality of this moment, even though the B3 retained in the viola adds dissonance. The root status of C is dissipated almost immediately, however. The viola moves to A♭3, which will henceforth accrue root status (reconfiguring the bass C2 as its third) and dominant harmonic function. These changes begin to induce D♭ as a latent tonal goal,

[24] The sensation of tonality in suspense increases toward the end, since the last *three* chords are all whole-tone subsets (alternating between the two whole-tone fields). Nonetheless, that sensation can quickly be dispelled by resolving the last chord to C major.

[25] Of course, large segments of the String Trio completely suspend tonality, but there are also numerous moments of tonal emergence—especially in the episodic sections—that recall earlier musical idioms and that also engage other modes of recollection, as described near the beginning of this essay.

Example 5

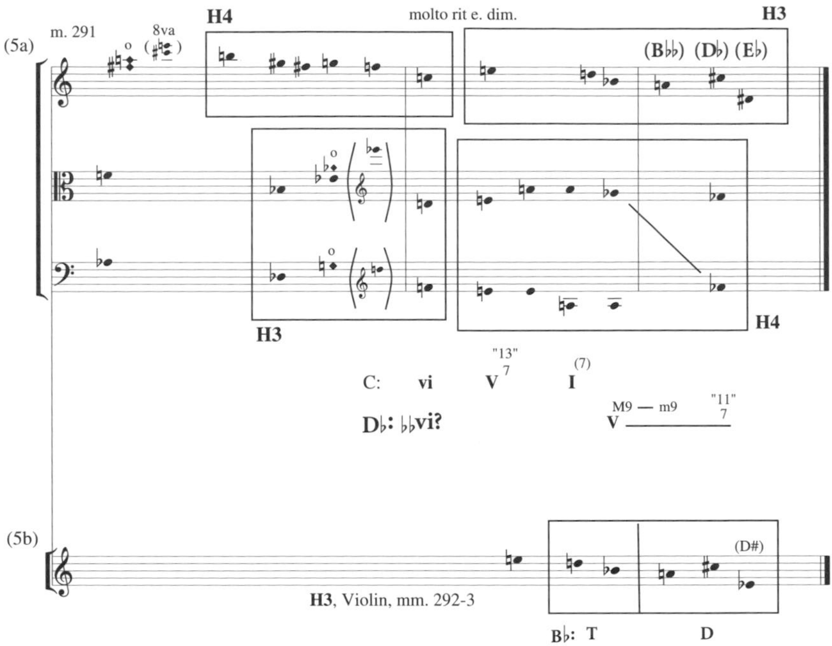

Reduction of Schoenberg, String Trio, mm. 291–293.

so that C and D♭ will be juxtaposed as transitory tonal centers (much as they were observed to be in Example 1). The root status and dominant function of A♭ markedly increase when the cello takes A♭2 as its last note, and the viola G♭3 projects the minor seventh above it; the last four violin pitches also contribute to this extended dominant sonority, projecting (in sequence) a major ninth (B♭4), a minor ninth (A4 = B♭♭4), an "eleventh" (C♯5 = D♭5), and the fifth (D♯4 = E♭4).[26] The so-called eleventh (C♯5 = D♭5) actually articulates the latent tonic D♭, but it also displaces the chordal third C (recently heard in the bass); in fact, because the violin's C♯5-cum-D♭5 is approached by leap, one also senses a linear connection back to the violin's C5 in m. 292 (suggesting

[26] Because of its temporal position, the violin's D5 in m. 292 makes an interesting "pivot" tone between the latent keys of C and D♭, changing from scale-degree 2 in the former to scale-degree ♭2 in the latter: it appears slightly too late to function clearly as the fifth of dominant harmony in the momentary C major cadence in m. 292, and slightly too early to function as a diminished fifth (E♭♭5) in the dominant of D♭ that steadily takes shape after the D5 has ceased to sound.

that the A minor triad might also function as a B♭♭ minor triad in the key of D♭). Just as the extended dominant of D♭ takes shape in m. 293, slightly diffuse but perceptible, the piece simply breaks off. Even so, the implied D♭ tonic harmony is almost the more vivid for remaining unstated.[27] The tonal implications of the last few measures, though clear enough, simply dissipate, unrealized except as acts of memory and imagination. They become pure idea.

The sense of transitory—but closing—tonal implications in C and D♭ is largely determined by hexachord H4, from which the relevant roots appear in the lower register, while H3 in the violin contributes harmonic dissonances characteristic of Schoenberg's earlier tonal idiom. On the other hand, H3 also complements the tonal potencies of H4. Example 5b rewrites the violin's final statement of H3 (and identifies the pentachordal subset it shares with H1 from the Fourth Quartet), to show how the violin also projects a latent half cadence in B♭ at the end of the String Trio.[28] The interaction of the two complementary hexachords is different from what we observed earlier in the Fourth Quartet's first movement, where the relevant complementary hexachords alternated and H1 alone prevailed at the last. In the String Trio, however, the hexachords are set in counterpoint, so that the simultaneously *schwebende* tonal potencies of H3 and H4 become *aufgehoben* through their contrapuntal interaction. The music breaks off just as the hexachords project unresolved dominants in both D♭ and B♭, thereby preventing either latent key from emerging unequivocally. The final measures make several tonal areas latent through an imbalance in the "pantonality," but they also ensure that tonality (in the conventional sense) is *aufgehoben* through a carefully calibrated interaction of collective and individual voices.[29]

[27] In fact, the downbeat of m. 291 presents the pitch classes {C♯ = D♭, E = F♭, F, A♭}, suggesting a D♭ harmony with both major and minor third. The cello A♭3 is in the bass of that sonority, and even moves directly to D♭3.

[28] A premonition of this tonal implication appears only a bit earlier, in m. 290, where the violin plays the pitch sequence D6-B♭5-E♭6 A5, suggesting tonic and dominant in B♭. In m. 291, B♭3 in the viola arrives simultaneously with the cello D♭3 mentioned in note 28, and is also approached from the fifth above.

[29] It is striking, and perhaps more than coincidental, that Examples 1c and 5a both involve the keys of C and D♭, as well as senses of repose on A and B♭. The latency of semitone-related key-pairs is a recurring pattern in Schoenberg's music. Christopher Wintle ("Schoenberg's Harmony: Theory and Practice," *Journal of the Arnold Schoenberg Institute* 4 [1980]: 50–67) and Christopher Lewis ("Mirrors and Metaphors: On Schoenberg and Nineteenth-Century Tonality," *Nineteenth-Century Music* 11, no. 1 [1987]: 26–42) have examined the cogency of semitone-related keys in several of Schoenberg's songs. Walter Frisch (among others) has discussed the large-scale relevance of the keys E and F in Schoenberg's Chamber Symphony, op. 9, in *The Early Works of Arnold Schoenberg, 1893–1908* (Berkeley and Los Angeles: University of California Press, 1993), 220–247. For a

IV

Schoenberg concludes "Problems of Harmony" with an extraordinary and convoluted sentence that reads like a legal document, full of clauses and provisos. I conceive it as his attempt to draft a "Constitution" for his ongoing approach to the fundamental problems of composition (twelve-tone or otherwise):

> Since, as I have pointed out, the logical and artful construction of a piece of music is also secured by other means, and since the lack of tonality only increases the difficulty but does not exclude the possibility of comprehension; and since further proof of lack of tonality has not yet been adduced but as, on the contrary, probably much that today is not regarded as tonal, may soon be so accepted; and since dissonances need not in the least disturb tonality, no matter how increasingly difficult they may make the understanding of a work; and inasmuch as the use of exclusively tonal chords does not guarantee a tonal result, I come to the following conclusion: music which today is called "tonal" establishes a key relationship continuously or does so at least at the proper moment; but music which is today called "not tonal" *never allows predominance of key relationships.* The difference between the two methods is largely in the emphasis or non-emphasis on the tonality. (284, emphasis added)

There is certainly no outright denial or abandonment of tonality here; it is merely a matter of "emphasis or non-emphasis," and the concept of tonality, in some expanded or sublimated form, is never in any doubt. A music that "never allows predominance of key relationships" (but which also does not entirely abandon them) would realize Schoenberg's concepts of *schwebende Tonalität, aufgehobene Tonalität,* and *Pantonalität,* especially if we conceive the latter as superseding the two earlier concepts through their combination and systematic extension to all keys equally and "simultaneously." There is no reason to assume that Schoenberg's twelve-tone compositions were intended to demonstrate the impossibility of this "pantonality"; I expect, instead, that they were his attempts to realize it.

study of tonal structure in the First Quartet, with extensive discussion of semitone-related keys, see Lynn Marie Cavanagh, "Tonal Multiplicity in Schoenberg's *First String Quartet,* op. 7" (Ph.D. diss., University of British Columbia, 1996). William Benjamin analyzes the Orchestra Piece, op. 16, no. 5, in terms of semitone-related keys in "Abstract Polyphonies: The Music of Schoenberg's Nietzschean Moment," in *Political and Religious Ideas in the Works of Arnold Schoenberg,* ed. Charlotte M. Cross and Russell A. Berman (New York: Garland, 1999). Schoenberg himself harmonized the theme from his Variations for Orchestra, op. 31, juxtaposing F major and G♭ major; this harmonization, and Schoenberg's remarks about it, are reproduced in Glenn Watkins, *Soundings: Music in the Twentieth Century* (New York: Schirmer, 1988), 334–335. Schoenberg also discusses semitone-related keys in connection with *schwebende Tonalität* in *Theory of Harmony,* 384.

Schoenberg's twelve-tone music can thus be heard as an attempt to refine "tonality" into a pure idea, to attain a state in which tonality—or more accurately, the *representation* of any individual tonality—is *aufgehoben* in the fullest Hegelian sense. Indeed, "*Pantonalität*" and "*aufgehobene Tonalität*" are different names, but they identify the same concept, one that is fully Hegelian in tone. Transitory and multivalent moments of tonal potency in such music would not have the real structural force or formal responsibility they once had in earlier forms of tonality. Nor need they, apparently, for Schoenberg professes the belief that "one may sooner sacrifice logic and unity in the harmony, than in the thematic substance, in the motives, in the thought-content" (280). That belief is surely necessary if one is to attempt, in good faith, to suspend tonality completely. In music that makes such an attempt, it is essential that transitory and multivalent tonal potencies are *not* fully reified, for only through *Aufhebung* can *Pantonalität* be realized. All the same, moments of tonal latency are also essential, for only they can reveal what *Aufhebung* has subsumed.

A sublime and supplementary aesthetic effect therefore arises at those moments of closure when fluctuating tonal latencies can no longer be kept in a state of balanced suspension. The latency of one or several individual tonalities is then revealed, through a kind of supplementary immanence in which tonal potency is heightened, and itself becomes an attribute of closure, in moments that are characterized by vivid qualities of incipience and expectancy. Somewhat paradoxically, closure at such moments ceases to be about balance and completion, and becomes instead a state of imbalance, of latency, of possibility and expectation, of suspense rather than suspension. These moments of closure are sublime because they evoke unrealized but intense objects of memory, imagination, and possibility; they unveil a multitude of latent continuities that can be imagined, but that would produce an incommensurable effect if actually heard, and that must therefore remain unattainable in a paradoxical mixture of future and past modes of hearing. Above all, these moments are sublime because they briefly freeze a moment of *Aufhebung* and reveal, in a momentary tonal representation, how tonality is suspended and becomes pure idea in the pantonality of Schoenberg's twelve-tone music.

Despite Roger Sessions's sometime influence, recent music theory in North America has been extremely circumspect about the tonal specters in Schoenberg's twelve-tone music. In part that may be due to the fact that tonal latencies are indeed essentially irrelevant in the music of Milton Babbitt, under whose influence North American music theory has largely developed.[30] We will need to put aside our recent disciplinary investments and assumptions if we are to assess the formerly new as it recedes into the past. We might heed the unbiased response of a writer who, though not a professional musician or music theorist, is evidently a profoundly sensitive listener:

> Schoenberg's considerable output is always organized not independently of tonality, but by a constant refusal of it; tonality continually solicits him and returns to haunt him, and it is to this that his work owes a great part of its pathetic quality, for all his phrases constantly suggest others of which they are merely shadows and from which they turn aside at the last moment. They are sketches which are continually reworked.[31]

We will need to internalize—as Schoenberg himself did—the extraordinary tonality of the earlier masterworks in order to understand his later twelve-tone compositions in their proper context, and in order to hear the sublimated implications of their sonorities. We would gain some closure for his achievements, understand them better as events in a continuous development, and also *reopen* them to a much-needed understanding of how Schoenberg suspends tonality in his twelve-tone compositions.

[30] As Schoenberg himself remarked, "usually when changes of style occur in the arts, a tendency can be observed to overemphasize the difference between the new and the old" ("My Evolution," in *Style and Idea*, 87–88). That was done by casting the recent (Schoenberg) in terms of the new (Babbitt), at the expense of the continuity between Schoenberg and his own past.

[31] Michel Butor, "Music as a Realistic Art," trans. Donald Schier, *Perspectives of New Music* 20 (1981–1982): 461–462. Butor stresses the pathetic, while I have emphasized the sublime; both are powerful aesthetic forces in Schoenberg's extraordinary music.

MARTIN BOYKAN

The Schoenberg Trio: Tradition at an Apocalyptic Moment

I

In an interview on the occasion of the first performance of the Symphony in Three Movements, written around the end of the Second World War, Stravinsky acknowledged that for the moment, at least, he had turned his back on a quarter century of Italianate neoclassicism to revive the techniques of the *Sacre du printemps:* possibly, he thought, he had been influenced by "the apocalyptic times through which we are living." Thomas Mann seems to have experienced much the same thing even more intensely while writing *Doktor Faustus;* his little memoir *Die Entstehung des Doktor Faustus* describes how he began to doubt the value of everything he had written with the exception of *Buddenbrooks,* the novel of his youth. He also acknowledges his indebtedness to Schoenberg's description of the recently completed String Trio, in which the composer made a special point of its singularity. He had not wanted to write chamber music, Mann reports him as saying, but rather a novel; in fact, the Trio was a very detailed and realistic narrative of his recent heart attack, including the doctors, the nurses, the injections.

For Schoenberg, then, the apocalyptic moment was personal, not public, an encounter with his own death. But it is hard to believe that in the year 1946 he was not thinking also of that larger apocalypse that had just swept across Europe. He too seems to have instinctively cast a backward glance, at least in a few pages that suggest a nostalgia for old Vienna. Far more striking than any occasional reminiscence, however, is the novelty of the Trio; it represents a dramatic departure from the kind of music he had been writing for twenty years. Gone are the traditional forms—sonata, rondo, and so forth—the wide-arched Brahmsian themes, the classical methods of transformation and development. In its place we have little fragments, one after the other. Much of the material is quite disparate with improbable juxtapositions. The continuity is marked by interpolations, interruptions, even non sequiturs, so that at times Schoenberg seems to be poised at the edge of incoherence. And that is probably why this piece has exerted a peculiar fascination ever since it was written.

But the composer who thought of himself as the great conservator of the Western tradition was hardly about to indulge in nihilist fantasies. I think that it is precisely because of its intractable material that the Trio became Schoenberg's most deeply excogitated work. I am afraid I cannot begin to explore its highly complex narrative within the limits of the present essay; when I teach the Trio it takes an entire semester to do it justice. I shall attempt only to throw some light on the meaning of its bizarre continuity and, in the end, raise some questions about its program.

Example 1

II

Let me begin with four measures from the middle of the Trio (mm. 148–151, Ex. 1). I imagine that every listener is particularly struck by the quiet of this moment. The players put on their mutes, and we hear a succession of soft diatonic sonorities, not for the first time in the Trio, but never before with such consistency. And the motivic surface is here reduced to the utmost simplicity: a single idea sequenced measure by measure.

It may seem surprising that music of such commonplace regularity should be so memorable. But this simplicity is, in fact, deceptive; it disguises a multiplicity of references to music we have already heard. We can learn a good deal about the continuity of the Trio by tracing these references, but a listener who has not understood the long-range harmonic planning of the piece is likely to miss them altogether. And so I am obliged to touch on a few structural matters before considering this passage in detail.

Example 2

Example 2 is the row of the Trio. We have here Schoenberg's usual pairing of prime and inversion, with invariant hexachords. The idea is that a transposition of the hexachord signals a new harmonic area, though Schoenberg is actually more flexible than this crude generalization would imply, and a transposition may serve a variety of other purposes. Note also that the first and last trichords of the row are the same, a useful technique Schoenberg had explored in the Fourth Quartet. So far we are on very familiar ground. But there is one feature of this row pair that is absolutely unique to the Trio: the harmony produced by prime and inversion together. Example 3a shows the two complementary collections formed by the first trichords of P and I and by the second trichords of P and I. These famous collections are so symmetrical that they transpose and invert into themselves. In fact, they exist in only two complementary pairs; the alternative is shown in Example 3b. Schoenberg was very familiar with these pairs, having used them in the Suite, op. 29, and the *Ode to Napoleon* (as had Webern in the Concerto for Nine Instruments). In the Trio, however, they are no longer in the foreground; instead they have become a structural background for the unfolding of the real row forms. If there are only two pairs, then half the row forms will yield one pair as in Example 3a, and the other half as in Example 3b. Schoenberg conceives these pairs as harmonic regions, remotely analogous (one imagines him thinking) to the dominant and subdominant regions of tonality. And so the Trio as a whole divides into two regions; Part 1 and the First Episode are assigned to Region I (as I shall call Example 3a) and Part 2 to Region II (Ex. 3b). Since the Second Episode is upbeat to the recapitulation, it avoids playing the prime and inversion together so as to withhold a regional commitment until the end, where Region I is restored. The recapitulation in Part 3 unfolds, of course, in Region I.

Example 3

(a) (Region I)

(b) (Region II)

This scheme allows Schoenberg to provide a rather precise calibration of his harmonic space. We hear a passage as inhabiting a particular region, and within that region a particular harmonic area. At the moment that the region is defined by the simultaneous presentation of prime and inversion, Schoenberg tends also to indicate the area by emphasizing the first note of each. I should add that at times we are on the move, of course, and then we lose the certainty of area or region.

Let me illustrate how this works in the music. In the very first bar of the Trio, we hear the region before we know the basic row. The music of Part 1 is highly agitated, with exaggerated upbeats that intensify the anxiety, but after the "confusion" lifts, the fourfold repetition of a single motive in mm. 41–44 provides a focal point. Once again, we have a statement of Region I, this time in a short "elaboration" (Ex. 4), and now the harmonic area is indicated by downbeats on the pitches D and G (prime on D, inversion on G). This area

Example 4

has, in fact, already been suggested, not only by the row statements in mm. 12ff. but also by the melody (Ex. 5), which moves from D to G, and by the chords immediately preceding the focal point (mm. 37–40, Ex. 6), with a top voice again moving from D to G and a stepwise ascent in the lower voice into the G of m. 41.[1]

Example 5

Example 6

The First Episode maintains Region I but shifts the harmonic area to the prime on B♭ and the inversion on E♭. If we compare the downbeat of m. 57 with the downbeat of m. 71 (Ex. 7), we will find that together they form a regional collection identical to Part 1, but with the outer voices now playing B♭ and E♭. It may seem quite a stretch to connect two chords that are fourteen

[1] From the beginning, Schoenberg's language was remarkably free of historic tonal associations, but in a homophonic passage like mm. 37–40 I think the outer voices remain privileged, if only for acoustic reasons.

bars apart, and it would not have occurred to me if Schoenberg had not gone to great pains to enforce this connection. Both of these downbeats are placed at the beginning of parallel phrases, and both receive powerful accents from extended upbeats that incidentally privilege the pitch E♭. Later in the episode, the region is expressed in a much more obvious way.

Example 7

The recitative in mm. 81ff. is the only exception to the regional plan I have outlined above. I doubt that listeners are really jolted by the sudden intrusion of Region II here, but for Schoenberg it clearly represents an issue, and so he provides an elaborate transition leading to a fairly literal restatement of the recitative, transposed to the correct region (mm. 105ff.). It is characteristic of Schoenberg that this resolution of the issue only occurs after a direct confrontation between the two regions (mm. 101–103)—a special moment in which the background geometry becomes part of the dramatic narrative on the surface.

Part 2 begins with a restatement of the focal measures of Part 1, now in Region II (mm. 133–134), and in a harmonic area defined by the prime on G and the inversion on C. Both region and area are confirmed in the following passage (mm. 135–141) with the melody of Example 5 now moving from G to C, and with the interval C–G emphatically placed at the phrase beginning and ending.

III

At this point we have sufficient context to return to the four bars with which I started (Ex. 1). The first thing one is likely to note about this passage is the diatonic hexachords, whose derivation from the row need not detain us here. Another obvious feature is the ubiquitous motive stated at first in violin and cello, which is quoted from the very beginning of the Trio (Ex. 8). But a listener is also likely to be struck by a curious resemblance between the violin and viola in m. 148 and the trichordal theme of the First Episode (m. 57). If we conceive the short notes of the violin (F and E) to be something like appoggiaturas, then we will hear row trichords registered exactly as in the episode (Ex. 9). Now this is an extremely rare instance in Schoenberg's music; appoggiaturas are hardly possible where there is no distinction between consonance and dissonance, except perhaps where row trichords have become powerfully referential since the beginning of the piece. If we interpret the viola and cello in m. 148 in the same way, we will once again hear row trichords (Ex. 10). Since the following bars are clearly sequential, we can now block out the harmony for the whole passage (Ex. 11), and we find that Schoenberg has simply been arpeggiating the collections that define Region II.

Example 8

Example 9

Example 10

Example 11

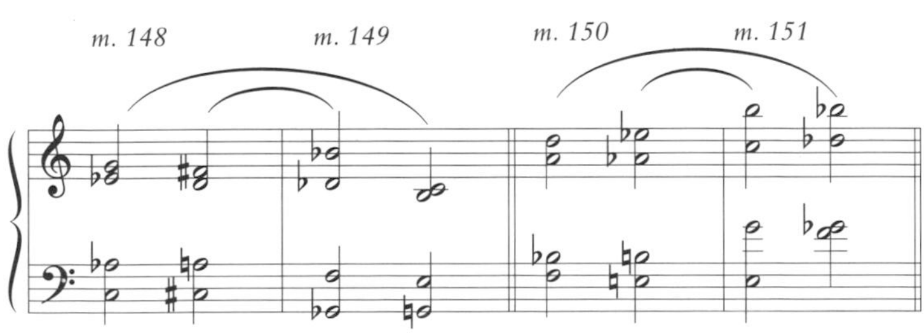

In short, we have two different ways of hearing these measures. Conceive the pitches as equal in importance, and the reference to the little motive from Part 1 will be obvious. If the F and E or the B♭ and B♮ of m. 148 play a supportive role, as the rhythm would seem to suggest, then the reference to the First Episode theme and the Region II chords emerges. I would argue that both interpretations are essential and that Schoenberg has paced this music slowly enough so that we can grasp them together.

Nor are these the only forces shaping this passage. The first two bars are bracketed by a voice-exchange between C and G in outer voices (assuming the "appoggiaturas"), thereby securing the connection with the earlier music from Part 2 (though this harmonic area begins to shift as the phrase proceeds). The motives from Part 1 freely retrograde at the halfway mark to provide some sort of articulation in the fourth bar as they return to their origins, but at the same time there is another pattern in the transpositions of the diatonic hexachords which requires five bars for its completion. Finally, it is hard not to be surprised by the odd registral disjunction of the violin in m. 150 and the quick embellishments that follow. Certainly another reference is intended here, and we can trace the source of this deformation of the motive to a pregnant moment earlier in the Trio.

Measure 63 (Ex. 12) is the beginning of the second phrase of the First Episode. In response to the unproblematic presentation of the first phrase, we would expect a fairly smooth continuity, but any hope of this is blocked by the non sequitur in the next bar. The three conjunct notes B♭–B♮–C that are interrupted here remain in our consciousness, to demand their share of the narrative at some later point. We first hear them again in an altered harmonic context at the beginning of Part 2 (m. 133, Ex. 13), and now it becomes clear that the purpose of the registral and rhythmic variation in mm. 150–151 is to confer a privilege on the same notes. They associate with m. 133 but also look forward to the lyric melody at the heart of the Trio, and beyond that to a further history in the Second Episode.

Example 12

Example 13

IV

I have focused so intently on four bars from Part 2 to show some of the subterranean streams that connect fragments in the Trio. For my present purposes, though, it is also important to note how many references can be suggested by a surface that appears to be of the utmost simplicity. It would not be true to say that motives intertwine because they are similar (in the manner of *Tristan*, for example). On the contrary, Schoenberg's motives retain their distinct profiles; it is only by *varying interpretations*, by privileging certain notes at the expense of others, that the various meanings emerge. It is tempting to think of Joycean puns, but even this analogy is not quite accurate, because the polysemy of Schoenberg's music is a function of the narrative. Meanings accrue as the work unfolds; the texture of memory continues to thicken until the recapitulation in Part III, where everything becomes memory.

This recapitulation is surely one of the strangest in all of music. It is far too truncated to provide architectural balance in the classical manner. Nor does it resemble the symmetrical designs of Liszt or Bartók, if only because it involves the *entire Trio* (except for the Second Episode, which can hardly be repeated, since it functions as upbeat to the recapitulation itself). I would suggest that Schoenberg has reconceived the idea of recapitulation. No longer a matter of formal balance, it has become invested with a psychological aura. The unprecedented idea occurs to Schoenberg to play the Trio twice: *once as narrative, and once as memory.*

It seems to me that there is no other way to understand the particular abbreviations (and occasional expansions) in the recapitulation of Part 1. This music is so violent and agitated that I imagine most listeners connect it to the autobiographical crisis: the heart attack, the ride in the ambulance, or something of that kind. And just as a trauma etches itself indelibly in the mind, so Part 1 receives the most literal recapitulation of any music in the Trio. But if the facts of a crisis are remembered with peculiar clarity, the angst is no longer felt, and Schoenberg renders this altered state of mind by a series of adjustments that serve, as far as possible, to regularize the phrasing.

Later, his memory leaps from one "high point" to another, omitting connective passages. But he makes no attempt to render the cuts seamless, as in a formal reprise. On the contrary, he composes his recapitulation so as to direct maximum attention to the cuts themselves. Compare, for example, the first period of the First Episode to its severely compressed memory in Part 3. Twenty-two bars have been reduced to eight. The first 4-bar group (mm. 238–241) presents a regularized version of the main theme, but the 4-bar response, even though it appears to balance it, seems very odd. We are offered the aborted incipit of m. 63 (which I have discussed above; see Ex. 12), the non sequitur that follows (m. 64), and two measures of cadence quoted from the end of the period. The first half of the phrase finds no real continuation; there is no music that would lead to the cadence or justify it, and so we are left with the disturbing sensation of a gaping hole.

Unlike a classical recapitulation, which transposes everything into the tonic (or with reference to the tonic), Schoenberg remembers the Trio as it happened. Only when the lyrical melody from Part 2 reappears is the music firmly transposed back into the original harmonic area. Introduced by a relatively connected upbeat, this melody signals the end of the work; all of the compositional issues seem resolved, and a noteworthy calm descends on the music—a calm that is to prove deceptive, however, for Schoenberg reserves his most surprising idea for the last few seconds.

After two statements of the melody in a balanced pair of phrases, repetitions of the cadential figure in the usual manner of codettas, and a final reference to the focal point of Part 1 (end of m. 290 and m. 291), a hemiola infects the entire texture at the very last instant, transforming triple meter into duple, while the harmony becomes peculiarly unreferential. No amount of ritardando will prevent the Trio from ending on an upbeat. It is precisely because this piece has been so powerfully ordered, because the end had seemed so secure, that these last seconds are so wrenching. At this point, it is hard not to become aware of a programmatic intent. Does Schoenberg mean to say that one incident is over, but only a little time remains before the next heart attack that kills? Perhaps, but a story of this kind strikes me as trivial, and Schoenberg was not a trivial man.

V

It is widely known that the Trio is a narrative of Schoenberg's heart attack. But it is seldom remarked how uncharacteristic this program really is. Schoenberg grew up, of course, at a time when program music was popular, and he tried his hand at it in early works like *Verklärte Nacht.* But the essential Schoenbergian program is the one he devised for the Second Quartet, a pilgrimage out of the banalities of ordinary life (as represented by a street song like "O du lieber Augustin") to that lonely and exalted place where the artist can breathe the air of other planets. Schoenberg's thought is drenched in the Symbolist currents of the later nineteenth century, where life and art are understood to be incommensurable. "Denn irgendwo ist eine alte Feindschaft / Zwischen dem Leben und der grossen Arbeit,"[2] as Rilke wrote in the *Requiem*. Or as a French Symbolist famously said, "As for living, we can let our servants do that for us." Schoenberg, after all, is the author of *Moses und Aron*, a heavy Symbolist trip, in which the young man who protests the worship of the golden calf does so with the words "Gedankenhoch waren wir erhöht / ...Lebenstief sind wir erniedrigt."[3]

Lebenstief: life as humiliation. Is it not astonishing to find Schoenberg at the end of his life composing a story about doctors, nurses, injections? What can all that have to do with the ascent to "pure idea" celebrated in *Moses und Aron?* We can only speculate, but I would suggest that for Schoenberg the apocalyptic moment shattered the thinking of a lifetime. After a near-fatal illness, after the destruction of Europe and the first reports of the Holocaust, it was no longer possible to conceive of ordinary life as a humiliation; somehow it had begun to seem precious. I do not know how else to interpret Schoenberg's remark to Thomas Mann that he wanted to write a novel rather than a piece of chamber music. A novel, after all, is the story of a life, and the Trio would seem to be an attempt to reproduce the texture of life as we know it, with its disjunctions, its interruptions, its fragmentation—all the "dreadful sundry of this world," in Wallace Stevens's phrase. We hear it unfold along with a gathering web of reminiscences, and in the end relive it once again in memory. And through it all is the iron will to make it cohere.

But life is notoriously resistant to finalities. I think there are times when the Trio seems to acknowledge this. I have called attention to that moment in the First Episode where the recitative is finally quoted in the correct region. This is an important point of arrival, and a classical composer would certainly have celebrated it with a fanfare of trumpets and drums, or at least with a dramatic hush in the manner of Beethoven. Schoenberg is able to direct his music toward its goal with the clarity and the compelling purpose of any classical composer, but at the last moment (m. 104) he seems to back away, casting a shadow on the whole incident.

And so the end of the Trio also appears to be provisional; the composer who looks back on his life is after all still alive. Eduard Steuermann once told me that Schoenberg complained that the students who imitated his Six Piano

[2] For somewhere there is an old enmity between life and the great work.

[3] We were elevated to the heights of thought...[now] we are humiliated to the depths of life.

Pieces, op. 19, were really writing long pieces which they didn't bother to finish. There is no question that the Trio is finished. A complex and powerful design connects all the fragments, resolves all the compositional issues, and provides a deep coherence to the narrative as a whole. It is only in the last few seconds that Schoenberg poses a question, and this is arguably the most radical and disturbing idea he ever had.

Epilogue

STANLEY CAVELL

Philosophy and the Unheard

The invitation to participate in this celebratory weekend has sent me back to a pair of disorienting, and orienting, facts of my life: first, to the intellectual or spiritual crisis—which led me to dedicate myself to the study of philosophy—in discovering that music was no longer my life's work, something I could no longer disguise from myself the year after I graduated with a major in music from the University of California at Berkeley; second, to my knowledge that, although I have written very little explicitly about music over the ensuing decades, something I have demanded from philosophy has been an understanding precisely of what I had sought in music, and of what demanded that reclamation of experience, of the capacity for being moved that called out for, and sustained, an accounting as lucid as the music I loved. It was in returning to Berkeley a decade later to begin a lifetime of teaching that this recognition of music as, let's say, a figure for the mind in its most perfected relation to itself, or to its wishes for itself, was confirmed for me (contrary to so much in the formation of professional philosophy in those years), in conversations with and in the musical analysis classes of Seymour Shifrin and David Lewin, colleagues and friends whose passion for music expressed itself in such different as well as in such similar forms. Whatever bouts of intellectual loneliness I may since then have been tempted to, have been attended by the memory of those scenes of instruction—sublime instances of tracking the work that art does, of the rigor and the beauty one looks and listens for.

It was in that same period that I discovered, after some years of resistance to it, the liberation in the teaching of Wittgenstein's later work, centered in his *Philosophical Investigations*. I was not exactly surprised to learn eventually of

Wittgenstein's remark, "Who can understand my philosophical work who does not know what music has meant in my life?" but it makes me wonder the harder why he actually says so little about music. He does, it is true, say a few things; for example, in the *Investigations* there is this: "Understanding a sentence is much more akin to understanding a theme in music than one may think" (§527).[1] Perhaps the reason Wittgenstein surmises one may avoid this thought is that one imagines the understanding of a sentence to be a matter of understanding and combining the meanings of its constituent words, and that this in turn is a matter of knowing what objects they refer to. A pervasive purpose of the work of the *Investigations* is to trace and to awaken, as if from a trance, each of the interminable consequences of what Wittgenstein calls this primitive picture of human language, and its hold upon philosophical thought. Thus the very invocation of the understanding of a musical theme as a guide to philosophical understanding, among the reorientations in this traumatic breakthrough of philosophical imagination—call it the promise of an understanding without meanings—is a utopian glimpse of a new, or undiscovered, relation to language, to its sources in the world, to its means of expression.

The strangeness of Wittgenstein's power, if that is what it is, is tied to the abruptness of his difference from the expected sound of philosophy, say of its pitch sequences (within which, of some fascination for the Schoenbergian ambience of this weekend, the idea of a series, as in the instance of following a rule, plays a notorious role), manifested in the apparent poverty of Wittgenstein's philosophical means. He describes what he does in the *Investigations* as "returning words from their metaphysical to their everyday use"—hardly, it would seem, the stuff of trauma, until perhaps we notice how often modern philosophical advance, or the claim to it, turns not on seeking to refute or to continue its past but on wishing to turn its back on that past, and then see that Wittgenstein's unheard-of directness in this dissociation is nevertheless in service of philosophy's perpetual discovery of the strangeness of our lives to ourselves—a discovery that reaches from at least the Cave in Plato's *Republic*, through the entrance to the dark wood at the opening of *The Divine Comedy*, to the antics of self-torture that Thoreau perceives in his fellow inhabitants of Concord, to the couch in Freud's study. The first three images (cave, dark wood, self-torture) are meant as figures of our everyday lives; the last (the couch) is a new response to that life; all demand of us a journey. In Wittgenstein's album (a title he gives to his *Investigations*), the topics of

[1] Ludwig Wittgenstein, *Philosophical Investigations*, trans. G. E. M. Anscombe (Oxford: Basil Blackwell, 1968), 143.

understanding, meaning, sentence, rule, privacy, consciousness, and so forth are bound up with a vision of the human as caught between a sense of inexpressiveness suggesting suffocation and a sense of uncontrollable expressiveness threatening exposure.

May such a formulation be seen as an initial Wittgensteinian response to the work of Schoenberg—his older, equally displaced compatriot—even knowing that Wittgenstein in person shunned most forms of modernism in the arts and in modern intellectual life generally? I report being struck, rereading in Schoenberg's letters to prepare for the mood of this weekend, at how punctual and fervent Schoenberg's recurrence is to the wish for, or the despair of, his music's being understood. But the various instances intersect somewhat oddly. In 1926 he writes: "To me it matters more that people should understand my work than that they should take an interest in it."[2] Is this because an interest may be based on an illusory understanding, for example, on an account of what the twelve-tone system is in the absence of the capacity for judging its successes? Later in his life Schoenberg expresses his gratification in being shown that his "music can speak distinctly to a musician, that he can know and understand me without explanation." Naturally I think here of a fundamental methodological remark in Wittgenstein's *Investigations* (§109), that "there must not be anything hypothetical in our considerations. We must do away with all explanation"[3]— in favor of a certain form of what he calls a perspicuous presentation of philosophical material. Earlier Schoenberg had written to Kandinsky: "I forgot, it's no use arguing because of course I won't be listened to; because there is no will to understand, but only one not to hear what the other says."[4] Instead of requiring a "will to understand," Wittgenstein speaks of philosophical problems as kept in place by "an urge to misunderstand" (§103)—, namely to misunderstand what for Wittgenstein should be closest to us: our every word. It is only fitting that Schoenberg should link understanding with hearing; and since he speaks of a composer's responsibility both to performers and to audiences, we have to ask how one may prove (if only to oneself) that one does hear apart from demonstrating it in performance, where communicative virtue depends upon virtuosity, a sparsely distributed property.

If it is in Beethoven that music most famously comes to take on its terrorist aspect, causing anxiety over whether one hears what is happening, it is in

[2] Schoenberg to Max Butting, 4 February 1926, in *Arnold Schoenberg Letters*, ed. Erwin Stein, trans. Eithne Williams and Ernst Kaiser (Berkeley and Los Angeles: University of California Press, 1987), 118.

[3] Wittgenstein, *Philosophical Investigations*, 47.

[4] Schoenberg to Wassily Kandinsky, 4 May 1923, in *Arnold Schoenberg Letters*, 93.

Schoenberg that this anxiety reaches its purest pitch, seeming to offer nothing unless it provides everything. In confronting it, each is abandoned to his or her conscience to tell whether to go on with it. This strikes me as a description of an effect of philosophy as well (as it matters most to me), which also chronically creates an anxiety in proving that one understands. Conceivably for this reason modern philosophers who are moved to think recurrently about music tend to regard it as an image of or an inspiration to the philosophical task, hence they tend to appeal to music for its representation of an idea fundamental to their thought, which they may well sense they have otherwise failed to realize unmistakably in their philosophical prose. I think here, beyond the instance of Wittgenstein, of Schopenhauer's sense of the world as will, of course of Nietzsche's perception of the union of the Dionysian and the Apollinian, of the philosopher Ernst Bloch's sense of sustaining hope in the imagination of Utopia—examples that surely lie behind Theodor Adorno's interpretation of Schoenberg's intervention in the history of music (and secondarily of Stravinsky's) in his *Philosophy of Modern Music*.[5]

I do not know what standing Adorno's views have with thinking musicians these days. Charles Rosen in his 1977 Modern Masters book on Schoenberg does not cite Adorno, and in the preface to its 1996 reprinting Rosen mentions Adorno only to dismiss his treatment of Stravinsky as disgraceful and of Schoenberg as unconvincing.[6] But among intellectually inclined nonmusicians it is my impression that Adorno remains a dominating presence in the image of what a philosophy of music may be. Before taking very brief steps into two of Adorno's texts I am glad to recall some sound advice offered by Carl Dahlhaus in his collection *Schoenberg and the New Music*, in which Adorno's is by far the most frequently cited name (except for the names of Wagner and of Schoenberg). Dahlhaus's advice is that "we should only call upon philosophy if it proves impossible to proceed without its help."[7] The soundness of the advice is that philosophy, to be helpful, must always be called upon—it must not seek to have the first, any more than the last, word to get you to listen to it. It should first show that it can listen. But the difficulty with Dahlhaus's advice is that it is bound to come too late; by the time we call upon philosophy we have already subjected ourselves to its

[5] Theodor Adorno, *Philosophy of Modern Music*, trans. Anne G. Mitchell and Wesley V. Blomster (New York: Seabury Press, 1973).

[6] Charles Rosen, *Arnold Schoenberg* (Chicago: University of Chicago Press, 1996), viii.

[7] Carl Dahlhaus, *Schoenberg and the New Music*, trans. Derrick Puffett and Alfred Clayton (Cambridge: Cambridge University Press, 1987), 275.

forces, turned ourselves into philosophers. Then it is up to each of us to find our way to intelligibility.

Is there a more extreme example of an artist attempting to make himself intelligible than that of Schoenberg, in his music no less than in his theoretical works? And, as I have had occasion to say about philosophical ambition, someone whose motive is absolute veracity is likely to be very hard to understand.

The young David Lewin, in a remarkable discussion of act 1, scene l, of *Moses und Aron*, opens with some general remarks, which begin with the observation: "The dramatic idea of the work hinges on the paradoxical nature of God: the *Unvorstellbares* [Unrepresentable] that commands itself to be *vorgestellt* [represented]."[8] Lewin goes on to propose that "the musical metaphor that reflects (or better defines) the dramatic idea is the nature of the twelve-tone row and system as 'musical idea' in Schoenberg's terminology. The 'row' or 'the musical idea' is not a concrete and specific musical subject or object to be presented for once and for all as referential in sounds and time; it is, rather, an abstraction that manifests itself everywhere ('allgegenwaertiger') in the work.…It remains unrealized and unfulfilled until it is manifested and communicated…by means of material sounds…in all its manifold potentialities.…God demands that His order be communicated to the Volk. Yet how can they be taught to love and understand the immaterial and Unvorstellbares (the true musical experience)?"[9] When Lewin alertly qualifies the idea of the musical idea of the row as defining the dramatic idea, he throws the intellectual burden of understanding these sublime matters all but entirely upon the work of the music, which he thereupon undertakes to articulate. But this does not deny, it may be taken to assert, that the idea of representing the unrepresentable in all its manifold potentialities has itself innumerable manifestations (Moses' stammer, for example, or the burning bush), which the musical may contest or confirm.

It is when Adorno interprets what he calls Webern's "fetishism of the row" as (still) maintaining dialectical force that Adorno has recourse to the idea of expressing the inexpressible. He amplifies this claim by saying: "One aspect of the situation is that twelve-tone music, by force of its mere correctness, resists subjective expression. The other important aspect is that the right of the subject itself to expression [i.e., the right to expression of the individual consciousness in late capitalism] declines.…It has become so isolated that it can hardly seriously hope for anyone who may still understand it.…Its

[8] David Lewin, "*Moses und Aron*: Some General Remarks, and Analytic Notes for Act I, Scene I," *Perspectives of New Music* 6 (fall–winter 1967): 1.
[9] Ibid.

melancholy disappearance is the purest expression of its terrified and distrustful withdrawal.... However, it remains incapable of expressing the inexpressible as truth."[10]

Three more sentences from Adorno will help to underscore how his intellectual allegiances allow him, or demand from him, formulations that in moments are close and yet are immeasurably far from those I have cited from David Lewin. Adorno continues: "The possibility of music itself has become uncertain.... That certain freedom, into which it undertook to transform its anarchistic condition, was converted in the very hands of this music into a metaphor of the world against which it raises its protest.... To a certain degree it places itself at the disposal of the world-spirit which is, after all, not world-logic.... [But] the decline of art in a false order is itself false. Its truth is the denial of the submissiveness to which its central principle...has driven it."[11] It is in Adorno's efforts to express or to portray as it were the experience of this crisis of expression (as if music now speaks only of speechlessness) that his book is punctuated with notations of loneliness, melancholy, withdrawal, despondency, anxiety, shock, and at the same time declares the continuing impossibility or denial of one's own experience. But the full credibility of this effort—whose importance I should not wish to be neglected—depends upon a fuller trust or interest in Adorno's clarity of experience, together with his articulation of it in a further Hegelian process of concepts, than I find I can lend to it. Is there some alternative philosophical path through which to explore what I am calling this crisis of expression?

Adorno's characteristic appeal to the negative in his dialectical opposition to the present ("The decline of art in a false order is itself false," which I take to say: the apparent decline of art has something in it that opposes decline) is something that, it seems to me, Thomas Mann had particular trouble with, for all the usefulness Adorno's manuscript on Schoenberg may have had for him in composing *Doctor Faustus.* Adorno writes, in his extraordinarily admiring "Toward a Portrait of Thomas Mann" (1962), of an encounter in which he describes himself as rebelling against the way Mann proposed, in the ending of his book, to describe the composer Leverkühn's last work, his Faust oratorio. "I found," he reports himself saying to Mann, "the heavily laden pages too positive, too unbrokenly theological in relation to the structure not only of the *Lamentation of Dr. Faustus* but of the novel as a whole. They seemed to lack what the crucial passage required, the power of determinate negation as the only permissible figure of the Other.... Two days later

[10] Adorno, *Philosophy of Modern Music*, 112.
[11] Ibid., 112–13.

[after a dinner to which the Adornos had been invited by the Manns]...the author...read, clearly excited, the new conclusion which he had written in the meantime. We could not hide how moved we were."[12] It is true that the published version of that passage (I assume it now constitutes the last pages of chapter 46)—even without the chance to compare it to its former draft—seems to revel in negations, beginning with the "revocation," in the oratorio's competition with the Beethoven Ninth, of vocal jubilation, and climaxing with the "deliberate reversal of the 'Watch with me' of Gethsemane," Christ's offer of shared suffering leading to what Faust now rejects as a false salvation. But in the next paragraph, the last of this late chapter, the narrator of Mann's *Dr. Faustus*, in describing the "hope beyond hopelessness" of the oratorio's concluding sound, comes to plead with his reader: "Listen with me." Is this transfiguration of the Gethsemane "Watch with me," from the visible into the ineluctable modality of the audible, endowing unheard music with the power of redemptive suffering—is this transfiguration a match in good faith for philosophy's negations? Adorno reports that he was openly moved. But by what? With what right? Was it by the dramatized effectiveness of dialectic's negation, or was it by an artist's attestation of art's contesting at once of religion and of philosophy? Mann's narration, if one grants its success here, has, as we used to say, "earned" its conclusion, morally, artistically, intellectually. Does dialectic provide an explanation of what "earning it" consists in? Is this what the injunction means, that we are to believe *in order to* understand? Whom does one believe?

In conjunction with David Lewin's account of the communicability of the omnipresence of the idea or row, I go back for a moment to Wittgenstein's unpredictable *Investigations*, specifically to its claim that in his break with philosophy, more specifically with his own past, Wittgenstein continues to follow the aim of logical investigation—the urge to understand the basis, or essence, of everything empirical—but now not by moving to a new language but by turning ourselves to understand what is already in plain view, retrieving the ordinary from the metaphysical. Or rather, this ordinary will seem to have been already in plain view when we determine what will constitute understanding what we are precisely fated to pass by, which in practice begins with the realization that we do not understand (and yet we are obedient enough to be mastered by) the basis upon which we speak as we do, our responsiveness to the world in what Wittgenstein calls our everyday language,

[12] Theodor Adorno, "Toward a Portrait of Thomas Mann," in *Notes to Literature*, vol. 2, ed. Rolf Tiedemann, trans. Shierry Weber Nicholsen (New York: Columbia University Press, 1992), 17–18.

our initial tongue—the same old words, the same old tones. Philosophy is to liberate us—without renouncing our speech—from the false intensities, the falsely conceived dissonances, that philosophy and convention drive us to impose upon ourselves (which are already measures of renouncing). We must recognize the ordinary world of our constructions and of our destructions to be as mysterious (Freud says uncanny, finding a new familiar in place of an old; so, more or less, does Heidegger)—as mysterious as the things of faith once were.

My suggestion is that the Schoenbergian idea of the row with its unforeseen yet pervasive consequences is a serviceable image of the Wittgensteinian idea of grammar and its elaboration of criteria of judgment, which shadow our expressions and which reveal pervasive yet unforeseen conditions of our existence, specifically in its illumination of our finite standing as one in which there is no complete vision of the possibilities of our understanding—no total revelation as it were—but in which the assumption of each of our assertions and retractions, in its specific manifestations in time and place, is to be worked through, discovering, so to speak, for each case its unconscious row.

If this allegory of the *Investigations* through Schoenbergian practice is illuminating, then one may be encouraged to reflect further on why, as I have variously sketched the question, the philosophical subject of the *Investigations*, the modern ego entangled in its expressions of desire (Wittgenstein speaks of our urge to understand as well as of our equally pressing urge to misunderstand), is specifically characterized by Wittgenstein in its moments of torment, sickness, strangeness, self-destructiveness, perversity, suffocation, and lostness. If these qualities rhyme with ones that musicians call upon to notate their experience of Schoenberg's expressiveness (Charles Rosen, claiming for Schoenberg's music that it "is among the most expressive ever written"—and not just in the period of its expressionism—specifies the qualities he hears as anxiety, anguish, horror, terror, violence, as well as charm), then it may well be in the paths and grounding of Wittgenstein's *Investigations* that we can learn a new responsibility with such concepts.

But is this a way to envision what a philosophy of music should be, one that is itself illuminated by musical procedure? It seems to me—to begin with—a promising way to keep open the question of where and how we must claim to understand, and where and how we must prepare ourselves not to.

I conclude by citing a source for the appeal to, or the demand for, understanding cast both as hope and as despair, a source surely known to all the figures I have invoked here, namely Friedrich Schlegel's great romantic essay "On Incomprehensibility." Having introduced almost at once what he calls the fascinating question whether the communication of ideas is actually possible, Schlegel soon announces: "Now, it is a peculiarity of mine that I absolutely detest incomprehension, not only the incomprehension of the uncomprehending but even more the incomprehension of the comprehending." I note for our interest on this occasion that in appending a poem of his to conclude his essay, Schlegel expresses the wish that a composer will set it to music. The inspiration of this essay, and I would even say, of this wish, come to me, to close my circle of proposals for this day, by way of Ralph Waldo Emerson's once monstrously famous essay "Self-Reliance," which I take as in general a meditation on human understanding (notably of the relation of inspiration to communication, or of what he calls intuition to tuition), and (since we know Emerson read Schlegel) specifically on Schlegel's questioning of understanding, as Emerson relates anecdotes of understanding and misunderstanding to ones concerning standing and standing for; and he includes, in his working through, the idea of following the standard of what he calls the true man, where standard's standing is that of providing a measure but may also pick up, as a flag, the overtone or image of a page turning in a true book. Such readings take Emerson into regions and rigors of thinking that he of course is not normally asked, nor generally granted the power, to reach, but I find his achievements to be lucid and provocative music to my ears.

Notes on Contributors

MARTIN BOYKAN is the Irving G. Fine Professor of Music at Brandeis University. He has composed extensively for a variety of chamber ensembles, for voice, and for orchestra. Most recently a solo sonata for violin was premiered in Boston and New York, and a new CD of his work was released by CRI, including the *Piano Trio No. 2, Echoes of Petrarch and the Second String Quartet.*

REINHOLD BRINKMANN is James Edward Ditson Professor of Music and Director of Graduate Studies at Harvard University's Music Department. He has written extensively on the history and aesthetics of music from the eighteenth to the twentieth centuries. His most recent publications include *Late Idyll: The Second Symphony of Johannes Brahms* (1995, pb. 1997); *Schumann and Eichendorff. Studien zum "Liederkreis," Op. 39* (1997); and, co-edited with Christoph Wolff, *Driven Into Paradise. The Musical Migration from Nazi Germany to the United States* (1999).

STANLEY CAVELL is Walter M. Cabot Professor of Aesthetics and the General Theory of Value, Emeritus at Harvard. He has some evidence that retirement will allow him to push further his work in the regions where philosophy and literature attract and reject one another, for example the region of music. Recent books include *Contesting Tears; The Hollywood Melodrama of the Unknown Woman* (1996) and *Philosophical Passages: Wittgenstein, Emerson, Austin, Derrida* (1995)

MICHAEL CHERLIN is Associate Professor of Music at the University of Minnesota. His principal areas of research have been Schoenberg studies and relations of music to text. Recent publications include "Memory and Rhetorical Trope in Schoenberg's String Trio," *Journal of the American Musicological Society*, Fall, 1998 and "Dialectical Opposition in Schoenberg's Music and Thought," *Music Theory Spectrum*, forthcoming.

RICHARD KURTH is Associate Professor of Music at the University of British Columbia where he teaches music theory. His research and writings have focused primarily on the music of Arnold Schoenberg and on relations between music and poetry, especially in the nineteenth century. His recent publications include "Partition Lattices in Twelve-Tone Music: An Introduction," in the *Journal of Music Theory*, (volume 43, no. 1); and "On the Subject of Schubert's 'Unfinished' Symphony: Was bedeutet die Bewegung?" in *19th Century Music*, (volume XXIII, no. 1).

Lewis Lockwood is the Fanny Peabody Professor of Music at Harvard University. His fields of special interest in music history are the Renaissance and Beethoven. In the latter field his publications include the book, *Beethoven: Studies in the Creative Process* (1992) and numerous articles. He serves on the Editorial Board of the yearbook, *Beethoven Forum*.

Jeff Nichols is an Associate Professor of Composition at Harvard University. His music is published by Theodore Presser and C.F. Peters, and has been performed by new-music ensembles throughout the U.S. His theoretical work includes analyses of Schumann's *Dichterliebe* and several late works of Beethoven.

Karen Painter, a musicologist on the faculty at Harvard University, specializes in German music, aesthetics, ideology, and musical thought from the late 18th century to the mid 20th. Her publications include reception studies of Mahler, Mozart, Hindemith's *Mathis der Maler* and Pfitzner's *Palestrina*. She is completing a book under the working title *Symphonic aspirations. German music and thought in the twentieth century.*

Stephen Peles is a composer and theorist who currently teaches at the University of Alabama School of Music. He has published on both tonal and post-tonal topics, and is a contributor to the recent *Cambridge History of American Music.*

Judith Ryan is the Robert K. and Dale J. Weary Professor of German and Comparative Literature and Harvard College Professor at Harvard University. She has written widely on early twentieth-century and on contemporary literature, concentrating on lyric poetry and the novel. Her most recent publications include *The Vanishing Subject: Early Psychology and Literary Modernism* (1991) and *Rilke, Modernism and Poetic Tradition* (1999).

Christoph Wolff is William Powell Mason Professor of Music at Harvard University. A music historian with special interest in the seventeenth- and eighteenth-century music, he includes among his recent publications; *Mozart's Requiem: Historical and Analytical Studies, Documents, Score* (1994); *The New Bach Reader* (1998); co-edited with Reinhold Brinkmann, *Driven Into Paradise. The Musical Migration from Nazi Germany to the United States* (1999); and *Johann Sebastian Bach. The Learned Musician* (2000).

Index

Index